T0388414

HOW GOVERNMENT BUILT AMERICA

How Government Built America challenges growing, anti-government rhetoric by highlighting the role government has played in partnering with markets to build the United States. Sidney A. Shapiro and Joseph P. Tomain explore how markets can harm and fail the country, and how the government has addressed these extremes by restoring essential values to benefit all citizens. Without denying that individualism and small government are part of the national DNA, the authors demonstrate how democracy and a people pursuing communal interests are equally important. In highly engaging prose, the authors describe how the government, despite the complexity of markets, remains engaged in promoting economic prosperity, protecting people, and providing an economic safety net. Each chapter focuses on a historical figure, from Lincoln to FDR to Trump, to illustrate how the government–market mix has evolved over time. By understanding this history, readers can turn the national conversation back to what combination of government and markets will best serve the country.

Sidney A. Shapiro is the Frank U. Fletcher Chair in Administrative Law at the Wake Forest University School of Law. He is the author of *Administrative Competence: Reimagining Administrative Law* (2020) and *Achieving Democracy: The Future of Progressive Regulation* (2014). Previously, he was a distinguished visitor at Oxford University, University of Padua, and School of Public and Environmental Affairs, University of Indiana, Bloomington. He is a founding member and Vice-President of the Center for Progressive Reform.

Joseph P. Tomain is Dean Emeritus and Wilbert and Helen Ziegler Professor of Law in the University of Cincinnati College of Law. He is the author of *Achieving Democracy: The Future of Progressive Regulation* (2014) and *Clean Power Energy Politics* (2017). He was a distinguished visitor at the American Academy in Rome, the University of Notre Dame, Stanford University, and Oxford University and served as Fulbright Senior Specialist in Cambodia.

How Government Built America

SIDNEY A. SHAPIRO
Wake Forest University School of Law

JOSEPH P. TOMAIN
University of Cincinnati College of Law

Shaftesbury Road, Cambridge CB2 8EA, United Kingdom

One Liberty Plaza, 20th Floor, New York, NY 10006, USA

477 Williamstown Road, Port Melbourne, VIC 3207, Australia

314–321, 3rd Floor, Plot 3, Splendor Forum, Jasola District Centre, New Delhi – 110025, India

103 Penang Road, #05–06/07, Visioncrest Commercial, Singapore 238467

Cambridge University Press is part of Cambridge University Press & Assessment, a department of the University of Cambridge.

We share the University's mission to contribute to society through the pursuit of education, learning and research at the highest international levels of excellence.

www.cambridge.org
Information on this title: www.cambridge.org/9781009489355

DOI: 10.1017/9781009489386

First published 2024

A catalogue record for this publication is available from the British Library

Library of Congress Cataloging-in-Publication Data
NAMES: Shapiro, Sidney A., 1947– author. | Tomain, Joseph P., 1948– author.
TITLE: How government built America / Sidney A. Shapiro, Wake Forest University School of Law; Joseph P. Tomain, University of Cincinnati College of Law.
DESCRIPTION: Cambridge, United Kingdom ; New York, NY : Cambridge University Press, 2024. | Includes bibliographical references and index.
IDENTIFIERS: LCCN 2023056528 | ISBN 9781009489355 (hardback) | ISBN 9781009489386 (ebook)
SUBJECTS: LCSH: Administrative law – Political aspects – United States. | Administrative law – Economic aspects – United States. | Federal government – United States. | Capitalism – United States. | Democracy – United States. | United States – Politics and government – History. | United States – Economic policy – History.
CLASSIFICATION: LCC KF5402 .S525 2024 | DDC 320.973–dc23/eng/20231214
LC record available at https://lccn.loc.gov/2023056528

ISBN 978-1-009-48935-5 Hardback
ISBN 978-1-009-48937-9 Paperback

To civil servants and their many contributions toward "a more perfect union."

Contents

Preface

As college students in the 1960s and law students in the 1970s, we believed with countless others that government service was a noble calling. After law school, one of us worked as a government attorney, and since the mid-1970s, we have been teaching and writing about government. Gradually, the mood in the country shifted to skepticism about the government. Nowadays, many Americans regard government, civil servants, and the people who see government as important to the country as an enemy.

About fifteen years ago, the authors were at a bed and breakfast (B&B) in Asheville, North Carolina, to discuss the writing of our previous book. At a late afternoon wine and cheese reception, one of the other guests at the B&B was railing about how the government was ruining the country. Considering how the mood in the country had shifted to suspicion about the government, we did not find this remark surprising. Yet, like many who seek to avoid an argument in a setting like this one, one of us kept quiet. The other author politely responded with the following question – "do you like your insurance company?"

The anecdote captures a misunderstanding among many people who only see government as a negative force in American life. The guest complaining about the government overlooked how an unregulated insurance company is an open invitation to cheat customers and refuse to pay claims.

This experience, and others like it, prompted us to write a book about the many ways that the government has made America a better place. The market system has also been important in building a more prosperous and successful America, and the book describes this history. But we focused on the many contributions of the government because they are less well known and appreciated. Like Rodney Dangerfield, a comedian popular in the 1980s and 1990s, who organized his jokes around the phrase, "I don't get no respect," the government does not get the respect it is due.

We also focus on the history of government for a second reason. Like the guest we experienced in Asheville, it is easy for Americans to overlook the limitations of markets. The book therefore explains in a nontechnical way how markets have failed the country and its fundamental political values.

We see the history of government as relevant to another challenge – the current political polarization. As in the past, the country has a way past the angry rhetoric and finger-pointing. It is necessary for enough Americans to turn the national conversation back to what mix of government and markets will best serve the country. This change does not take everyone. But it does require understanding that a debate about the proper mix of government and markets has been at the heart of American democracy since the founding of the country.

We focus on the government for one more reason – it is not perfect. Never has been, never will be. History, however, demonstrates that it has not been the basket case that political rhetoric often makes it out to be. We have not idealized the government, and we have not idealized markets. Our intent has been to provide a truer account – one that acknowledges the achievements and limitations of both government and markets, which is why the country has always relied on a mix of the two.

We want to acknowledge that our book reflects years of scholarship about government and the country by other academics and writers. We are also appreciative of the support of the law schools where we work, the many students who have helped with research and thoughtful questions during class, and the scholars who have offered comments about our book. And we thank our families for their patience as we have been distracted by our research and writing.

1

Introduction

The Historical Necessity of Government

The United States has come through one of the darkest periods in our history. Close to one million people died from COVID-19, and millions more became ill and were out of work. Yet the reaction to this scourge varied widely depending on where you live in the United States.

New York adopted some of the strongest regulations in the country including a mandatory requirement for mask wearing when the virus surged. According to then Governor Andrew Cuomo, "No one wants to enforce a law because then you make the other person unhappy and nobody wants anyone unhappy. You know what makes people really unhappy? Dying makes people really unhappy…. Loss of a loved one makes people really unhappy."[1]

As the pandemic swept across South Dakota, Governor Kristi Noem had a different approach in mind: "The state hasn't issued lockdowns or mask mandates. We haven't shut down businesses or closed churches…. That isn't the government's role."[2] In Florida, Governor Ron DeSantis imposed financial penalties on school districts that required children to wear masks.[3] Texas Governor Greg Abbott even prohibited private businesses from requiring them.[4]

The attitudes about government in those states reflect two visions of the country that go back to the founding. Both are so fundamental to the way we understand ourselves that they have been captured by popular entertainment. Both, it turns out, are mythical. They are myths because, while they reflect important aspects of our history, neither gives a true account of it.

1.1 TWO VISIONS OF AMERICA

When the authors were growing up, *The Lone Ranger* was a staple of Saturday morning television. The Ranger, who wore a mask to hide his identity, rode through the West with his Native American colleague, Tonto, saving people beleaguered by bandits. After a successful rescue, someone would ask, "Who was that masked man," as the Ranger rode away. In the movie westerns, the settlers and the lawmen who helped them were portrayed as models of self-reliance, individualism, and self-sufficiency. The government is nowhere in sight in this vision of America. What made America great, the story goes, is for the government to get out of the way and let people make their own decisions. When this happens, good things happen.

This vision of America was even adopted by the Marlboro brand of cigarettes. Advertisements featured a strapping cowboy pictured riding his horse through a beautiful Western scene. The slogan "Come to Marlboro County" offered male smokers the opportunity to associate themselves with the iconic rugged cowboy and the self-reliance and independence of this romanticized version of the West.

Frank Capra's 1939 classic movie, *Mr. Smith Goes to Washington*, portrayed another American myth popularized in the movies and television. Jefferson Smith, played by Jimmy Stewart, comes to Washington handpicked by political bosses back home. Once there, the naïve Smith first falls in line and introduces a bill for a boys' camp only to learn that the land was part of a graft scheme. When he tries to expose the graft, the DC corruption machine tries to vote him out of the Senate. In his defense, he mounts a twenty-four-hour filibuster. Aided by a network of boy scouts and his politically savvy secretary, played by Jean Arthur, the movie is a story about people and politicians coming together in a democracy to do what's best for the nation.[5] It reflects a "democratic wish of the direct participation of a united people pursuing a shared communal interest."[6] As Smith says on the Senate floor:

> I wouldn't give you two cents for all your fancy rules if, behind them, they didn't
> have a little bit of plain, ordinary, everyday kindness and a – a little lookin' out for
> the other fella, too. That's pretty important, all that. It's just the blood and bone
> and sinew of this democracy that some great men handed down to the human
> race, that's all![7]

In 1943, Norman Rockwell captured the idea of pure democracy in a painting of a New England town meeting in which a man was standing up and talking and his fellow community members were listening respectfully.[8] As a painter and illustrator, Rockwell was well known for his iconic portrayals of American culture painted for *The Saturday Evening Post*, a popular national magazine from 1920 to the 1950s.

The New England town meeting remains an icon of American democracy. In the "Hartsfield Landing" episode of the TV series *West Wing*, viewers learn that all forty-two adults living in Hartsfield Landing, New Hampshire vote at midnight of the day of the state's presidential primary. Allison Janney, who plays the President's press secretary, C. J. Cregg, observes, "'I think it's nice. I think it's democracy at its purest. They all gather at once.... At a gas station.'"[9] In the long-running TV series, *Gilmore Girls*, the colorful residents of the fictional New England town of Stars Hollow gather to discuss the issues facing the town, often disagreeing but listening to each other as Rockwell had pictured.

A prominent American philosopher, John Dewey, defined democracy as a discussion about the type of country in which we wish to live.[10] And Richard Andrews sees government as the "central arena in which members of society choose and legitimize ... their collective values.... through representative democracy."[11] Politics in this country has often been less noble than these depictions, but that does not mean this myth does not capture an important insight about the country. While democracy may not resemble a polite New England town meeting, many Americans aspire to an idealized vision of government "lookin' out for the other fella, too" captured by Rockwell, the *West Wing*, and *Gilmore Girls*.

1.2 THE MYTHS OF AMERICAN HISTORY

These two visions of America exist side by side because both support the fundamental values that define us as a nation. A nation consists of how we see ourselves as bound together as a people.[12] The fundamental values we hold in common make us a community of communities. After the United States fought for independence from Great Britain, the country was ruled under the Articles of Confederation. Each state was recognized as semi-sovereign; there was no conception of the "United States." The new Constitution, along with the Declaration of Independence, created that identity by expressing, albeit imperfectly, the country's commitment to liberty, equality, fairness and the common good, and these aspirations have continued to guide us ever since.

When Tony Kushner, who wrote the 1993 Pulitzer prize-winning play "Angels in America," which examined AIDS and homosexuality in America, he spoke about those values:

> [T]hese bonds, what Lincoln called the mystic chords of memory, the bonds of affection that ... held the union together, I don't think they're broken irrevocably. I think it's always been the sort of secret of democracy that it depends on a kind of secular religion. And the religion is the union.... But the union can only cohere if people are believing that what they're promised in the Declaration is still possible, life, liberty, and the pursuit of happiness.[13]

Americans share these values even as we hold diverse ideological and political opinions. Individualism, self-reliance, and small government are part of our national DNA, but so are democracy, vibrant government, and a people pursuing their communal interests. Neither vision of America is wrong, but both are incomplete. History demonstrates it has taken both to fulfill America's fundamental aspirations.

Achieving some of these values will inevitably come into conflict with others.[14] This conflict can be seen in the tale of the states presented earlier. As in the movie westerns, South Dakota prizes self-reliance, individualism, and self-sufficiency. Government mandates are understood as an unnecessary limitation on individual liberty. In New York, while the government limited freedom by requiring mask wearing, it expanded liberty and freedom by enabling people to live a longer and better life in exchange for this reasonable limitation.

Those favoring leaving mask wearing to individual choice are fond of misquoting Benjamin Franklin, "Those who would give up essential liberty, to purchase a little safety, deserve neither safety nor liberty." Franklin, however, was not opposing the government, he was supporting it. The quote is from a letter supporting increased taxation to fund security on the Pennsylvania frontier. Franklin was saying that the tax opponents were seeking a "little safety" for their property, but he objected that such short-sighted behavior meant opponents of the tax were the opponents of "essential liberty." As a result, the tax opponents deserved "neither safety nor liberty."[15] Or as Justice Louis Brandeis pointed out in a Supreme Court case, "It is true … that every exaction of money for an act is a discouragement to the extent of the payment required, but that [must be] seen in its organic connection with the whole. Taxes are what we pay for civilized society…."[16]

1.3 HOW GOVERNMENT BUILT AMERICA

The chapters that follow tell the story of government throughout American history starting with the colonies and continuing through the first two years of the Biden administration. Each chapter focuses on the additions to government that occurred at the time, how those changes promoted the nation's fundamental values, and how the politics of the time promoted or prevented needed additions to government.

We focus on the government because its role in building the country is often overlooked and misunderstood. Some historians have discussed a national consensus that the government, by and large, should leave individuals alone to pursue their self-interest.[17] And it is common for Americans to think of the United States as dedicated to free markets with government regulation being an occasional and unwelcome exception.

Each chapter is focused on a person who personifies the historical events at the time. Some were politicians, some were writers, and some were political activists. All of them share the fact that they had an outsized influence on their times in ways that affected the mix of government and markets. They are not the only ones. The history of government is chock full of colorful and influential people, and the book includes others as well.

1.4 HISTORY'S LESSONS

The history of government leaves us with six lessons about government. The first, and perhaps most significant lesson, is that the government has played a crucial role in building the country in ways that are truer to our national values. Small government is in the eye of the ideologue; it has no historical precedent. The nation can substantially shrink government as those entirely hostile to it prefer, but history establishes that the problems with markets will not go away.

Government, while essential to achieving those values, did not do it alone. A second lesson is that it has taken both government and markets to achieve the country by supporting its values. Markets have contributed to those values even as they have limited and subverted those values as well.

Another lesson is that although the government is big and complex, it is big and complex in response to changes that were occurring in the economy that sent the country in directions inconsistent with its national values. As the economy has grown and become more complex, so has the government. By way of example, industrialization dramatically changed the relationship between employers and workers with the result that employers failed to provide safe working conditions.

Yet, the fourth lesson is that the government, despite its size and complexity, undertakes the same three essential functions it has undertaken over the history of the country. First, the government has been necessary to create, sustain, and expand markets. As readers will learn, markets do not generate all the investments from which the country can benefit for reasons that will be explained. Second, as the previous example indicated, the government has also protected individuals from market activities that harm them or discriminate against them based on race and other immutable characteristics. Markets with unlimited liberty, as also will be explained, cannot and have not protected Americans from exploitative business behavior, physical harm, and discrimination. Finally, the government has established a social safety net that improves the lives of vulnerable Americans and Americans experiencing poverty. Markets expect and encourage self-reliance, but as will be examined, many Americans have experienced extreme poverty through no fault of their own.

Over the arc of American history, there is a positive story to tell. Still a fifth lesson is that the pathway toward achieving America's fundamental political values has been littered with mistakes and regrets. The nation tolerated slavery because of its economic benefits, and it subjugated Native Americans for the same reason. Women were regarded as inferior to men as a matter of law and society for much of the nation's history. The LGBTQ community was driven underground by the nation's prejudices. The government, at the behest of voters, has aided and abetted all of these failings. It is also true however that our understanding of the nation's values – particularly equality – has evolved over time. What makes us a nation has changed to encompass those who had been excluded and marginalized.

1.5 THE NATION IS THE FIGHT

A final lesson is that employing the government to be true to America's values has never been easy. When the government intervenes to promote the country's values, it will reduce some people's freedom and liberty, which was the point that Benjamin Franklin was making. Those adversely affected fight to block the government from acting, and they are often in a powerful position to do so.

And people will disagree about the need for government action to restore or promote the country's values. The myth of individualism and self-reliance has a strong hold on many Americans. The idea of small government is a powerful idea. It is easy to see how markets promote freedom and more difficult to see how they restrict it. And the political forces that benefit from stopping government intervention have misled the public about the need for government.

To have a nation truer to its national values, Americans must fight for it as they have done in the past. "That's what this place is" observes the New York Times columnist, Carlos Lozada, "This is a fight. This is a constant ... fight ... over which stories predominate."[18] As the historian, Jill Lepore, sums up the American experience, "The nation, as ever, is the fight."[19]

2

The Founders' America

Government and Markets

In 1776, two publications changed the world and defined the United States. The Declaration of Independence proclaimed the superiority of democracy as a form of government, and Adam Smith's *The Wealth of Nations* proclaimed the superiority of markets to order our daily lives. Together these works asserted that an effective society was one that took the mix of government and markets seriously as Smith noted: "Commerce and manufactures ... can seldom flourish in any state in which there is not a certain degree of confidence in the justice of government."[1]

This idea that our country is based on a mix of government and markets, while true, is not especially inspiring. Instead, like all societies, we tell ourselves an origin story that is compelling, often told, and reverently repeated. It connects us to our history, and because it also connects us to our values, it is exceedingly important to tell the story accurately as best we can. Our origin story relies on famous moments of history, a veneration of our sacred documents, and a pride in the American way of life. There is truth in each of those beliefs, and together they yield a picture of a content and exceptional America, whether we prefer an America of the small "d" democratic New England Town Hall or of the rugged independent West.

The problem is that the origin story is partial. There never was a time when Americans went about their business unfettered from the hand of government as the story of the independent West imagines. Nor does a society as pluralistic as ours function like a small-town democracy painted by Norman Rockwell. Rather, the nation's history tells a story about the ebbs and flows between those two visions, and the story is considerably bumpier and more complex than we might like. We must accept these complexities as we try to balance the mix of government and markets because, at any point in our history, the mix defines us.

2.1 THE FOUNDING MIX

The mega-hit *Hamilton* revolutionized American musical theater by grafting rap onto the range of musical styles used on Broadway. It also made a significant political statement. The final song – "Who Lives, Who Dies, Who Tells Your Story" – is sung after Alexander Hamilton's death as the result of a duel with Aaron Burr. The song is about whether Hamilton's contribution to the founding will be remembered or forgotten. The song answers how history is remembered depends on who is telling the story.

The often-told story is that government started out small and limited, and today we need to return to that guiding principle. According to this account, the Constitution and the Bill of Rights established the Framers' commitment to small government and free markets. This is not how the founders pictured the future of the country. What may seem remarkable to today's critics of government is that both sides in this controversy agreed about the need for government.

The colonies were well-regulated societies. The actors playing Aaron Burr, John Laurens, Marquis de Lafayette, and Hercules Mulligan, for example, meet early in the musical with Alexander Hamilton in a tavern to toast the Revolution.[2] Colonial governments closely regulated taverns and most other businesses. The historian Lawrence Friedman has pointed out, "A century before Adam Smith, the proprietors, squires, and magistrates of America certainly did not believe that government was best that governed the least."[3]

At the conclusion of the American Revolution, the new country grappled with the issue of where the locus of power to govern ourselves should reside. This is this question that divided the Federalists and the Anti-Federalists as well as the Hamiltonians and the Jeffersonians. The fight, then, was about the extent to which a central government would augment state government. Hamilton and the Federalists won that debate with a powerful argument. He famously argued in Federalist Paper No. 1 that "the vigor of government is essential to the security of liberty."[4] To that end, he led the federal government's efforts to manage the economy and invest in infrastructure including the construction of canals, bridges, and roads. To this day the federal government is involved in the same or similar investments to promote economic prosperity.

2.2 EARLY REGULATION

Regulatory activities in the colonies were widespread and extensive.[5] A 1788 law, as an example, besides requiring a license to run a tavern, required:

> That every innholder or tavern-keeper, shall, within thirty days after obtaining his or her permit, put up and fix a proper sign on or adjacent to the front of his or her house, with his or her name thereon, and keep such sign up during the time he or she shall keep an inn or tavern, under the penalty of ten schillings for every month's neglect thereof.[6]

And this: "That if any inn-holder or tavern-keeper, shall be convicted of being drunk in his own inn or tavern, besides the penalty consequent on the crime of drunkenness, his license shall immediately thereupon become void."[7]

Such laws were written for the benefit of society; the colonial governments did not let the "free market" reign. Tavern owners must be responsible, taverns must be visible and open to the public, and the number of taverns was limited by the number of licenses that were issued. These early regulators were concerned about the effects of commerce on society with, perhaps, a bit of moral scruples thrown in for good measure. After all, states still issue liquor licenses.

The regulation of markets was as detailed as it was commonplace. Boston in the 1730s adopted a municipal ordinance to regulate the newly built marketplace at Faneuil Hall, which today is a popular tourist attraction. City officials established the location of stalls, set the prices of goods, oversaw their quality, enforced regulations concerning weights and measures, and licensed butchers.[8] When the carpenter hired by the city to build stocks to punish rule breakers charged excessive fees, he was the first one clamped into his handiwork.[9]

Colonial governments also engaged in extensive controls concerning private behavior including drinking, gambling, theater going, prostitution, vagrancy, and even kite flying.[10] The close supervision of commercial and social behaviors indicates the extent to which the public interest was privileged over the private interest in early America.

The states continued their close regulation of markets after the Constitution was signed. A history of the nineteenth century finds there was an "overwhelming presence of the state regulation in nineteenth century American life."[11] There were "a plethora of bylaws, ordinances, statutes and common law restrictions regulating nearly every aspect of early American economy and society, from Sunday observance to the carting of offal."[12]

2.3 THE DECLARATION OF INDEPENDENCE

In 1817, John Turmbull completed a painting of the presentation of the first draft of the Declaration of Independence to the Second Continental Congress in the Pennsylvania State House, now Independence Hall, in Philadelphia. The painting, which is now displayed in the Capitol Rotunda, is printed on the reverse side of the two-dollar bill and appears in several series of stamps. Jefferson, portrayed as the principal author, is presenting the draft to John Hancock, the president of the Congress, who is seated at a table surrounded by the other members of the drafting committee. Trumbull captured a nice moment, but it was painted after the event, and he imagined how it occurred.

The Declaration of Independence was a way for the Continental Congress to share with others throughout the colonies the reasons for the breaking from England and restoring the right of the people to self-government. At a time when communication in the colonies could take months, it was a document that could be passed around to ensure everyone was on the same page regarding the reasons why a revolution was necessary and proper.[13]

Signing the Declaration was not taken lightly. Representatives needed clear authorization from their states, and some received that authorization only shortly before they added their signatures to the document. Even though tension between Britain and its colonies had been building over the previous decade and more, the colonists largely would have preferred fair representation in Parliament. When Parliament balked and thwarted the colonists' desire for self-government, they exercised their political right to "dissolve the political bands," which connected them with Britain.[14]

This declaration has become a foundational statement of the country's fundamental political values – the values that define our collective identity as a nation. As it famously declares: "We hold these truths to be self-evident, that all men are created equal, that they are endowed by their Creator with certain unalienable rights, that among these are life, liberty and the pursuit of happiness." Those declared principles were neither then nor now fully realized. However, defining those principles was a task, and an important and enduring one.

Notably, the Declaration defines inalienable rights as "life, liberty and the pursuit of happiness" rather than adopting John Locke's definition of inalienable rights in *Two Treatises of Civil Government*.[15] Locke, a prominent English physician and philosopher, envisioned the appropriate role for government by starting with the "state of nature" – a place where there was perfect freedom and equality and no government. From this equal beginning, men (as it was then) acquired property by dint of their labor and effort, and having done so, they mutually agreed to create a government for the purposes of maintaining order and protecting the property that they owned. For Locke, then, the government existed to guarantee "life, liberty and property."

But Jefferson chose the phrase "life, liberty, and the pursuit of happiness" instead of Locke's triad. The Founders' views about government were complicated and not limited to Locke's ideas.[16] In particular, they were influenced by a political philosophy, republicanism (not to be confused by today's Republican party), which dates to the 1500s in Italy[17] and was adopted by the Renaissance authors, such as Machiavelli, who are still read today.[18] Republicanism understands the furtherance of the public good as a primary characteristic of good government, and it therefore puts the government in charge of organizing economic and social activities.[19] As such, it prioritizes the public good over individual rights.[20] Drawing from this tradition, Jefferson substituted the pursuit of happiness for property because property could be regulated by the civil government and could be included under the concept of happiness.[21] Notably, "property" was explicitly protected in the Constitution.

Jefferson's substitution of "happiness" for Locke's choice of "property" in the Declaration of Independence signals that he believed "people empower government in the expectation that it will help them realize or achieve security and happiness."[22] As Jefferson explained in another document, "[t]he only orthodox object of the institution of government is to secure the greatest degree of happiness possible to the general mass of those associated under it." George Washington added, "The aggregate happiness of society is or ought to be the end of all government."[23]

2.4 THE CONSTITUTION

We tend to forget that after the Revolution, the "United States government failed miserably before it succeeded."[24] The first attempt at governing the country – The Articles of Confederation – soon proved to be totally inadequate. The Articles formed a confederation of sovereign states that, like a treaty between independent countries, bound the states to cede to the national government a limited set of powers. As the Articles stated, the states were in "a firm league of friendship with each other," and each state "retain[ed] its sovereignty, freedom, and independence" except for those powers expressly delegated to the Continental Congress.[25]

By 1787, it was evident that Articles did not permit the Continental Congress to coordinate the states for national purposes, and there was no President or Executive Branch that could fill the gap. On top of this, elected leaders were worried that a weak federal government could not handle the political unrest across the country. By way of example, public leaders feared that an armed resistance of about 1,000 men, known as Shays' Rebellion, protesting high taxes and a poor economy in Massachusetts, could lead to a takeover of a state government.[26] George Washington wrote in a warning letter to James Madison, "No day ever dawned more favorably than ours did; and no day was ever more clouded than the present…. We are fast verging to anarchy and confusion!"[27] There were also difficulties collecting the revenue needed to run the national government and pay off the Revolutionary War debt; the states were engaged in protectionist and retaliatory trade restrictions that hobbled national commerce; they individually pursued their own foreign policies; there was neither a single currency nor a monetary system to unite the colonies; and the national government lacked any means to require the states to abide by its decisions.[28]

After the states called for a constitutional convention to establish a more effective federal government, the challenge for the framers was how to fulfill the government's role to ensure life, liberty, and the general welfare, but still avoid the government tyranny that led to the war of independence. James Madison's plan to separate the executive, legislative, and judicial powers into three separate branches, which had never been tried before, was his answer to how to ensure both effective government and self-government.

These checks and balances among the three branches have led some historians to conclude that he intended that the separation of powers would produce "a harmonious system of mutual frustration" to protect liberty.[29] But Madison, along with Washington and Hamilton, was a vigorous proponent of a strong national government. He intended that the separation of powers would guide or focus the strong government he favored rather than throttle it.[30]

Additionally, he wanted to ensure that the public interest prevailed over private interests by promoting small and numerous interest groups.[31] He reasoned that the separation of powers would ensure that the government acted to benefit the entire nation rather than concentrate power in favor of the few. He believed "the structure of institutions that he and the other framers had constructed would bring forth representatives of enlightened views and virtuous sentiments."[32]

What Madison achieved was a three-branch government that addressed the outstanding problems with the Articles of Confederation. The Constitution authorized the federal government to provide for the common defense and the general welfare, to raise taxes to be able to pay the war debts and pay for the operations of government, to enact laws that preempted state laws that were inconsistent with national law, and that could nationalize state militias in defense of the country. Madison, to sum up, "shifted the United States from a meeting house of diplomats into a single nation."[33]

2.5 THE RATIFICATION

Madison then joined Hamilton and John Jay in campaigning for the ratification of the Constitution by the states. They wrote eighty-five essays in support of the Constitution known as the Federalist Papers and published them anonymously using the fictional name "Publius." Because of illness, Jay had to drop out of the project early on leaving Hamilton to write fifty-one of the essays and Madison to write twenty-nine more. Madison believed that by restricting public power through three branches of government, bicameralism, and federalism, and by restricting private power by encouraging a proliferation of separate interests, the United States government could be formed for the good of the nation and protect individual liberty as well. As Madison wrote in Federalist No. 10: "Extend the sphere, and you take in a greater variety of parties and interests. [Y]ou make it less probable that a majority of the whole will have a common motive to invade the rights of other citizens[.]" He then argued that this was the way to achieve the strong government that was necessary and yet protect individual liberty. "If men were angels, no government would be necessary," Madison wrote memorably in Federalist 51.

The Anti-Federalists – those who were suspicious of a strong national government – were not satisfied because the Constitution had been adopted without specific provisions to safeguard individual rights from invasion by the federal government.[34] Prior to 1787, several state constitutions contained bills of rights, and "We the people" did not want to see those rights reduced or extinguished. After the lack of a bill of rights became a rallying point for the Anti-Federalists – states balked at ratifying the Constitution –Madison's response was to add a "Bill of Rights" as the first ten amendments to the Constitution. After the Federalists vowed to support this change, the amendments were ratified in 1791.[35]

2.6 THE REST OF THE STORY

So far, this history of our early years, like other histories, understands the country's origins to be its founding documents – the Declaration of Independence and the Constitution, which contain the fundamental values of liberty and equality.[36] But there is more to the story. While the country aspired to liberty and equality, it failed to live up to those values. The treatment of indigenous people and the enslavement of Black Americans are part of the founding story as well.

About 15,000 years ago, after the last Ice Age ended, small groups of Stone Age hunters lived on and then crossed a land bridge from Asia onto a new continent. Eventually, those wanderers spread throughout every corner of what would become the United States of America. Then, about 1,000 years ago, a group of Vikings landed in Newfoundland, and they too found the new continent. They did not stay long.

On October 19, 1492, under the flagship of Queen Isabella and King Ferdinand of Spain, Christopher Columbus landed somewhere in the Bahamas, and the European conquest of the Americas began. As the United States was colonized by Europeans and grew into its current boundaries, the indigenous peoples who had arrived much earlier were displaced by acts of conquest, or as some recent historians name it "genocide."[37] As Chapter 2 develops, the government was responsible for this conquest, and it did so to develop markets and the prosperity of the Americans who were moving westward as the country expanded.

The story of government and markets is also a story of the enslavement of Black Americans. The first importation of about twenty enslaved people from Africa to the shore of Virginia occurred in 1619. From this time until the Civil War, government and markets worked singularly and uniformly together to maintain slavery. In the South, slavery was written into the laws that made the southern economy possible. Government, through law, prohibited enslaved men and women from marrying, owning property, reading, voting, and more. Astonishingly, Southern laws made Black children the property of their masters whether they were born from slave parents or were the offspring of their white masters. Thomas Jefferson's children with Sally Hemings were his property and were treated as such. Southern governments made slaves a subordinate caste because the government made them a subordinate people.[38] It is likely that forty-one of the fifty-six signers of the Declaration, including John Adams and Benjamin Franklin, owned enslaved people.[39] More potently, Northern banking and insurance interests financed the slave trade, and Ivy League and other universities were funded in part by slave trade money.[40]

The acceptance of racial slavery was the price the North was willing to pay for political union and national economic prosperity. The historian, Jill Lepore, reminds us that the Declaration of Independence was an "act of extraordinary political courage," but it was also "a colossal failure of political will, in holding back the tide of opposition to slavery by ignoring it for the sake of a union that, in the end, could not and would not last." She continues, "The Constitution would not lift this curse. Instead, it tried to hide it. Nowhere do the words 'slave' or 'slavery' appear in the final document."[41] Instead, in compromising on the issue of how slaves would be counted for purposes of allocating the number of representatives a state would have in the House of Representatives, the Constitution provided that each slave would count as three-fifths of a person, a ratio proposed by James Madison. A delegate, Gouverneur Morris, called these arrangements "the curse of Heaven."[42]

The founders supported another form of "big" government – the one that conquered the indigenous people and enslaved Black Americans. In the summer of 2019, the *New York Times* published an essay by Nikole Hannah-Jones entitled "The Idea of America," which was awarded the Pulitzer Prize.[43] The essay was part of *The 1619 Project*, which aimed to remind Americans that Black Americans have played and continue to play a central role in realizing a better version of a democratic union than the standard story tells.[44] Despite the newspaper's reporting of historical events, the Trump administration published a rebuttal under the title *The 1776 Report*, seeking to deny the centrality of race as a defining factor of America since before the founding.[45] By erasing stories about Black and indigenous Americans, the country downplays the inevitable connection between markets and government and the impact of this mix on our national values.

2.7 "TO RUN A CONSTITUTION"

Woodrow Wilson, in 1887, the centennial year of the Constitution, who was then a professor at Princeton and later president of the United States, observed, "It is getting to be harder to run a constitution than to frame one."[46] More recently, the historian Jill Lepore noted: "I once came across a book called *The Constitution Made Easy*. The Constitution cannot be made easy. It was never meant to be easy."[47] The founders quickly learned this lesson.

The ink was barely dry when the Federalists, led by Alexander Hamilton, who supported a strong federal government, and the Anti-Federalists, led by Thomas Jefferson, engaged in heated debates about the role of the federal government under the new Constitution. Hamilton's side won out, and the country embarked on the combination of markets and government that have marked our history ever since. Quite simply, a strong central government is necessary for a strong economy. Our political economy is neither all government nor all markets. It is a complementary combination of both. Jefferson and Madison, once they were elected President, supported key parts of Hamilton's ideas about the role of government despite their earlier opposition.

2.8 AT THE BEGINNING

The framers of the Constitution anticipated the need for a public administration, but they did not have a lot to say about it. The Constitution authorizes the president to appoint "Officers" of the United States with the approval of two-thirds of the Senate, and Congress can vest the appointment of "inferior" officers in the president, heads of departments, or courts of law.[48] Nevertheless, faced with the prospect of conducting foreign policy, operating a military, and managing the territory that was now the United States, Congress quickly acted.

In 1789, Congress established the Departments of War and Treasury, and the Department of Foreign Affairs was soon renamed the Department of State. Secretaries were authorized to appoint "inferior officers" to assist them in conducting the government's business. In the same year, Congress also created a customs service, the post office, and a system of patent appeals to be administered by various departments. The Office of the Attorney General was established in 1792, and Congress added a Navy Department in 1798. By 1801, some 3,000 federal employees were working for the federal government.[49]

One reason that the Articles of Confederation failed was the inability of congressional committees to manage the country's affairs. The nation's first leaders, a historian of the period notes, therefore had a "deadly fear of government impotence."[50] According to Alexander Hamilton, "Energy in the Executive is a leading character in the definition of good government. It is essential … to the steady administration of the laws."[51] This led to two developments.

First, Congress did not try to work out in detail how laws were to be implemented but instead delegated that job to the administration. A 1789 law, for example, authorized military pensions "under such regulations as the President may direct."[52] A 1790 law established disability payments for invalided military personnel, and it authorized the President to adopt regulations for this purpose including setting the amount of such payments.[53] Another law gave the President the authority to fix the amount of those pensions if it was no more than the maximum amount that Congress had established.[54]

Second, the founders looked for ways to ensure that the government employees who were going to fill in the details were competent to do so. Both Congress and the president worked on this issue. Congress in its very first legislative act required government officials to take an oath in which they swore to uphold the laws of the United States and to carry out the duties of the office to which they had been appointed. It also enacted conflict of interest legislation to prevent employees from making decisions based on personal financial considerations.[55] Taking an oath might not seem like much of a guarantee of competence today, but at that time it was considered an important aspect of personal behavior.

When President Washington hired government employees, he considered a man's reputation – his standing in the community, his neighbor's respect, and his electoral success in running for office – as a guide to his future behavior. Washington did not depend entirely on reputation, however.[56] He and his cabinet officials required subordinates to file reports and other correspondence to ensure that they were paying attention to their jobs and to help them supervise other employees under their responsibility.[57]

President Jefferson also understood the need for competent public administration. As he explained, "In government, as well as every other business of life, it is by division and subdivision of duties alone that all matters great and small, can be managed with perfection."[58] After taking office, he not only refused to fire the people who Washington had hired, when he hired a new employee, he also asked "is he honest? Is he capable? Is he faithful to the Constitution?"[59]

2.9 THE AMERICAN SYSTEM

When George Washington appointed Hamilton as the first Secretary of the Treasury, the national government owed $40.1 million to domestic creditors and another $11.8 million to European creditors that it had borrowed to fight the War of Independence. Interest payments were $4.5 million per year, which was four and one-half times greater than the entire budget of the new federal government. To make matters worse, the states had outstanding debts of another $25 million.[60] It is hardly surprising that no one was willing to lend any more money to the federal government or to indebted state governments.

Hamilton boldly proposed that the federal government should refinance its debt and only pay interest on the debt instead of trying to pay it off right away. He also understood that the federal government had to pay off the states' debts if his plan to refinance the federal debt was to work.

Those states that had already paid off their debts, such as Virginia, objected to paying for the states that had not done so. There was also a strong reaction to Hamilton's plan to pay the full value of the bonds – 100 dollars for a 100-dollar bond. Most bonds had been purchased by speculators who stood to make a large windfall when the bonds were redeemed for their full value since they paid only a few dollars for each bond. But Hamilton insisted that unless the federal government paid full value, it could not provide a strong credit reputation for the new country.

In a deal known as the "dinner table bargain," Jefferson, Madison, and Hamilton engaged in political horse trading to reach a compromise. What was said at this famous closed-door dinner is lost to history. As a song in the musical Hamilton points out, there was no one else in the room.[61] The result, however, is not lost to history. Hamilton agreed to move the capital of the new federal government to what is now Washington, D.C., from Philadelphia, and Jefferson and Madison agreed to the assumption of the state debt on Hamilton's terms.

Like the musical itself, Hamilton's refinancing of the public debt was a smash hit. The new country was able to borrow money at lower interest rates; the states, which were no longer struggling to pay off their bonds, were able to cut taxes as much as 85 percent, and a $100 federal bond was again worth $100, encouraging investors to lend money to the new country.[62] It is not an overstatement to conclude that the country may not have survived without Hamilton's rescue plan. If state and federal debts had been left to the "free market," then "Americans" would most likely be enjoying afternoon tea, crumpets, and clotted cream along with the King.

But that was not the only problem the new government faced. There was no national currency, and although the states each had a rudimentary state monetary system, one state's money was not valid in another state. As Hamilton recognized, it would be impossible to have markets in which goods were exchanged across the nation without a common currency. Economic development was also hampered by the lack of a national banking system, which meant businesses could not readily borrow money to expand. Some state banks did exist, but they were unreliable and insufficient to sustain reliable economic expansion.

Hamilton therefore proposed that the federal government establish a national bank to make it possible to create a national currency and lend money to new businesses. He defended his proposal in a "ground-breaking" document, *The Report on the Bank*, which carefully explained those and other advantages and drew attention to the role of a national bank in other countries.[63]

Hamilton was not done investing to promote economic progress.[64] Congress established a system of tariffs on imported goods and imposed a set of domestic taxes to reduce and manage the debt load. The tariffs generated needed revenue and offered protection for fledgling domestic manufacturing. Because the tariffs were paid mainly by the wealthiest of Americans, who were generally the only ones who could afford imported goods at the time, the Federalists largely avoided having to tax others with far less money.

Hamilton's role for the new federal government included financing infrastructure and protecting fledgling industries together with central monetary controls. Henry Clay, a prominent national politician, who served as Senator, Secretary of State, and the Speaker of the House of Representatives,[65] recognized these practices as so fundamental to the economy and the country that he described them as the "American System."

2.10 THOMAS JEFFERSON

Thomas Jefferson became an Anti-Federalist based on his belief that the federal government was more likely to be corrupted by the influence of power and wealth than by keeping government local and closer to home. His vision saw America as a land of small farms where people would be self-sufficient farmers who as property owners would be less likely to be corrupted as they engaged in self-governance. By comparison, because the industry and manufacturing favored by Hamilton were crowded into cities where people were less likely to own substantial property, Hamilton's plan, thought Jefferson, would more likely sacrifice the common good as corruption spread.[66]

Jefferson, as President, nevertheless continued to use the federal government as an instrument to create economic opportunity despite his misgivings about central authority. Famously, he purchased the Louisiana Territory from the French government, a significant national commitment, to open the territory for American settlement, leading to greater economic opportunity. He also refused to close the National Bank because it had been chartered by Congress for a set number of years. After the bank's charter expired in 1811, Jefferson's successor as president, James Madison, renewed its charter as the Second National Bank in 1816 for another twenty years. Madison became convinced about the need for the bank because of economic difficulties related to the War of 1812 and the cost to the nation of Jefferson's Louisiana Purchase.[67]

2.11 MAKING MARKETS WORK BETTER

What the early leaders recognized is that investors in private markets will hesitate to pay for investments in roads, canals, and other similar ventures if people can take advantage of the investment regardless of whether they pay for it. To avoid this free-rider result, the private owner of a highway or canal could charge people to use it, but it is still true that many other people will benefit from better transportation who do not pay to use the highways or canals. Highways and canals generate new economic activity by making transportation easier, and the private investor has no way to charge all those who benefit from this new business activity. Government solves the problem by requiring everyone to pay taxes for the joint benefits they receive from economic infrastructure, and that infrastructure makes markets work better.

The legal system itself is the most fundamental of these infrastructures. Without a legal infrastructure, a market economy cannot exist. Law defines the ownership of property that makes it possible to sell land, goods, and services. The legal rules for buying and selling are established by contract law. And tort (or nuisance) law establishes the legal rules for the protection of persons and property by requiring compensation if either is wrongfully damaged. A government-funded court system ensures that those rules are followed. Law, in other words, establishes the conditions needed for market exchange and for the protection of persons and property in those markets.

In early America, the Post Office is a good example of how the government created incalculable benefits for the new country. There had been a limited postal system in the colonies that connected coastal towns, and some states had tried to set up post office services, but these did not reach outside of a state. Recognizing this limitation, the Constitution authorized Congress to establish a national postal system, which it did in the Post Office Act of 1789 and the Post Office Act of 1792.[68] As one historian concludes, the Post Office became "part of the very fabric that constituted the market for both goods and information."[69] The National Bank is another example. Once there is a central bank to manage the money supply and provide a standard currency, everyone will get the benefit of this investment regardless of whether they paid for it or not.

2.12 CONCLUSION

The founders, while fully realizing the dangers of autocratic government, were not anti-government. They accepted the extensive market regulation practiced in the colonies and continued it in the states. Historians credit Hamilton's initiatives with creating the conditions for growth and prosperity in the United States for the next 200 years. According to a prominent legal historian, James Willard Hurst, Hamilton was "a prophet of public policy 100 years or more ahead of this time."[70]

Even Hamilton's Anti-Federalist critics understood that government investments in infrastructure can promote economic prosperity and opportunity. Lin-Manuel Miranda, the author of the musical *Hamilton*, has the actor playing Thomas Jefferson admit the genius of Hamilton's financial system, even though he opposed it at the time.[71] In the musical, James Madison likewise celebrates Hamilton's contribution to the country when he recognizes that but for Hamilton, the United States would have been in bankruptcy.[72]

The mix of government and markets at the founding of the country could not and did not last in perpetuity. Politics prevents such stasis. Indeed, it is a hallmark of a democratic politics that we fight over how much power can be exercised by the government and how much power can be exercised by markets. That fight produced a pro-market preference that lasted from about 1828 through 1880. In between, however, the Lincoln administration returned to activist government to fight a civil war and reestablish many elements of Hamilton's American Plan. And the government, despite the preference for markets over government, engaged in additional infrastructure investments during the rest of this time. The mix of government and markets was adjusted, but also continued, as the next chapter takes up.

3

Abraham Lincoln's America

A Fair Chance

A group of historians was trying to find a way to recognize Abraham Lincoln's legacy for President's Day in 2012. Their problem was how to honor someone who was already one of the most revered leaders in American history. They decided to build a tower of books that had been written about Lincoln – 7,000 in all – and place it in the lobby of Ford's Theater, where President Lincoln was assassinated, which is now a national historical site in Washington, D.C., administered by the National Park Service. The tower was thirty-four feet tall, but it contained only about one-half of the approximately 15,000 books that had been written about Lincoln at the time. The stack has grown since, and more books have been written about Lincoln than any other person in the world except Jesus Christ.[1]

And there is more. There are 4,000 or more pieces of music about Lincoln including Aaron Copeland's magnificent work, A Lincoln Portrait,[2] which contains a narration of some of his most famous speeches. Narrators include "who's who in American life" such as Bill Clinton, Edward Kennedy, Samuel L. Jackson, and Barak Obama. There are dozens of movies that include Lincoln as a character including fictional biographical films about him, such as Henry Fonda's 1939 movie, Young Mr. Lincoln, and Daniel Day Lewis' 2012 film, Lincoln.

As the President, who saved the nation, fought the Civil War, and ended slavery, Lincoln stands tall, literally and figuratively, among American presidents and leaders. What is often less appreciated is that he is the father of the "American Dream." The phrase "American Dream" was coined in 1931 by an historian, James Truslow Adams, who spoke of a "dream of a social order in which each man and woman shall be able to attend to the fullest statute of which they are innately capable, and recognized by others for what they are, regardless of the fortuitous circumstances of birth or position."[3] Long before that formulation, Lincoln recognized that economic opportunity is a defining feature of America,[4] and that it was the government's responsibility to promote this goal. In a eulogy for Lincoln, the poet Ralph Waldo Emerson observed "This middle-class country has got a middle-class President, at last."[5]

Despite his actions, Lincoln retained the racial prejudices of white people at the time. But he also understood that the nation's commitment to liberty required the government to eliminate the barriers, particularly slavery, that denied people the opportunity to better themselves. For him, it was a matter of ensuring a "fair chance in the race of life."[6]

3.1 ANDREW JACKSON

Lincoln's views about the role of government differed from the understanding that prevailed for much of the nineteenth century. Andrew Jackson's victory in the 1820 presidential election ended the Hamiltonian policy of looking to the government as an engine of national power and economic growth. In its place, the political order favored small government and fostered the frontier ethic described in Chapter 1. Apart from the Lincoln administration, presidents and other political leaders were, for the most part, advocates for individualism and limited government until the 1880s.

Jackson became a nationally recognized war hero after he commanded the troops that recaptured New Orleans after the British had occupied the city during the War of 1812. Jackson's forces, about 4,500 regular Army troops, and a group of Black Americans, frontier militiamen, Choctaw Native Americans, and New Orleans aristocrats faced off against some 8,000 experienced British troops led by General Sir Edward Pakenham, brother-in-law of the Duke of Wellington. In the ensuing 30-minute battle, the British were soundly beaten and suffered over 2,000 casualties, while Jackson's troops lost fewer than 100 men.[7]

Jackson's status as an American war hero persists. A song sang by Johnny Horton, *The Battle of New Orleans*, about Jackson's victory was number one on the Billboard charts in 1959 for six weeks and is ranked number 28 in Billboard's top 100 songs from 1958 to 2008. It can still be heard from time to time on popular media.[8]

The election of 1828 offered voters a stark choice. Jackson, the war hero, was a self-made frontiersman, a country lawyer, an enslaver, and a supporter of individualism and local government. The incumbent, President John Quincy Adams, was an intellectual, the son of the second president, John Adams, and an enthusiastic supporter of the American System that he inherited from his presidential predecessors. He had been educated at Harvard, had been a Senator, and had served as a diplomat. Adam's ideas about government were organized around achieving the common good; Jackson stood for a simple, frugal, and unintrusive government.[9]

Jackson opposed the American System as seeding power to banks and wealthy individuals over the "common men" he represented. He claimed that "all such measures invariably aided the rich, the privileged, and the idle—the aristocracy—against the humble yet meritorious ordinary working people."[10] Jackson had reason for his antipathy toward the Bank and to those politicians and financiers that supported it. By way of example, Senator Daniel Webster was on the Bank's retainer list and was not embarrassed to remind the Bank to remit its fees to him if it wanted his continued support.[11]

Acting on these beliefs, Jackson refused to extend the charter of the National Bank started by Hamilton, and the economic stability it had provided, like "ballast in a ship's hull, floated away."[12] As an elite, Eastern, and powerful institution, the Bank was anathema to Jackson. He had a particular dislike of Nicolas Biddle, the head of the Bank, who was an urbane, sophisticated, renaissance man accomplished in literature as well as finance and not known for his excessive modesty.[13] Jackson also opposed the federal government's support of national infrastructure develop- ment. His veto of a National Road from Maysville to Lexington, Kentucky, ended federal road construction until the early twentieth century.

Jackson's emphasis on laissez-fairism was popular with many Americans. The American system that preceded Jackson had underwritten an economic expan- sion that was widely shared among farmers, small merchants, and others, who were engaged in entrepreneurial activities. The fact that the government had played a role in creating this relative equality was not readily visible to these voters. Instead, when Alexander de Tocqueville visited the United States, he found that Jackson's constituency saw their society as egalitarian and individualistic. Americans, he noted, "are apt to imagine that their whole destiny is in their own hands,"[14] not in the hands of the government.

3.2 HIDDEN GOVERNMENT

The Jacksonians' retreat from the American System, it turns out, did not end the government's efforts to promote economic prosperity. While some of the most vis- ible governmental efforts were curtailed, the federal government still had a signifi- cant impact on economic growth and individual opportunity. It is easy to lose sight of this effort, historian Brian Balogh notes, because it was a government "out of sight."[15]

During Jackson's time, the government licensed hundreds of government- chartered private companies for the purpose of constructing thousands of miles of turnpikes that facilitated the movement of goods and people in return for a toll charged by the company that constructed the road. The government also invested in canals that offered transportation services.[16] The 363-mile-long Erie Canal, which was constructed between 1817 and 1824, became the longest artificial waterway and the greatest public works project in North America.[17]

The federal government's efforts to ensure orderly development of Western lands were one of the most significant of these "hidden" investments. The 1783 Treaty of Paris ended the Revolutionary War, recognized several eastern states, and identified the largely uninhabited lands west of the Appalachians as U.S. ter- ritory. Americans, including George Washington, sought to develop these lands, and property disputes were common. To resolve conflicting claims and settle the territory, a committee of the Continental Congress, chaired by Thomas Jefferson, drafted the Northwest Ordinance of 1784. The Ordinance was later amended and paved the way to statehood for several states, protected land titles, and opened trading opportunities.[18] Surprisingly, perhaps, the Ordinance also outlawed slavery in these new lands.

As westward expansion continued, Jackson and his successors recognized that "[a]cquiring, exploring, surveying, and ultimately selling land was crucial to the nation's future and essential to most Americans."[19] The government was involved in exploring newly acquired lands, determining the price and quantity of the land to be sold, distributing land to individual settlers, financing their purchases, setting up a system of governance for the territories, and establishing when a territory could qualify for statehood.[20]

The Jacksonians also extended the postal system to the new territories, which facilitated Western expansion, employed thousands of workers, and constituted the country's first communications infrastructure. Regarding the Post Office, it has been noted that "[n]o other branch of government penetrated so deeply in the hinterland or played such a conspicuous role in shaping the pattern of everyday life."[21] The westward expansion of the Post Office was, if you will, the first Internet.

One action of the Post Office – the Pony Express – became the stuff of legend and was symbolic of the rugged individual's frontier mentality. Starting in 1925, Hollywood filmed no less than ten movies about the Pony Express and countless other westerns had scenes about this unique mail service. About 80 riders carried the mail between Missouri and California in ten days or less between 1860 and 1861. Riders switched from horse to horse at stations set up along the way for this purpose. When the first rider arrived in San Francisco, he was met with "tumultuous excitement as the streets filled with people cheering the event."[22]

Ignobly, the government also facilitated western expansion by using the military to relocate Native Americans and battle against the tribes that resisted relocation. The tribes were defending their land and their way of life, but most Americans perceived their resistance as a threat to the country's destiny. The legitimacy of their claims was lost in a sea of racism that reached the highest levels of government.

Before Jackson became a military hero because of the Battle of New Orleans, he gained a national reputation for leading military campaigns against Native Americans, and he made their removal from tribal lands one of his priorities as president. He signed the 1830 Indian Relocation Act that led to the removal of more than 70,000 Native Americans between 1830 and 1840 from millions of acres that their ancestors had occupied for generations in Georgia, Tennessee, Alabama, North Carolina, and Florida so the land could be used by white settlers to grow cotton. Those removed were forced to walk hundreds of miles to an area across the Mississippi River, which had been designated as "Indian territory." So many died on the way that the relocation has become known as the "Trail of Tears."[23]

3.3 THE LIMITED LIABILITY CORPORATION

Among the contributions of hidden government in the Jacksonian Era, the creation of the modern business corporation, has had the longest lasting impact on private sector development, growth, wealth, and power. Corporations are not natural persons. Rather they are creatures of government that have been at the forefront of shaping and growing the economy.[24] The 1937 celebrated book by Adolf Berle and Gardiner Means about the modern corporation observed, "Corporations have ceased to be merely legal devices through which the private business transactions of individuals may be carried on at…. The corporation has, in fact, become both a method of property tenure and a means of organizing economic life."[25]

Some form of business entity had existed for centuries, but companies began taking their modern form in seventeenth-century Britain when the Crown began issuing charters to firms to undertake certain businesses. These charters granted monopolies, such as the one granted to the East India Company on December 31, 1600, for the purpose of participating in the spice trade. The East India Company was more than a business firm; it was an arm of government. As a business, it was immensely successful and operated until 1873. During that time, it became the symbol of British colonialism, particularly in India and later in China where it established a monopoly of the opium trade in India which it then used to purchase much-desired tea, silk, porcelain, and other goods from China.

In colonial America, the Crown continued to grant charters to American businesses. After the Revolution, state legislatures granted these charters. Initially, the states issued corporate charters one by one, and they often followed the British model of granting a monopoly to sell a product or service to a corporation.[26] Beginning in the 1820s–1830s, however, there were two significant changes. The states passed laws establishing a general process for businesses to obtain a corporate charter, and those laws provided for the limited liability of the corporation after it was formed.[27]

Limited liability is the *raison d'être* of the corporation, and it is an attractive one. For persons who start a business, without corporate charter protection, all their personal assets are available to pay creditors or pay damages. Corporate charters, by comparison, limit payments to creditors to the amount of investment made into the corporation. No investor can go bust unless they put all of their money into the corporation.

Despite its importance to economic development, the creation of the limited liability corporation was hidden from public view because of the tendency to believe that property is natural, that its distribution follows a foreordained path, and that beneficial economic results flow from that natural state.[28] But the basic constituents of the corporation – property and capital – are not natural phenomena. They are social constructs fortified by law. In essence, publicly granted government charters protect the accumulation and concentration of private wealth.[29]

3.4 THE SPOILS SYSTEM

Andrew Jackson represented a break with the past. As this chapter related, he was the first president who was not from the upper-class Americans who occupied the presidency, and he considered himself as a man of the common people. He thought that previous hiring practices perpetuated an "aristocracy" who ran the government. He therefore fired almost one-half of the government's employees and replaced them with men from his political party.[30] He was unconcerned with expertise or experience because he believed the "duties of all public officers are, or at least admit of being made, so plain and simple that men of intelligence may readily qualify themselves for their performance."[31]

He was wrong about this. As one history of the period aptly put the matter, the "marriage of mass politics and public employment was happier for politics than for the public service."[32]

This system of party patronage became known as the "spoils system" after one of Jackson's supporters quipped, "To the winners go the spoils." Because of the lack of experienced and expert employees, the government stumbled in carrying out its functions. The situation became so bad that Jackson and his successors started to worry about the political consequences of having an unreliable workforce. They therefore retained or hired competent people to run what they regarded as essential governmental functions. The mail had to be delivered, pensions paid, and taxes collected.[33] It wasn't a failure all the way down, but it wasn't an effective government either.

The spoils system also created massive government corruption. Party workers appointed to government jobs were required to make contributions to the party as a condition of retaining employment to the point where their contributions accounted for up to 75% of all campaign contributions in the post-Reconstruction era.[34] As an additional source of funding, the parties openly sold public jobs.[35] The presidential election became a quadrennial "event," a historian has observed, "with [patronage] as the prize."[36]

3.5 FAIR CHANCE IN THE RACE OF LIFE

Lincoln returned the federal government to more visible efforts to promote economic development. He signed the National Banking Act of 1863 to revive the National Bank, killed off by President Jackson in 1833.[37] The new legislation made the national currency the only money supply by prohibiting the states from printing their own money. It also created a system of banks chartered by the federal government to promote the stability of the financial system. The Morrill Tariff of 1861 reestablished tariffs to protect domestic manufacturers from foreign competition.[38] And Lincoln's decision to charter the first transcontinental railroad to link the entire United States has been called the "greatest 'internal improvement' up to that time."[39] The government also invested directly in individual economic opportunity. The Homestead Act of 1862 made it possible for individuals and heads of families to own 160 acres of "unappropriated public lands" if they farmed the land for five years and paid a small fee.[40]

The opportunity to own land turned out to be a mixed blessing, however. Much of the land distributed under the Homestead Act was semiarid, making the small family farms that people homesteaded an "environmental impossibility."[41] While Laura Ingalls Wilder's fictional stories in *Little House on the Prairie* pictured the homesteads as a version of Lincoln's American Dream, the reality for many settlers was less than mythic. A biographer of Wilder documents how her father and husband went broke on multiple occasions, attempting to eke out a living on the small farmsteads in the Dakotas where the author grew up.[42]

Congress allocated the best lands to the railroads that they sold off to wealthier farming interests in large tracts that made farming more feasible and profitable.[43] Western homesteading and agricultural development sound friendly to family farming, but these early practices set the stage for large-scale farming and for the agribusinesses of today.

On a more egalitarian note, the 1862 Morrill Land-Grant College Act set aside 30,000 acres of public land for each senator and representative from a state to be used to create and support at least one college dedicated to agriculture and the mechanical arts.[44] One hundred and twelve universities were created because of the original legislation. A second Morrill Act passed in 1890 provided financial support to states for the creation of nineteen historically black universities.[45] The 1890 Act forbade the states from racial discrimination in admissions policy, but it allowed them to create "separate but equal" universities for Black Americans.[46] We will have more to say about public education below.

Hamilton saw the government's promotion of the economy as necessary to create the economic prosperity that was needed to pay off the country's debts, to finance the military in defense of the country, and to make the United States an important player in world affairs. Lincoln had a different motive. His starting point was Jefferson's identification of "the pursuit of happiness" as a fundamental political value and as a responsibility of government. As Lincoln explained, "The legitimate object of government is to do for a community of people, whatever they need to have done, but cannot do, at all, or so well do, for themselves in their separate, and individual capacities."[47] The government's central purpose, as he liked to put it, was to "clear the path" for Americans to achieve economic success.[48] Lincoln's American Dream, a historian observes, "was of a nation in which every man, by which he came almost to mean men and women of every color, had an unobstructed chance to rise in society by dint of their own preparation, strength and effort."[49] He sought to bring "economic opportunity to the widest possible circle of hard working Americans."[50] In Lincoln's own words, he wanted to give all Americans a "fair chance in the race of life."[51] That chance needed government initiative and support to succeed.

3.6 NEW BIRTH OF FREEDOM

The Civil War became the government's most significant and profound investment in equal opportunity. The North prevailed but at a cost of over 650,000 dead on both sides. In his address honoring the Union soldiers who died at the Battle of Gettysburg, Lincoln memorably linked the North's fight to win the Civil War with the quest to ensure a true equality:

> Fourscore and seven years ago our fathers brought forth, on this continent, a new nation, conceived in liberty, and dedicated to the proposition that all men are created equal. Now we are engaged in a great civil war, testing whether that nation, or any nation so conceived, and so dedicated, can long endure…. It is for us the living … to be here dedicated to the great task remaining before us— … that this nation, under God, shall have a new birth of freedom, and that government of the people, by the people, for the people, shall not perish from the earth.[52]

Lincoln became a national figure after a series of debates in a senatorial race in Illinois against Senator Stephen Douglas. The first debate in Ottawa, IL, drew about twelve thousand people who stood for three hours as Lincoln and Douglas debated. Douglas supported having each new state decide whether it would permit slavery or not when it entered the Union. Lincoln opposed this option because it would spread the denial of opportunity from the South to other parts of the country. The debates have been described as "the greatest argument over the American experiment since the constitutional convention."[53]

Lincoln's position in the debates was complicated. Using a word in common use at the time, he maintained that "there is no reason in the world why the negro is not entitled to all the natural rights enumerated in the Declaration of Independence, the right of life, liberty and the pursuit of happiness."[54] Yet he denied that he supported political and social equality between the races or that he intended to eliminate slavery in the Southern states, which was not politically feasible at the time because Southern members of the Congress would block the repeal. But he also believed that slavery would become abolished if it was prohibited in the new states because eventually there would be more votes in Congress for abolition than Southern votes to retain slavery.

The debates made Lincoln a leader in the Republican Party, and anti-slavery proponents were successful in making him the Republican candidate for president in 1860. His election prompted the South's secession prior to his inauguration, and when Southern forces fired on Fort Sumpter in Charleston, NC, the Civil War began.

In 1863, Lincoln used his power as Commander in Chief to issue the Emancipation Proclamation, ending slavery in the nation. Historians have debated why he waited three years to end slavery. Whatever twists and turns are found in his words and actions, it remains true that he rallied Northerners to fight a bloody civil war to prevent the South from preserving slavery by becoming an independent nation.[55] As Frederick Douglas remarked on the eleventh anniversary of Lincoln's assassination:

> It must be admitted … Abraham Lincoln was … in his associations, in his habits of thought, and in his prejudice, … a white man…. Our faith in him was often taxed and strained to the uttermost, but it never failed…. We … came to the conclusion that the hour and the man of our redemption had somehow met in the person of Abraham Lincoln.[56]

When the South surrendered at Appomattox, the United States had redeemed Jefferson's declaration that "all men are created equal." There would be a long road ahead to achieve that end – a road that this country is still on – but Lincoln's leadership started this journey toward a truer equality. This is his enduring legacy, but not the only one.

In pursuing a "right to rise,"[57] he created "a blueprint for modern America."[58] Government from this time not only found ways to make markets work better, work started by Hamilton, but it has also been committed to Lincoln's "right to rise." Lincoln revived the country's commitment to "all men are equal," and he notified the country that equality requires "equal opportunity." As the authors have pointed out, "Lincoln's presidency forever changed the contours of our country as well as the constitutional rules by which we live in favor of individual equality."[59]

3.7 PUBLIC EDUCATION

Public education – free schools open to all children, run by the government, and paid for by taxpayers – has been an instrumental part in achieving Lincoln's "fair chance in the race of life." Public education has not only benefited the children who have received it but it has also delivered economic and democratic benefits to the entire country. As the authors of a history of public education observe: "The American Dream … holds out a vision of both personal success and the collective good of all…. The public schools are where it is all supposed to start—they are the central institutions for bringing both parts of the dream into practice."[60]

The concept that education was important to both individuals and to the public at large dates to the colonies. Public provision and funding were slower to develop, but it is possible to find examples in colonial New England. In 1642, for example, the Massachusetts General Court, which despite its name was the legislature for the colony, required parents and guardians to ensure that children could read and understand religious principles and civil laws. In 1647, the colonial government in Massachusetts required towns consisting of fifty families or more to appoint a teacher of reading, and towns consisting of 100 or more families were also required to appoint a Latin teacher. The Court also mandated that the teachers' wages were to be paid "either by ye parents or masters of such children, or by ye inhabitants in general."[61] By the mid-1660s, some local communities in Massachusetts offered free classes.[62] By 1671, every New England colony except Rhode Island had adopted some form of compulsory public education "as a means of preserving their religious, social, and political beliefs by transmitting them to their children."[63]

Students living in the Middle Colonies attended a mix of private or parochial schools, but there was little or no general education for children in the South. Social class distinctions and the long distances between plantations stymied the development of a public school system.[64] Because wealthy planters used tutors to educate their children, they did not contribute to the education of the children of poor whites, and the education of those children was largely informal where it existed. Formal education of slaves was prohibited by law, and plantation owners provided little or no education for them because they regarded it as unnecessary and counterproductive to maintaining slavery.

After the Revolution, national political leaders supported public education to nurture democracy and spur economic progress. In the Land Ordinance of 1785, which addressed the distribution of land that original 13 states ceded to the federal government under the Articles of Confederation, the Continental Congress provided funding for local schools. The Ordinance, which was written by Thomas Jefferson, gave one section of land to each local township to sell and then use the money to establish a school for the children living there.

Jefferson had an extensive vision for education in the new country.[65] He proposed plans for an entire school system in Virginia, from elementary schools to colleges and universities. Public elementary schools would be open to all, regardless of the ability to pay. High schools, referred to by Jefferson as "academies," would be open to all able boys. William and Mary College, at the highest level, would offer scholarships to needy boys that could benefit from higher education.

Benjamin Rush, the most prominent physician in the country and a well-known public figure, argued that a free and uniform system of education would "render the mass of the people more homogenous and thereby fit them more easily for uniform and peaceable government."[66] This was of concern because the new nation was populated by immigrants from different countries with different customs, religions, and social understandings. The idea was to promote a democratic culture by fostering reverence for the laws and the Constitution. For Rush, education mattered not only for nurturing the infant democracy but also for economic growth and prosperity. Public support of education, according to Rush, would lower taxes because it would increase "the profits of agriculture and [promote] manufacturing."[67]

3.8 HORACE MANN

Despite this early and prominent support, progress was slow and sporadic in creating a nation of public schools funded by taxpayers. Battles over tax support and making the schools nonsectarian slowed the movement toward some form of public education at the elementary level.[68] A campaign by Horace Mann, the nation's most dogged advocate for free, universal, and nonsectarian schools, eventually overcame those and other obstacles.

Horace Mann, despite growing up in poverty, graduated from Brown College and became a practicing attorney, which in those days involved an apprenticeship rather than law school. He became a successful politician in Massachusetts, rising to be President of the Senate. He then became the administrator of the newly formed state Board of Education. From this position, Mann became a nationally known advocate for "common schools." The phrase "common school" referred to the fact that the schools for children six to fourteen were publicly maintained and financed, belonged to a community, and could be attended by all white boys and girls, all of which made the schools "one of all the people and 'common' to them."[69] For Mann and other advocates, the common schools could socialize children concerning respect for the law and other democratic norms, as well as equipping them to work in the economy.

Mann "sought to develop a school system and curricula that would diminish strife among a pluralistic people, supplant it with a common and universal patriotism, and instill respect for law and order."[70] He considered education as the "antidote to a plethora of social ills—poverty, crime, poor health, ignorance, sloth, and greed."[71] In a 1839 report, for example, he pointed out, "[i]t would, indeed, be most lamentable and self-contradictory, if, with all our institutions devised and prepared on the hypothesis of common intelligence and virtue, we should rear a class of children to be set apart, as it were, dedicated to ignorance and vice."[72]

Mann also set out to demonstrate that an educated public spurred economic development because educated workers were more productive, using a "surprisingly modern methodological argument."[73] Mann interviewed factory owners in Massachusetts and asked them to compare the productivity and usefulness of workers who were more educated to those who were less educated. Based on the information he gathered, he reported that more educated workers were 50 percent more productive. An educational historian points out that "the economic case for education was strong and consistent with the moral argument. Both required not random charity for the poor, but a systematic and universal commitment."[74]

The design of the common school reflected these goals. Public funding made education available without regard to parents' ability to pay for it. The inclusion of boys and girls meant that more of the population would be educated. At a time when women were second-class citizens in many ways, public schools offered an equal opportunity for boys and girls. By the middle of the 1850s, and likely before, boys and girls received about the same type of schooling until they were about 15 years old.[75]

The campaigners stressed that the universal nature of the common schools was the engine that drove the previous benefits. Since the schools were financed by the government, they were available to everyone, regardless of their financial situation. Since the schools also had no religious affiliation, they did not exclude children because of their religion. Finally, the schools were meritocratic in that they did limit access to higher grades to the most successful students, which was the model in some European countries.

Today's fights over textbooks and curricula challenge and confirm Mann's vision of a common school. The controversies challenge the vision by interjecting partisan politics into public education. The controversies confirm the vision as a matter of public interest worth fighting over.

3.9 EDUCATION AND THE RIGHT TO RISE

The common school movement fused together the governmental functions of making markets work better and supporting equal opportunity. Mann, like Hamilton, recognized that the government's investment in infrastructure was necessary when it was unlikely that markets would generate the level of investment that would benefit the country. Private schools can charge tuition, but they have no way to get the rest of the people in the country, who also benefit from having an educated citizenry, to pay for their education. And given the high costs of private education, too many children would be left out of the system. Correspondingly, private markets will not generate the amount of education that can benefit the country.

Having the government make the investment using tax dollars addresses this problem. As two historians of public education in the United States note, "America's approach to schooling was critically important to its technological dynamism, rapid economic growth, more equal income distribution, assimilation of great waves of immigrants, and transition to mass college education."[76]

The country's commitment to public education can be clearly seen during Reconstruction. After the Civil War, newly democratized state legislatures provided funding for public schools that benefited both the newly emancipated enslaved people as well as poor whites in the South since education there was restricted to the wealthy few. Unfortunately, Reconstruction ended almost before it began, and with its end, school segregation based on race was manifest.

These developments acted on Lincoln's recognition that the government should do for the people what they cannot do for themselves. By the start of the 1900s, more children in the United States received a basic education than anywhere else in the world. As compared to Europe at the time, where secondary schools were costly and often unobtainable, schools in America were free and generally accessible. The country experienced an expansion of high school and college education in the twentieth century that continued the basic premises of the common school movement: a commitment to basic demographic and egalitarian principles and to equality of opportunity. The public schools were becoming government by the people, for the people.

This success was incomplete, however. Black children and teenagers were restricted to segregated schools in the South, which were not equal, and in many cases not close to being equal, to those available to white children despite the 1896 Supreme Court case, *Plessy v. Ferguson*, which held that separate facilities for Black Americans were constitutional only if they were equal.[77]

3.10 CONCLUSION

The full play of American values was on display in the first two-thirds of the nineteenth century. With Andrew Jackson's election, voters indicated their preference for markets over government as individualism became a dominant value. This preference would continue until the 1880s, except for the Lincoln administration that returned the country to the American system of relying on government to stimulate economic prosperity. The history of this time reveals two additional significant developments.

The country's preference for relying on markets for economic development and opportunity slowed, but it did not end with using the government for this purpose. The federal government invested in developing economic opportunities as the country expanded westward, and state governments developed the system of corporate chartering that became the backbone of the American economy.

Lincoln linking the government's role in creating individual economic opportunity with the political value of equality was the second development. He recognized that "a fair chance in the race of life" required the government to do for individuals what they could not do for themselves. For the North, this commitment required fighting a Civil War to create a nation that did not enslave its Black Americans. It also meant supporting public schools – the common schools – as an engine of individual economic opportunity. This opportunity could only be realized if public education was provided by the government and not private markets.

Lincoln's definition of equality became a powerful idea – one that remains as significant today as when he articulated it – because it offers a vision of the country that fuses individualism and democracy. Two Lincoln biographers point out that it is "through the middle class 'dream' that Americans come to share common aspirations – aspirations that help mute the differences in wealth, culture, races, and ethnicity" and establish a "community bound by shared values."[78] At the same time, Lincoln's commitment to equality of opportunity requires both markets and government. When markets limit opportunity, the government's role is to do what individuals cannot do themselves – restore the American Dream.

4

Ida Tarbell's America

Markets for Everyone

The power of markets to change and build the American economy was in full display in the last half of the nineteenth century, but so was the potential to create social and economic ills for millions of workers and residents. As if the Civil War with 620.000 dead was not cataclysmic enough, the forces of industrialization, urbanization, northern migration, and immigration changed the face of America forever. The United States evolved from a localized, rural, and primary agricultural country, where people depended on local artisan-made goods, to a country with large cities, an urban population, widely available manufactured goods, and a national market.

The remarkable economic changes that occurred warrant the definition of an "Industrial Revolution," but this progress also had additional impacts.[1] The rapid growth of the cities quickly outpaced efforts to make them livable. Individual workers, let alone individual consumers, could not protect themselves from dangerous workplaces and products. Monopolists exploited their control of entire economic sectors to become very wealthy, and this concentrated and ostentatious wealth stood in dark contrast with urban slums and growing poverty. Journalists and thinkers like Ida Tarbell brought these changes to public attention.

Beginning in the 1880s, Populist and Progressive reformers campaigned for the government to respond to the social and economic challenges. The Populists, mostly Midwestern farmers, were squeezed by monopolies at both ends. As we describe in more detail below, they fought the high prices that monopoly railroads charged for shipping their grain and suffered the low prices offered by monopoly grain elevators to buy and store their grain. The Progressives, mostly urban activists, sought health and safety reforms to combat the threats to life brought on by increasing urbanization. Both groups sought common cause against Big Business, Big Finance, and Big Industry and were backed up by journalists, political writers, and lawyers who persuaded Americans that a new arrangement between government and markets was necessary. The reformers stirred up public demand for the federal government to assume the role of policing business behavior.

The idea that the government should protect people from being harmed and exploited in markets was not new to the country. As covered earlier, regulation of markets dated back to the colonies and continued in the states after the Constitution was signed. The federal government stepped in at this time because it became obvious that the states could not cope with the dramatic changes in the national economy. Federal action regulated the railroads, dismantled the oil, sugar, and oil trusts that had monopolized key markets, protected consumers from dangerous foods and drugs, and safeguarded workers, especially children, from exploitation. The government's responsibility for protecting the financial and physical health of the public continues to this day.

4.1 THE INDUSTRIAL REVOLUTION

The invention of the stationary steam engine and new machines and techniques in textiles, ironmaking, and other industries changed the nature of labor markets in the 1820s–1830s. Once machines were powered by steam engines, factory owners were able to move to cities where there was more available labor since they no longer had to locate next to the streams and rivers that had been used to power the turbines that ran the machinery.

This relocation of jobs changed the location of labor markets. In 1790, more than 90 percent of all American laborers worked in farming, but by 1890, there were more non-farm workers than farm workers.[2] The number of Americans living in cities increased to 39.7 percent by 1900 as compared to about 15.3 percent in 1850. Between 1850 and 1900, New York grew from 500,000 people to 3.5 million, and Philadelphia expanded from 100,000 to 1.2 million. Chicago became the fastest-growing city in the world during this time.[3] In the 1880s alone, 101 American cities doubled in size.[4]

The railroads, with assistance from the government, became another backbone of economic development. A national system of railroads allowed manufacturers to move their goods further distances, more cheaply and more quickly, and move them to more remote villages and towns. It facilitated mail delivery and the delivery of newly invented mail orders, and together with agricultural specialization, the railroads facilitated the creation of urban markets for an array of farm products. And, because railroads were not constrained by existing waterways, they could connect any two points they chose and, in the process, create new towns. In 1880, with the invention of refrigerated rail cars, Midwest meat producers and California fruit and vegetable growers greatly expanded their markets.[5]

The invention of the telegraph coincided nicely with the development of the railroads in creating a nationwide marketplace.[6] Just as telephone and electric lines once ran together and into our homes, telegraphs and railroads shared the same pathways. Samuel Morse developed his code in 1838, and on May 24, 1844, that code traveled over a telegraph wire from the U.S. Capitol to a rail station in Baltimore with the message "What hath God wrought?" Morse had high hopes for his invention. He believed "that the laying of telegraph wires across the American continent would bind the nation together into one people…."[7]

That is what happened. The telegraph quickly replaced the pony express as people across the country quickly shared information. Over 2,000 miles of wire were strung from Portland, ME, to Chicago and New Orleans by 1846. Two decades later, wires carried messages from coast to coast.[8] During the Civil War, the federal government operated telegraph lines and laid thousands of miles of new ones. They were returned to the private companies after the war.[9]

The country was shrinking and expanding at once. People could travel and communicate more quickly with each other, and their circles of friends, acquaintances, and business associates grew accordingly. Speeding up the distribution of financial information was particularly significant because it allowed the formalization of trading floors such as the Chicago commodities exchange that opened in 1848.[10] News distribution was of singular importance. The Associated Press was formed in 1846 by a group of newspapers that wanted to share expenses covering the Mexican–American War. The AP and Western Union established a network of telegraph wires and offices that extended to the smallest towns and villages in America.

While the steam engine led to the growth of American manufacturing and the dramatic growth of American cities, it was coal mining that fueled the steam engines and provided a source of heat for many Americans. American industry relied on wood and whale oil well into the nineteenth century until coal marked the country's first energy transition. As steam engines dominated transportation, coal entered our energy portfolio and stayed there well into the twenty-first century. Pennsylvania mines became the major source of coal in the United States during most of the nineteenth century. Coal also powered the steam locomotives that revolutionized transportation in the country.

On August 27, 1859, the liquid black gold of Edwin Drake's first oil gusher in Titusville, Pennsylvania, joined coal as a fuel for the Industrial Revolution. Drake never capitalized on his discovery; he bounced around from job to job and lived in poverty. He returned to Pennsylvania in 1870 where the legislature rewarded him a pension. The birth of the modern oil industry also began in 1870 when John D. Rockefeller, together with his partner Henry Flagler, founded the Standard Oil Company in Cleveland, Ohio.

4.2 EDUCATION EXPANDS

The Industrial Revolution demonstrated the capacity of markets to generate tremendous economic growth and prosperity. Accompanying that growth and prosperity, the country experienced a new need for education. The "revolution" needed workers in the new markets and government answered. Government support for education became an infrastructure investment that fueled additional economic growth.

As Chapter 3 related, government support for public education dated to before the Constitution, but it was the common school movement that made public elementary education a national achievement. The Industrial Revolution had another significant impact on the country – it created a demand for high school educated workers. Workers with a high school education were needed for office jobs, known at the time as "business work," such as bookkeepers, clerks, and managers. These better-paid workers soon formed a new "middle class" in the country.[11] By the turn of the century, the growth in these and other white-color jobs created the opportunity for higher pay, and this in turn increased public support for expanding education.

Most Americans had six to eight grades of education by the middle of the 1800s because of the common school movement. As the economy developed, communities responded by building and staffing high schools. By 1920, there were high schools in most parts of the country including in rural and remote areas. By 1940, the average young person was a high school graduate.[12]

As with the common schools, the quality of education varied, and the South lagged behind other parts of the country. For the well-off, private schools and private tutors were available, and the rest of the students had to make do with schools that were largely inadequately supported. Black American students, who had to attend segregated schools, were the worst off, as Chapter 7 will cover in more detail. Despite these significant gaps in educational opportunity, the high school movement was "an extraordinary educational transformation" – one that would "make the United States the first national in the world to have mass secondary education."[13]

4.3 IMMIGRATION, TENEMENTS, AND SLUMS

The Industrial Revolution not only generated extraordinary wealth, it produced mass immigration, and the result was tenements, slums, and unlivable cities. There were three migrations. In one, a flood of people moved from rural areas to the cities to take advantage of the new manufacturing jobs that were created. Another migration witnessed Black Americans fleeing an oppressive Jim Crow South only to find slightly less oppression and segregation in the North.[14] Additionally, cities grew because of masses of Europeans who flocked to this country with the hope of finding a better living than in their home countries. Between 1865 and 1900, there were 13.5 million immigrants who moved into tenement neighborhoods in New York and other cities.[15] By 1910, more than 65 percent of those working in mining and manufacturing were foreign-born or the children of immigrants.[16] By 1910, immigrants made up about 40 percent of the population of the 12 largest cities and about 14 percent of the total population.[17]

Manufacturers were able to keep wages low because of the large pool of potential employees. Cheap labor fueled the rapid growth of manufacturing. It also fueled urban misery. The words "tenement" and "slum" became part of the country's vocabulary to describe the overcrowding, unhealthy conditions, inadequate sewage disposal systems, and desperate poverty in the cities.[18]

4.4 DANGEROUS WORKPLACES

The surplus of workers also left them unable to complain about harsh and often dangerous conditions in their workplaces. The results were grim. It is estimated that an average of about 35,000 workers died each year from 1880 to 1900 as the result of their work-related injuries, and another one-half million were injured.[19]

The fire at the Triangle Shirtwaist Company in March 1911 epitomized the dangers of slum manufacturing. As fire rapidly spread through the cramped garment factory, located on the 8th, 9th, and 10th floors of a building in lower Manhattan, 146 young women, many of whom were recent immigrants from Europe, were trapped and lost their lives. The building had only one fire escape; workers had trouble getting to it because managers had locked the doors on the floors to prevent theft; there were only a few buckets of water to put out fires, and firefighters did not have ladders tall enough to reach the fire. When the building finally collapsed, the fire became the deadliest tragedy in New York history until September 11, 2001, when terrorists destroyed the World Trade Center buildings.[20]

Child labor was also routine and legal as industry grew after the Civil War. Children as young as 10 years old or younger worked in factories and mines, but also on farms, in retail stores, and in home-based industries. According to the 1900 census, more than one in five children were employed, up from one in eight children in 1870.[21] Children routinely had working days of 10 to 14 hours, worked with machinery that ran so fast that small fingers, arms, and legs could easily be caught, leading to serious injuries and deaths, and they worked in factories full of fumes and toxins dangerous to the health of young children, leading to illness and chronic conditions suffered later in life.[22]

Some years ago, one of the authors and his children ran across an unexpected demonstration of the dangerous working conditions of children when they visited the Eckley Miners' Village. The village is a replica of a mining town at the foot of one of the coal mines in eastern Pennsylvania that operated in the 1850s–1880s. It was built as part of a 1970 Hollywood movie, *The Molly Maguires*, which portrayed the miners' efforts to fight the oppressive and unsafe workplaces. The film depicts the efforts of a Pinkerton detective, played by Richard Harris, to infiltrate the Molly Maguires, a secret society of Irish American coal miners, who were led by Jack Kehoe, played by Sean Connery. The miners were engaged in a violent struggle against the mine owner to obtain better pay and working conditions.

In a museum in the village, there was a set of two pictures, one on top of another, taken when the miners and their families lived in the company town at the foot of the mine. In the top picture, there is nothing but a fog that obscures whatever the photographer was photographing. In the bottom picture, there is a conveyor belt full of coal, and children, some quite young, are sitting on each side of the belt. The caption explained that the children were employed to sort the pieces of coal by size as they came down the conveyor belt. The caption also explained that because the belt was running in the top picture, the coal dust obscures the scene almost entirely. The bottom picture was taken after the photographer asked that the conveyor belt be shut down.

4.5 CONSUMER GOODS

The development of factory manufacturing and national markets provided millions of consumers with lower-priced goods, but it also increased their danger of eating contaminated food or taking either useless or dangerous medicines. In unregulated marketplaces, merchants were free to lie and mislead the public about the goods that they were buying and to substitute cheaper and more toxic ingredients in foods and medications.

Merchants peddled hundreds of types of patent medicines high in alcoholic content or fortified with dangerous amounts of morphine, opium, or cocaine. Remedies were advertised and sold for about any ailment including venereal diseases, tuberculosis, colic in infants, indigestion, dyspepsia, and even cancer. As the Smithsonian Museum of American History recounts, "Unscrupulous manufacturers greatly exaggerated the curative powers of their remedies, selling them as 'panaceas' or 'cure-alls.' The aptly named Swaim's Panacea purportedly cured all 'blood diseases' including scrofula, chronic rheumatism, ulcers, old sores, boils and carbuncles, diseases of the spine, catarrh, and wasting."[23] Physicians and medical societies warned the public that the so-called medications did not work and could be dangerous, but despite these warnings, sales were brisk, and adults and children died after taking some of them.[24]

4.6 MONOPOLIES

The industrialization of the country was related to the development of the business corporation in the early part of the century. As the last chapter related, states developed laws that replaced individual legislative chartering of businesses with laws that allowed individuals to take on the corporate form of doing business more easily. The primary asset – the very definition of a corporation – lies in its capacity to limit its financial liability. While this characteristic facilitated entrepreneurship and innovation, the lack of restrictions on corporations allowed them without restraint to engage in shady business practices and monopolize entire industries.

Matthew Josephson memorably described Jay Gould, Cornelius Vanderbilt, Henry Huntington, John Pierpont Morgan, and William Whitney as the "robber barons" for their ambition, dubious financial techniques, and business failures that twice dragged the economy into major depressions. John D. Rockefeller, another prominent robber baron, monopolized oil production in the country using "a catalog of collusion and corruption, harassment, intimidation, and outright thuggery."[25] For example, he made an alliance with the three major railroads that ran through Cleveland, and they agreed to reduce the cost of shipping oil to Rockefeller and pay for the reductions in price by raising the price that they charged independent oil producers to ship their oil.[26] This made it impossible for the independent producers to compete with Rockefeller and many sold out to him. Soon Rockefeller was in a position to control not only oil transportation but to gobble up the refineries as well. These maneuvers enabled Rockefeller to consolidate and monopolize the oil business.

Most state laws that chartered corporations did not allow one corporation to buy stock in another one, but Rockefeller and other robber barons got around that restriction using a legal "trust." Because a trust was not a corporation itself, it could own the stock of many other companies, which enabled the robber barons to own entire industries. For example, a handful of individuals, including Cornelius Vanderbilt, Leland Stanford, and Edward Harriman, controlled all of America's railroads, which accounted for 15 percent of the nation's business.[27] As another example, Rockefeller's Standard Oil Company controlled 90 percent of oil production and 85 percent of all petroleum sales.[28] More than 4,000 firms merged into 257 surviving entities from 1897 to 1904.[29] Trusts in railroads, tobacco, agricultural equipment, steel, and banking among others, "held 40% of US manufacturing assets and boasted a capitalization of $7 billion, seven times bigger than the US national debt."[30] The result was that 300 trusts held dominant positions in a variety of key industries by 1904. The trusts dominated markets; they dominated the economy; and their excesses needed to be addressed.

4.7 GILDED AGE

The monopolists became fabulously wealthy. At a time when there was no income tax, William H. Vanderbilt, Cornelius's son, had an income of $10 million in the 1880s ($339 billion today), while Rockefeller's income was around $100 million in 1907 ($2 trillion today). The average family income was under $500 during the same time. This lopsided distribution of wealth was reflected in an 1890 estimate that less than one percent of the country's families controlled more than 50 percent of the wealth of the country.[31] A more recent estimate found that only 200,000 people had control of 70 percent of the wealth in the country at this time.[32]

In 1873, Mark Twain and Charles Dudley Warner published *The Gilded Age: A Tale of Today*, a novel about American greed and corruption at this time in American history, and the name stuck as a description of the fancy carriages, top hats, ball gowns, debutantes, and disparities of wealth. Henry Adams' 1880 book, Democracy: An American Novel, criticized government to the same effect. Adams was a well-known American historian who was a descendant of two U.S. presidents. He published the book anonymously because of its not-so-veiled attack on the political corruption that was occurring.

Recently, a lavish HBO series, *The Gilded Age*, dramatized the extraordinary lifestyles of the rich. Julian Fellows, who wrote the series, also wrote the popular BBC series, *Downton Abbey*, about a rich aristocratic British family. Fellows explained that the Americans were "[n]o longer content to pattern themselves on European nobility, these capitalist barons began spending their money 'in an American way.' They didn't just buy country houses in the middle of 40,000 acres — they built vast palaces that were 15 feet away from the one next door' in New York and elsewhere."[33]

One country mansion, the Biltmore House in Asheville, NC, became and remains the largest single-family home in the country. As visitors to this 250-room French Renaissance chateau learn, it has four acres of floor space, 35 bedrooms, 43 bathrooms, and 65 fireplaces. The home was built by George Vanderbilt, Cornelius' grandson, who purchased 125,00 acres in the North Carolina mountains as his estate. The same family still owns the house and operates it as a tourist venue.

4.8 SURVIVAL OF THE FITTEST

A laissez-faire philosophy, which dominated political thinking from the 1820s to nearly the end of the century, was used to justify economic arrangements that made a relatively few very wealthy and led to a harsh and dangerous life for the many. As discussed in Chapter 3, support for limited government dated back to the 1828 election of Andrew Jackson as president. Jackson's enthusiasm for limited government was based on a belief that government efforts to make markets work better favored economic elites and the wealthy. The supporters of limited government during the Industrial Revolution had to find other justifications for limited government since they were the very economic elites that Jackson loathed as the enemy of the common man.

The success of a few and the misery of many others were defended by referring to Adam Smith's book, *Wealth of Nations*, published in 1776. These defenders asserted that Smith claimed the economy operated according to a "unified natural order, operating according to natural law, and if let to its own course producing results beneficial to mankind."[34] The author of a popular 1873 book extolling this claim defined these "natural" laws as based "on nothing less solid than the will of God."[35] Since the marketplace operated according to divine intervention, there was a natural morality that justified the extreme economic inequality that had occurred. Government intervention, it was said, could only make matters worse since it interfered in the natural order of things.

Another supporter of unfettered capitalism, Hebert Spenser, adopted an economic version of Charles Darwin's theory of evolution. While Darwin proposed that the organisms that survive in their environment are the ones most suited or "fit" to live and reproduce successfully, Spenser claimed that the same was true as a matter of economic competition. The success of the wealth industrialists was, according to Spenser, simply a natural process of the "survival of the fittest."[36]

These claims about competition, natural selection, and the survival of the fit meshed easily with the country's commitment to individualism, self-reliance, and small government as the keys to liberty. But they made a stronger claim to those commitments – unfettered markets were baked into the DNA of markets; any government regulation of markets would retard social progress; and, further, government interference was immoral because it contradicted the God-given nature of the way that the world works.[37]

Despite their professed belief in laissez-faireism, businessmen did not hesitate to accept government assistance when it was beneficial to them. As two historians note, "Social Darwinists produced an ideology tailor-made for business interests. Industrial magnates and the business community enthusiastically took up the slogans of laissez-faire—an irony since at the same time big business lobbied the federal government increasingly energetically for what amounted to millions of dollars in preferential treatment."[38]

A good example, noted earlier, was the free land the government gave the railroads in the early 1800s. There were even more extensive cessions of public land in the second half of the century. These grants and loans, which totaled tens of millions of dollars,[39] made it easier for the railroads to acquire the right of ways that they needed to construct their lines and then sell off unneeded land for a profit. As early as 1868, the railroads established departments to promote Western settlement.[40] Government also provided the troops that completed the eradication of Native Americans that had begun earlier in the nineteenth century, led by Andrew Jackson.[41]

"The exaltation of laissez-faire into a quasi-official creed," the historian Arthur Schlesinger notes, "was a conjuror's trick. Most of the worshippers at the shrine of undefined private enterprise found the new cult entirely compatible with government assistance to business."[42] According to another historian, laissez-faire capitalism simply meant hands off the capitalists, not hands off the economy.[43]

4.9 RETHINKING AMERICA

Beginning in the 1880s, political activists, muckraking journalists, political writers, and elected officials advocated for changing the mix of government and markets to address the social and economic challenges of industrialization. The reformers argued that monopolies, trusts, and other businesses not only undermined competition, but these practices also undermined democracy. Because the trusts were so large and able to dominate the economy, they also had overwhelming political influence. Reformers set out to take back democratic control by attacking laissez-faireism and by exposing the political corruption that kept elected officials from responding to the obvious economic and social problems that were occurring.

For the first time, the policing of business became a function of the federal government, giving birth to the modern regulatory state. In response to the Populist and Progressive political movements, the government transformed itself. Democracy functioned to redefine the relationship between government and markets. Elections and political pressure led to the government assuming the job of protecting people from the market and political misbehavior that was occurring.

4.10 THE POPULISTS

The Populist political movement in the 1870s led to the first significant change in the mix of government and markets. The Populists were farmers and local merchants who lived in areas of the country, mostly the mid-West, that were served only by one railroad. The railroad's monopoly allowed it to charge farmers high prices to ship their goods to distant markets. Adding insult to injury, because farmers typically only had access to one grain elevator that could store their grain and load it on railroad cars, the grain merchants also price gouged the farmers.[44] Then, at the other end of the line, railroads would charge high prices to local merchants, farmers, and consumers for transporting the goods they purchased from those more distant markets. What the Populists wanted, one historian explains, was "above everything else a form of government regulation that would eliminate these 'arbitrary' rate practices."[45]

The Populists turned first to state government, and the responses varied. Some states formed an agency headed by a single elected commissioner who had the authority to investigate the railroads, but any change depended on the state legislature passing new laws. Other states established an agency with a multimember commission that had ratemaking authority backed by substantial penalties.[46] Both systems failed because the Supreme Court held that a state could not regulate shipping that was part of interstate commerce, which meant that no state could regulate local traffic that eventually ended up outside of its borders.[47]

The failure of state regulation created pressure on Congress to act, and it responded by creating the Interstate Commerce Commission (ICC), which was authorized to hear complaints about railroad practices and to undertake investigations on its own initiative.[48] The ICC was largely ineffective because of legislative compromises necessary for its creation that limited its authority, and because of adverse court decisions that limited its power.[49] After Congress enhanced its oversight and enforcement powers in the Hepburn Act of 1906,[50] the ICC became the model for the regulation of business by the federal government. The ICC "provided the building block upon which the administrative state of the twentieth century subsequently rose."[51]

4.11 THE PROGRESSIVE MOVEMENT

The Progressive movement united religious and middle-class citizens, journalists, political writers, and politicians who battled against the business trusts, anticompetitive industries, and corrupt politicians. Both movements had a significant role in overcoming the survival of the fittest justification that claimed markets operated according to natural, or Divine, laws that could not be changed without harming the country. Assisting both groups were journalists – known as the muckrakers – who educated the public about the underhanded and monopolistic business practices of the robber barons and other unscrupulous corporations. These writers and the two movements influenced politicians, such as Theodore Roosevelt and Woodrow Wilson, who supported laws to address some of the worst aspects of the Industrial Revolution.

By recognizing that the country now had a national market system, the Progressive Movement taught the country that only a national government could protect the public from market behavior that injured their pocketbook and their safety. By emphasizing the connection between democracy and the mix of government and markets, the Progressive Movement reminded the country of how a national conversation about that mix was at the heart of achieving the nation's fundamental values.

4.12 THE MUCKRAKERS

Journalists, such as Ida Tarbell, were instrumental in puncturing the myth that wealthy industrialists were merely the beneficiaries of a natural order of competition in which the best and fittest businessmen prospered because they were the best and fittest businessmen. As these journalists established in detailed investigative articles and books, there was nothing divine about their success – they had cheated and clawed their way to great wealth using nefarious business practices.

Tarbell was on the staff of *McClure's*, a magazine first published in January 1903, which featured detailed journalistic investigations of the corruption and illegality, which accompanied the Industrial Revolution.[52] Her book, *The History of the Standard Oil Company*, first serialized in *McClure's*, catalogued how John D. Rockefeller monopolized oil production in the country using all available means of unfair and crooked competition. She described Rockefeller as a "living mummy," adding, "our national life is on every side distinctly poorer, uglier, meaner, for the kind of influence he exercises."[53]

Tabell and her family learned firsthand how Rockefeller's Standard Oil excelled at corporate concentration and monopolization. Tarbell's father was an independent oil producer in Hatch Hollow, which at that time was a prosperous Western Pennsylvania oil town, until "a big hand reached out from nobody knew where, to steal their conquest and follow their future. That mysterious hand belonged to none other than John D. Rockefeller...."[54] As related earlier, Rockefeller found a way to use the railroads to drive other oil producers, including Tarbell's father, out of business. Tarbell's father resisted selling to Rockefeller, but the struggle proved to be too great.[55] His business partner eventually committed suicide because he lost his business.[56]

As legend has it, when Harriet Beecher Stowe was introduced to Abraham Lincoln on Thanksgiving Day, 1862, his response was "So you're the little woman who wrote the book that made this great war." This dramatic story about the influence of one author on the course of U.S. history is not true, but Tarbell did have such an impact. After reading her book, Theodore Roosevelt, who as president led the fight to regulate monopolists like Rockefeller, took her to lunch at the Colony Club in New York to express his appreciation for the book and how it educated the public about the need for government intervention.

Upton Sinclair's famous novel, *The Jungle*, similarly educated readers and politicians about how food producers cheated them without regard for their health or safety. In telling the story of an immigrant who worked in Chicago's meatpacking industry, Sinclair exposed the intolerable working conditions in the plant, the deceptive practices the meat packers used to sell adulterated products, and the vermin, animal feces, human blood, and body parts that went into the meat people ate. The novel, which was translated into dozens of languages, was read by millions of people. One reader, President Theodore Roosevelt, appointed his own team of investigators, who supported Sinclair's "thinly disguised" fictional account of the risks posed by the packinghouses to employees and consumers.[57] Sinclair said he was attempting to call public attention to the working conditions and the horrible treatment of animals, but the public's outrage concerned their health risks. "'I aimed at the public's heart,' he said, 'and by accident I hit it in the stomach.'"[58]

Roosevelt described Tarbell, Sinclair, and other journalists as "muckrakers,"[59] which referred to their efforts to "rake" through the "muck" of the Industrial Revolution to expose the corruption and illegality that were all too common in the country's rapid evolution from an agrarian to an industrial society. Tarbell disliked TR's description, but there is little doubt her muckraking efforts inspired changes in the relationship between markets and government that have lasted to this day.[60] The muckrakers were joined by Progressive thinkers, and together they had an impact on the country's politics and policies.

4.13 HEBERT CROLY

The muckraking journals and books explained the ruthless suppression of competition that had occurred. Political writers, such as Herbert Croly, argued that economic arrangements are politically determined, and that as markets evolve, the government must evolve as well to preserve democracy and protect the American Dream.

Croly's book, *The Promise of American Life*,[61] contended that how Americans thought about government had not caught up with the Industrial Revolution. The quaint, mythic view of America pictured people living in small towns with neighbors who ran small, local businesses and were citizens and community leaders as well. If Americans ever lived that way, they no longer did. Instead, the country had become more of a Hobbesian world where businessmen faced a stark choice "between aggressive daring business operations, and financial insignificance or ruin."[62] Given such a choice, a businessman could either compete fairly and face ruin or could engage in the same tactics as the robber barons to try to survive.

Aggressive businessmen could pursue anticompetitive strategies because they were not constrained by state or local laws. The "net result" was "the establishment in the heart of the American economic and social system of certain glaring inequalities of condition and power." Large corporations became dominant "on a scale unprecedented in the economic history of the world."[63]

Croly saw a parallel development in the political sphere in which political machines came to dominate urban politics through specialization, organization, and illegal behavior. Rather than act as a constraint on the accumulation and concentration of corporate power, political machines facilitated its development; it needed to do so for its own survival. As Croly pointed out, "This alliance between the political machines and the big corporations – particularly those who operate railroads or controlled municipal franchises – was an alliance between two independent and coordinate powers in the kingdom of American practical affairs."[64]

Croly warned that the concentration of both corporate and political power posed a significant threat to democracy. His antidote was a new sense of the role of government as a countervailing force to the growing power of private organizations. If life in a modern political economy was a Hobbesian war of all against all, then public power should be brought to bear against, compete with, and balance private might. Croly was a writer and political thinker. The movement also needed lawyers.

4.14 LOUIS BRANDEIS

Louis Brandeis was a Boston lawyer, social reformer, and, later, a Supreme Court justice. He was also an important intellectual and synthesizer for Progressive thought. More than any other social reformer, he "stood as the opponent of big business and monopoly."[65]

In *Harper's Weekly*, Brandeis focused on the role of banking in facilitating the business and political dominance of the trusts, and those columns were then compiled into a book, *Other People's Money*.[66] The book noted how large businesses had turned to the large banks to borrow money because the smaller, local banks could not provide the necessary capital. The large banks used dispositors' money – "other people's money" – to exert control over the business decisions of the companies that borrowed money as a condition of lending them money. They saw the advantage of monopolization, and they found ways to become partners with the trusts in monopolizing the economy and making more money. The large banks owned stock in the companies, charged the businesses high commissions to lend them money, took control of companies using seats of the board of directors, and scripted the "great wave of mergers."[67]

Brandeis blamed banks for reducing competition by financing trusts, creating businesses that were too large to be effectively managed or innovative, and giving the business in which they were involved preferential treatment at the expense of other companies as well as consumers.[68] He also called the close link between banks and corporations "political despotism." Like Croly, he argued that the lack of regulation meant that these businesses had overwhelming political power and that the accumulation of political power was inimical to an effective democracy. The bottom line for Brandeis was that the "existence of large centers of private power" is "dangerous to the continuing validity of a free people" in a democratic society.[69]

4.15 CONGRESS RESPONDS

Congress responded to the Populist and Progressive movements by establishing for the first-time significant federal regulation that policed business behavior. The Sherman Antitrust Act of 1890 authorized the Justice Department to sue companies engaged in abusing competition.[70] The Food and Drug Act (FDA)[71] and the Meat Inspection Act,[72] both passed in 1906, attacked the problem of dangerous drugs and foods. Legislation in 1917 established the Federal Trade Commission (FTC) with authority to stop deceptive and unfair market practices.[73]

Each of these statutes was aimed at monitoring and managing industrial abuses of economic power that disadvantaged workers and consumers.[74] Along with the Interstate Commerce Commission (ICC), this legislation put the federal government into the business of policing national markets to protect the financial and physical well-being of consumers. As said earlier, this function of government was not new – the colonies and then the states had done the same thing. But now that there were national markets, a national government response was necessary, as Croly pointed out.

4.16 PRESIDENTS RESPOND

Political candidates also picked up on public agitation for a new mix of government and markets. Teddy Roosevelt, popularly known as "TR," campaigned for "genuine democracy" – a "democracy economically and politically." Recognizing the hold that laissez-fairism had on the country, TR told audiences, "This, I know, implies a policy of government interference with social and economic conditions in this country than we have yet had, but I think we have got to face the fact that such an increase in government control is now necessary."[75]

Roosevelt was known to the public as an outdoorsman. His time in the West, his African safaris, and his charge up San Juan Hill characterized him in the public eye as rough and ready. But Roosevelt was also a careful reader. Not only did he learn from books like Ida Tarbell's, but he also absorbed the lessons of Upton Sinclair's *The Jungle* and Herbert Croly's *The Promise of American Life*. Big business was perfectly legitimate; however, laissez-faire, as practiced by his predecessor, William McKinley, allowed too much room for corporate chicanery. Most notably, the dominance of the trusts threatened both capitalism and democracy from Roosevelt's perspective. For Roosevelt, the seizure of economic policy by the trusts was a "serious corruption of the democratic system" because private organizations were imposing a mix of government and markets that allowed them to unfairly extract wealth from small businesses and common citizens and illegally crush competition.[76]

Woodrow Wilson warned voters that the trusts and large corporate combinations had the motivation and means to capture democracy and make sure that public policy served their own interests, not the common good. In his inaugural address, Wilson promised that the government instead would be "at the service of humanity, in safeguarding the health of the nation, the health of its men, women, and children, as well as their rights in the struggle for existence." Invoking the nation's fundamental values, Wilson announced his intention to "square our every process of our national life with the standards we so proudly set up at the beginning and also have carried in our hearts."[77]

4.17 TR AND ANTITRUST

Roosevelt was wary of the power that a banker, JP Morgan, exercised over both the railroads and over Wall Street. With Morgan's help, rail magnate James J. Hill and some of his former rivals, including Rockefeller, formed the Northern Securities Company as a trust to monopolize western railroads. He ordered his Attorney General to begin legal action under the Sherman Act. The litigation was successful and upheld by the Supreme Court as the first great case prosecuted under the Sherman Act.[78]

Roosevelt had taken on Morgan; could he take on Rockefeller? Standard Oil was the country's first trust, and its control over the oil industry was near total. The oil giant had to be prosecuted because of its "Rockefeller rebates." "That single word, 'rebate,' one editorial observed, dominated Tarbell's chronicle of Standard Oil; every successful step Rockefeller took to 'corner the oil interest of the country' could be traced to the secret freight rates he obtained from the railroads."[79]

At Roosevelt's instigation, Congress passed the anti-rebate Elkins Act in 1903 to bolster the Sherman Act. Armed with both antitrust acts, Roosevelt's Justice Department sued Rockefeller under the Elkins Act for using illegal rebates. The case was tried by Judge Kennesaw Mountain Landis, who later became the first commissioner of major league baseball. Judge Landis ruled that the rebates were in fact illegal and for each of the 1,462 carloads of illegal oil that was shipped, a $20,000 fine was imposed for a total of $29,240,000. This was an extraordinary fine for the time. Yet, Rockefeller was blasé. "He was on a golf course when the word of the judgment reached him. 'Judge Landis,' he complacently predicted '[w]ill be dead a long time before this fine is paid.'" Rockefeller was right; Landis's ruling was overturned.

Rockefeller was less successful when the Department prosecuted him under the Sherman Act. Its lawsuit to break up Standard Oil was largely based on the facts in

Tarbell's history of the company.[80] The Department of Justice won, and the lower court's ruling to dissolve Standard Oil was upheld by the United States Supreme Court in 1911.[81]

If Rockefeller was not concerned about the Landis ruling, he could have been nothing but ecstatic about the Supreme Court's decision to break up his company into 34 separate units. Prior to the Court's decision, Rockefeller owned 25% of Standard Oil. After the decision, he then owned 25% of the 34 resulting companies, the effect of which was to see his wealth increase from $300 million to $900 million.[82]

Despite this irony, TR's Justice Department had accomplished what the Progressives set out to do – end the domination over the economy of the monopolistic trusts. From here on, the government had the authority to reign in the power of companies over markets when that power was acquired by anticompetitive methods. Entrepreneurs were free to make large fortunes by inventing new products and forms of business, but they could no longer do so by putting their competitors out of business using unfair and deceptive acts and practices.

4.18 POLITICAL CORRUPTION AND INFLUENCE

The Progressives were also concerned with political corruption and influence. To address legislative corruption, states adopted voter-registration laws, secret ballots, the direct primary, and an initiative and referendum process to give voters more say about legislation. The basic idea, as Al Smith, four-term Governor of New York famously explained was that "[a]ll of the ills of democracy can be cured by more democracy."[83]

The Progressives also attempted to protect the new regulatory agencies from being corrupted by political influence. Their solution was to make "neutral competence" the centerpiece of the regulatory system. The government would hire "experts" with problem-solving capacity using science, economics, and other bodies of expert knowledge. They would be protected by a civil service system that stopped administrators from replacing them except for legitimate work-related reasons. These steps would remove the field of administration "from the hurry and strife of politics."[84]

Woodrow Wilson, then a professor of government at Princeton, argued that "politics sets the tasks for administration" and the bureaucracy takes on the "detailed and systematic execution of public law."[85] Wilson saw this bifurcation as protecting public administration from the corruption that could be found in the legislative arena. He stressed that administrators must carry on a conversation with the public about what they are doing, but he also stressed that this conversation would be about the merits of public policy, rather than the doing of political favors. He, like other Progressives, wanted to separate the administration of regulation from "partisan politics" and foster a broader conception of politics that involved a more democratic conversation about a proper mix of government and markets.[86]

4.19 CIVIL SERVICE REFORM

Having supported legislation to require government employees to be hired based on expertise and experience, the Progressives turned to the concern that the founders also recognized: how do you ensure that government employees will be responsive to their political leadership and effective in carrying out their mission? The founders had depended on the character of those they hired and added political supervision and reporting requirements. The Jacksonians, by comparison, had relied on party allegiance and the threat of being fired from a job to keep employees in line with the administration's directions. Since the government was now too large to be supervised personally by the president and cabinet members, the Progressives had another idea.

The Progressive Movement demanded an end to government corruption and incompetence, but Congress routinely voted down reform legislation. Sixty-four civil service reform bills were introduced in Congress between 1864 and 1888, and all of them failed. Congress did not respond because the political parties simply did not want to give up the financial benefits to them of the spoils system.

It took the assassination of a president to get Congress to act. On July 22, 1881, Chester Garfield, the newly elected American president, was scheduled to leave Washington by train for an extended trip through New England. As the president entered the train station, he was shot by Charles J. Guiteau, a disappointed job seeker who had been hectoring President Garfield for a job. The President lingered for 80 days before dying from his injuries.

The Pendleton Act of 1883 that established the basic structure of the civil service is still used today. The Act banned mandatory political contributions by government employees, and it adopted a merit-based selection system to hire employees that involved testing a candidate's fitness for the job and hiring those with the best examination results. Although merit-based hiring originally applied only to 11 percent of government appointments,[87] it now covers all but about 4,000 of the two million federal employees.[88] About one-half of federal workers are hired based on competitive examinations, and the other one-half, such as lawyers and scientists, are hired based on their credentials and training.[89]

The idea that civil servants would be both competent and responsive to their political leadership based on training and professionalism may seem like a fanciful idea – more idealistic than practical. To the contrary, the creation of an institutional culture of responsiveness is basic to the management of corporations and is used every day by managers to ensure employees conform to the goals of a company.[90] Reliance on a corporate culture is particularly useful when it is not possible to give detailed instructions or monitor compliance with such instructions.[91] Government, like business, uses the norms that managers establish for appropriate and responsible behavior. The key expectation has been "neutral competence," and the government has successfully relied on this expectation since the Progressive Era.[92]

4.20 CONCLUSION

In the Industrial Revolution, the genius of markets in creating economic progress and prosperity was on full display. So was the potential of markets to limit the freedom and liberty of consumers and workers by subjecting them to financial and physical harm. The fact that the balance between government and markets was off-kilter became more and more apparent. Despite the undue influence of the wealthy on the political system, the Populist and Progressive movements led to a readjustment of that mix. For the first time, the federal government took responsibility for policing business behavior. There was no other choice. The country now had national markets, and it needed national regulation.

Despite the dominance of laissez-faire thinking for much of the nineteenth century, the government continued to invest in infrastructure, particularly the railroads and public education in the states. Both investments spurred the economic progress that was occurring. At the same time, the federal government's investment in infrastructure was corrupted in favor of large businesses that were only too happy to sing the song of market freedom but take favors from the government when it suited them.

The government's assumption from the states of policing business behavior set a precedent that continues to this day. As markets continue to change, posing new problems and issues, the response has been to change the mix to address the new developments. As taken up next, the failure of the market system in the Great Depression of the 1930s paralyzed the country, and people turned to the government for help.

Government is not intrinsically opposed to businesses or markets. Instead, the government creates and monitors markets, and it stays out of the way as transactions occur. To a point. Once businesses distort, manipulate, or cheat markets, then both competition and citizens suffer. So does the common good and so does the democratic values of equality, liberty, and fairness. To fix the balance, restore market competition, and promote the general welfare as asserted in the Constitution, the government steps in with its corrective hand.

5

Franklin Delano Roosevelt's America

Saving Capitalism

For most Americans, a commitment to the laissez-faire approach of the previous decades evaporated in the aftermath of October 29, 1929, known as Black Monday, when the stock market collapsed and sent the country into the deep, devastating Great Depression. Up to that point, the government was so strongly committed to a hands-off approach that it did not even keep statistics on unemployment.[1] Ironically, just before the crash, Jack Yellen and Milton Alger wrote the upbeat song *Happy Days Are Here Again*. With the crash, Americans really did need a reason to see that "the skies above were clear again" and that they could "sing a song of cheer again." Campaigning for president, with *Happy Days* as his theme song, Franklin Delano Roosevelt told desperate Americans, "I pledge you, I pledge myself, to a new deal for the American people."[2]

Millions of Americans, who were in desperate shape or feared they would soon be, elected FDR in a landslide that gave the Democrats control of both houses of Congress by substantial margins. As President and with an overwhelming majority in Congress, FDR engineered the largest expansion of government in the country's history up to that point in time. Between 1933 and 1938, the New Deal passed 30 significant pieces of legislation to support emergency spending, manage the economy, regulate banking, Wall Street, and labor markets, and establish income support programs for unemployed, elderly, and disabled Americans.[3]

Once again, democracy became the vehicle by which Americans adjusted the role of government to match the new economic and social conditions in the country. And once again, the Roosevelt administration relied on the old playbook. The government's investments in infrastructure and its reliance on management of the money supply updated Hamilton's actions at the start of the country. New banking and securities laws were a continuation of policing market behavior that the national government assumed in response to the Populist and Progressive movements. And the nationalization of social welfare programs augmented poverty assistance in the states and cities that dated back to the beginning of the country.

What was different between the late nineteenth and early twentieth century reforms and the New Deal was the scale of FDR's activities. There had been a colossal failure of the market system, and a colossal response by the government was needed. When much of the country was mired in deep poverty, most everyone lacked the freedom to better themselves. FDR's New Deal sought to bring back happy days as it harkened back to Lincoln's definition of government as doing for Americans what they could not do for themselves.

Nevertheless, many of the wealthy regarded the New Deal as a gross interference with "free markets" and FDR as a traitor to his upper-class background and wealth.[4] This sentiment was captured by a 1936 Peter Arno cartoon in *The New Yorker* that shows a fur-clad matron who says to her obviously affluent friend, "Come along. Let's go the Trans-Lux [a movie theater featuring newsreels] and hiss Roosevelt."[5] Most other people disagreed. As a historian points out, "his admirers vastly outnumbered his detractors. How else to explain his unprecedented four terms in the White House?"[6] By restoring a market economy that had all but disappeared, FDR did not betray capitalism; he saved the market system from destroying itself.

5.1 OUT OF WORK, OUT OF LUCK

Margaret Bourke-White one of the most famous photographers of her era, shot a picture in 1927 that shows a long line of Black men, women, and children lined up to get food and clothing from a Red Cross relief station after a devastating flood in Louisville, Kentucky. They are standing in front of a large billboard that pictures a white family in a car with beaming faces and a caption that says, "World's Highest Standard of Living. There's No Way Like the American Way." Burke's picture became one of the defining images of the Great Depression because of the irony of this juxtaposition, even though it was taken before the October 1929 stock market crash.[7] Later, Walker Evans' photographs of Dust Bowl families and impoverished tenant farmers in the South graphically showed the pains of the economic want suffered by millions.[8]

After Black Monday, the New York Stock Exchange began a three-year decline that lost nearly 90% of its value compared to its high point on September 3, 1929. During the Jazz Age, Americans were encouraged to buy stocks to an unprecedented extent, which led to a significant expansion of consumer debt during the 1920s. Then millions of investors were devastated when the stocks they owned lost most, if not all, of their value in the crash, and they had no way to pay back the money they had borrowed. National income fell from $312.6 billion to $217.1 billion in a little over a year, investment fell from about 15% of the gross national product to 1%, while unemployment increased to 25% of the workforce as compared to 3% before the crash. Over 10 million Americans were out of work, and one-half of those who had jobs were employed part time.[9]

A 1932 song, *Brother Can You Spare A Dime*, popularized by Bing Crosby, came to epitomize the fate of the country. The song, which was written for a Broadway show called *New Americana*, departed from other popular songs of the time, such as *Happy Days Are Here Again,* by focusing on the loss of the American Dream for millions of people. The lyrics ask "why the men who built the nation – built the railroads, built the skyscrapers – who fought in the war, who tilled the earth, who did what their nation asked of them should, now that the work is done and their labor no longer necessary, find themselves abandoned and in bread lines."[10] The authors, Yip Harburg and Jay Gorney, were at a loss for the title of the song until they took a walk in New York Central Park, when they were approached by a man who asked them, "Brother can you spare a dime."[11] By a stroke of fate, Harburg turned to song-writing after the appliance company he co-owed went broke in the beginning of the Great Depression.[12]

The economy can adjust to a mild downturn and recover without government intervention if investors and consumers take advantage of falling prices by making additional investments or buying additional goods and services. If, however, there is a steep and sudden decline, this self-recovery mechanism will not work. Investors and consumers will not be able to adjust their economic behavior in time to stimulate an economic recovery. Even if markets will eventually recover, it can take years to do so, and in the meantime, millions of people will face reduced economic circumstances, and many others will find themselves in deep poverty.

Knowing that the economy would not recover on its own any time soon, FDR promised "bold, persistent experimentation." As he explained, "It is common sense to take a method and try it: If it fails, admit it frankly and try another. But above all, try something."[13] He surrounded himself with a "brain trust," advisors from business, law, and academia who had different views about how to return the country to economic prosperity.[14] FDR, true to his promise of experimentation, adopted many of these ideas. One of the key innovations was the first successful application by a nation of the economic theory of Lord Alfred Keynes, a British economist.[15]

5.2 LORD KEYNES

John Maynard Keynes, who studied and taught at Cambridge, was hardly a dull academic. He was an early member of the Bloomsbury Group, a collection of writers and artists, including the painter Duncan Grant and the art critic Clive Bell, who lived near each other in Bloomsbury, an area of London. They gathered there and at the country home in the English countryside of Venessa Bell, a painter and interior designer. Privileged, wealthy, and rebellious, the writers and painters, including Keynes, the only economist, lived unconventional social lives including various liaisons with each other. Keynes ended up marrying a Russian ballerina. He became a savvy art collection whose collection, donated to Cambridge University, was valued at $70 million in 2013.[16] It may be that his participation in a group of radical thinkers encouraged Keynes to break with economic orthodoxy and redesign the economics of managing downturns.

The standard response to an economic downturn had been to reduce spending to avoid a deficit due to lower tax revenues. Keynes recognized that this step added to the decline in economic activity that was occurring. Instead of fiscal austerity, he recommended deficit spending to put more money in people's pockets that they could use to make investments as well as purchase goods and services. Keynes' insight was that deficit spending would spur an economic recovery, and as the economy recovered, increased tax revenues would reduce deficit spending. Keynes' plan was a new policy idea in a more complex economy, but it was consistent with Hamilton's plan for the government to invest in ways that would build economic opportunity and prosperity.

Following Keynes' prescription, the New Deal engaged in deficit spending to jump-start the demand for goods and services by providing consumers with money to spend.[17] Government initiated a wide range of stimulus efforts including lending money to homeowners to refinance their mortgages to allow people to keep their homes,[18] guaranteeing home loans issued by lenders that submitted to federal regulation to boost home sales and construction,[19] lending money to farmers to keep them in business,[20] and, as discussed in more detail below, hiring millions of workers to improve the nation's infrastructure including national forests and parks, highways and roads, public art, and to build dams to control flooding and generate electricity,[21] such as the Boulder Dam in Nevada and dams built by the Tennessee Valley Authority (TVA). The infrastructure investments provided millions of jobs.

True to Keynes' prediction, government spending spurred an economic recovery, but the country did not fully recover until World War II when federal defense spending put the economy back on its feet. One reason for the delayed recovery was that the Depression was so deep that the country was struggling to return to normality even with the government's infusion of money into the economy. It is also true that FDR, having engaged in a first round of Keynesian spending, reverted to the traditional economic policy of cutting costs and balancing the federal budget, but he abandoned this effort in 1937 when the economy fell back into a decline, which led to the "Second New Deal," an additional round of spending and investment.

5.3 SAVING THE BANKS

The first effort to improve economic conditions occurred days after FDR took office. By the time Roosevelt became president, more than 9,000 banks had failed because of the financial chaos triggered by the stock market crash.[22] Banks do not keep all the money that is deposited, but instead loan it to people, which provides the credit that the economy needs to grow. This is possible during normal times because not everyone with money in a bank will want to take it out at the same time. During a sudden downturn, though, people are afraid the bank will go broke, and they rush in to withdraw their money. The new administration feared this run on the banks would lead most of the banks in the country to fail.

This is the same fear of a bank collapse that George Bailey faced in *It's a Wonderful Life*. In this 1946 movie, a Christmas fantasy, Clarence, played by the British actor Henry Travers, is a neophyte angel who has been sent to earth to help George Bailey, played by James Stewart, after Bailey decides the only way to prevent a run on his bank is to commit suicide. Then, Bailey's widow could use the money from his life insurance to repay the $8,000 in deposits that George's uncle had accidentally lost.

Clarence stopped Bailey from jumping off a bridge by showing him what the world would be like without him. The fantasy demonstrates how George's life, including loaning money to townspeople to own their own houses, had made his family and his neighbors better off. Returning to reality, George returns to his business as the townspeople arrive with a laundry basket full of money and other valuables to keep the bank in business. The community knew George and his good works, and they trusted him. The movie, which the American Film Institute ranked as the most inspirational film of all time, is still a popular Christmastime favorite.

As in the movie, FDR knew he could only save the banking system if depositors trusted that banks in the normal course of business would have sufficient funds to allow them to withdraw money. FDR therefore declared a four-day bank holiday two days after being inaugurated. Three days later, Congress passed the Emergency Banking Act,[23] which authorized bank regulators to determine whether a bank was fiscally sound enough to reopen, authorized the Treasury to make loans to the fiscally sound banks, and enabled the Federal Reserve to issue currency to support the loans.[24] Having put the banking system on sounder footing, Roosevelt went on nation-wide radio the night before the banks were to reopen to explain why Americans could trust the banking system.

The president told the 60 million people listening, "I can assure you that it is safer to keep your money in a reopened bank than under the mattress." He asked Americans to have "confidence and courage," and not be "stampeded by rumors or guesses." This was the first of many such "informal" radio talks that were nicknamed "fireside chats" because FDR spoke from the White House Diplomatic Reception Room, sitting next to a fireplace. While conversational, his talk and those that followed were carefully scripted.[25] Roosevelt's address is seen as averting a widespread panic caused by a wide-scale bank run.

Having temporarily saved the banking system, the New Deal set out to prevent a recurrence of the banking crisis. The Federal Deposit Insurance Corporation (FDIC) was established in 1933 to insure individuals' bank accounts, initially for $2,500 in 1933 and increased to $5,000 the next year.[26] Today, depositors are covered up to $250,000 for each account. Because the insurance, paid for by a tax on the banks, reassured the public that their funds were safe from a bank failure, the legislation ended the threat of a run on the banks. In addition, the Banking Acts of 1933 and 1935 gave the Federal Reserve new and expanded powers to regulate banks and manage economic conditions as one way of avoiding another severe recession.[27] As covered later, the Fed used this authority to address the subprime mortgage crisis that occurred in 2007 from causing even more distressing economic damage.

5.4 THE ONLY THING TO FEAR IS FEAR ITSELF

The Great Depression hit hard; a hardness captured in the iconic photographs of Margaret Bourke-White and Walker Evans, mentioned earlier, together with those by Dorothea Lang Berenice Abbott and others. Those depictions show the pain and fear in the eyes of ordinary Americans who were sick, hungry, and uncertain about the future. Speaking to this despair, FDR told the country at his first inaugural, "[L]et me assert my firm belief that the only thing we have to fear is fear itself— nameless, unreasoning, unjustified terror which paralyzes needed efforts to convert retreat into advance."[28]

The films of Frank Capra during the 1930s spoke to people's fears, and like FDR's promise that "happy days are here again," the films reassured people that Americans would overcome the harms that were being visited on them through no fault of their own. His films, as a film scholar explained, show "compassion towards the common American" and demonstrate "that when people work hard and hold together," they can "help not only themselves, but one another."[29]

Three of his most popular films show those traits. *It's a Wonderful Life* contrasted the "good banker," George Bailey, with the "evil" bankers that had caused the Depression. In *Mr. Smith Goes to Washington*, described in the beginning of this book, the honest politician, Smith, takes on the corrupt political system and prevails. Good also prevails over evil in *Mr. Deeds Goes to Town*. Deeds, played by Gary Cooper, moves to a small town in Vermont and plans to share an unexpected inheritance with those in need. When a greedy lawyer attempts to stop Deeds from giving away his money by having a court to declare him insane, he is saved by a reporter, played by Jean Arthur, who was part of the original plot to get Deed's money but who decides instead to help him after becoming aware of his essential goodness.

In each of these films, Capra simplifies the struggles of Americans as a battle of good versus evil, and Capra maintains that good will prevail over evil if people have compassion for their fellow Americans as they find ways to help each other overcome those who selfishly think only of themselves. Capra was popular, in other words, because he was able to "disguise the social, political, and economic problems presented by the Great Depression and gave the people something they had lacked: hope."[30]

5.5 JOBS, JOBS, JOBS

Perhaps more than anything else, the vast unemployment in the country robbed people of any hope of a future. FDR acknowledged that "a host of unemployed citizens face the grim problem of existence, and an equally great number toil with little return," and our "greatest task is to put people to work."[31] Job creation was another form of government investment, an investment in human capital. Of the many responses to unemployment, several New Deal programs stand out, and, in many instances, we continue to enjoy their fruits.

If you live in the rural Pacific Northwest, then it is likely that you receive electricity from the hydroelectric projects at the Bonneville Dam or the Grand Coulee Dam. If you live on the East Coast and have visited Manhattan, you may well have traveled through the Lincoln Tunnel. If you live in Middle America, then you may have visited a local post office or federal courthouse. And if you have vacationed almost anywhere in America, you have probably enjoyed the beauty of a national park that dates back to the 1930s. In each instance, you have touched the physical reality of the New Deal because these projects were constructed as part of the Public Works Administration (PWA). The PWA was "authorized to spend $3.3 billion in pump-priming construction projects"[32] and it "oversaw tens of thousands of infrastructure projects, from repairing roads to building dams, as well as cultural and arts initiatives."[33]

A companion program, the Civil Works Administration (CWA), ultimately employed nearly 4 million workers who laid 12 million feet of sewer pipe, built or upgraded 500,000 miles of roads, 40,000 schools, over 3,500 recreation areas, and nearly 1,000 airports.[34] The CWA also employed 50,000 teachers for rural and adult education and hired 3,000 artists.

Additionally, the Federal Works Progress Administration (WPA) consisted of five job programs for unemployed artists in various media. As its director, Harry Hopkins, said of the artists, "they've got to eat like other people."[35] The WPA enabled many people in the arts to continue their careers and produce notable literature and art for years to come. The Federal Writers Project supported authors including Nelson Algren, Saul Bellow, John Cheever, Ralph Ellison, Zora Neale Hurston, Claude McKay, and Studs Terkel. The Federal Art Project, created to provide work relief for painters, sculptures, muralists, and graphic artists, employed among others the photographers mentioned earlier and painters such as Jackson Pollock, Lee Krasner, Mark Rothko, Arshile Gorky, Diego Rivera, and Louise Nevelson.[36] Those artists' New Deal work can still be seen, particularly in public murals. And the Federal Theater Project and the Federal Music Project provided jobs for out-of-work artists, musicians, directors, and actors, including the likes of Arthur Miller, Orson Welles, John Houseman, and Elia Kazan. It was a twofer. Artists were employed, and the public enjoyed their works and performances.

Another jobs effort, the Civilian Conservation Corps (CCC), employed 3 million young men ages 18 to 25 who were primarily on government assistance. They earned a dollar a day and were required to send $22–25 a month back home to their families, which supported many more people. To provide jobs for women, Eleanor Roosevelt established She-She Camps as a counterpart to the CCC. Government spending on constructing and running the camps became a significant source of revenue for nearby communities.[37] Yet the program did have an important downside. Although the CCC began as a racially integrated program, it eventually became segregated.

The Corps was principally engaged in reforestation and conservation and helped shape today's national and state park systems. Over the course of its tenure, the CCC planted over 3 billion trees, reforested many parts of the United States, and built over 800 state parks. The "CCC employees fought forest fires, planted trees, cleared, and maintained access roads, re-seeded grazing lands and implemented soil-erosion controls. Additionally, they built wildlife refuges, fish-rearing, water storage basins, and animal shelters."[38]

5.6 MANAGING SUPPLY AND DEMAND

The Great Depression was unprecedented in American history, and Roosevelt's advisors gave different advice about what to do about it. Some believed that deficit spending would not be sufficient to pull the country out of its economic tailspin because the economy had deteriorated to the point that it would not generate enough new demand to reverse the downturn. They proposed that the government directly control supply and demand.[39] FDR, having promised experimentation, did not settle on deficit spending as a response; he also tried a second approach to restarting the economy that involved economic planning.[40]

In 1933, Congress created the Agricultural Adjustment Administration (AAA) to address falling farm prices.[41] Despite the reduced demand for farm products, farmers continued to grow and sell their products to pay their mortgages and other expenses. Some money, even a small bit, was better than no money. This new agency was authorized to pay the producers of corn, cotton, hogs, tobacco, rice, and tobacco to reduce their output and compensate farmers for their loss of income. A tax was levied on processed food to pay for the subsidies.[42] A study of the results at the time indicated that the program did increase farm income in absolute and relative terms,[43] but the improvement was limited by the reduced demand for farm and other products that was occurring at the same time.[44] After the Supreme Court declared the AAA to be unconstitutional,[45] Congress replaced the 1933 AAA legislation with the Agricultural Adjustment Act of 1938, which functioned in a similar manner.[46]

The National Industrial Recovery Act of 1933 (NIRA) had the ambitious goal of preventing price cutting as business firms struggled to attract new customers.[47] The President and his advisers believed that this practice led to firms going out of business because they did not have enough revenue to operate. They were also concerned that it resulted in reduced wages being paid to workers, which reduced their ability to make purchases that would aid in economic recovery. To support industry, the NIRA suspended antitrust laws and required companies to write their own codes of fair competition.[48] Those codes facilitated fixed prices and wages, production quotas, and entry restrictions. In short, the NIRA promoted industry price-fixing.

As a biographer of Roosevelt put the matter, the NIRA had "birthing problems."[49] The code-writing process not only produced more than 500 overlapping codes that largely reflected the preferences of the largest companies and ignored input from workers and consumers, compliance was spotty, and the codes failed to end the price cutting that was occurring.[50] In 1935, the Supreme Court declared the law to be unconstitutional,[51] and the administration made no attempt to replace it. Government regulation of industry is one thing; government-authorized price-fixing by industry itself is another. The former is constitutional; the latter is collusion.

The AAA and the NIRA were outside of the historical purposes of the government. Never previously and never since has the government attempted to engage in such industry-wide economic planning to change supply and demand in the economy. The idea is entirely hostile to the mix of markets and government that is the basis for organizing the country to achieve our national values. The government invests in economic prosperity, regulates market conditions to protect people, and establishes help for those most in need. It is a mark of the desperation of the New Dealers and FDR's willingness to experiment with what works that this movement to industrial planning and away from markets occurred.

5.7 NEW DEAL REGULATION

While propping up markets, the New Deal also expanded government policing of market behavior by responding to business practices that contributed to the nation's economic woes. There was new regulation of stock markets, banking, and labor markets. The pre-New Deal regulatory initiatives rested upon the assumption that minor government policing could ensure a smoothly functioning market. If tainted meat or ineffective or adulterated drugs posed health problems, then a government agency was charged with fixing that limited, identified problem. But the Depression put to rest this constrained view of national power. By the time the New Deal was done, many areas of the economy came under government policing.[52]

After Congressional hearings revealed that state regulation had failed miserably to prevent financial institutions from the irresponsible and misleading behavior that led to the crash, Congress passed the Securities Act of 1933,[53] the Securities Act of 1934,[54] and the Public Utility Holding Company Act of 1935[55] to regulate the sale of securities and related activities that had led to the Great Recession.

Congress also passed the Glass-Steagall Act in 1933 to require the separation of commercial and investment banking.[56] Commercial banks held deposits from consumers, while investment banks arranged for the sale of securities to the public and invested in those securities as a way of making money. Congress separated the two so that the failure of an investment bank would not jeopardize the financial security of depositors in commercial banks. As readers will learn, Congress ended this requirement in 1999 at the behest of the Clinton Administration, and once again, the failure of investment banks in the subprime mortgage crisis of 2007–2010 threatened commercial banks. This time around, however, depositors knew that their accounts were safe because of the FDIC insurance.

The National Labor Relations Board, established in 1935,[57] set out to manage the tumultuous relationship between labor unions and employees that had led to prolonged strikes and considerable violence. One history of labor relations notes that labor violence "probably claimed several thousand lives and left countless others maimed and traumatized" from "beatings, lynching, chaotic riots and mob violence; arsons, bombings, and sabotage; assassinations; even military-style skirmishes between armed combatants."[58] By recognizing workers' right to form a union, the legislation intended to give employees the power to protect their own financial security and safety through collective bargaining.

5.8 ANOTHER KIND OF REGULATION

Just as nineteenth-century railroad regulations and federal financial support built out rail transportation, New Deal regulations built out the country's infrastructure in electricity distribution, natural gas distribution, air transportation, and radio communications. Harkening back to Alexander Hamilton, this was done by protecting new firms from possibly harmful competition that might prevent them from earning adequate revenues as these industries were developing. Following the example of the Interstate Commerce Commission, the government also regulated the prices that regulated entities could charge consumers. The aim was to prevent these businesses from taking advantage of the limited competition by charging exploitive prices.

In 1920, Congress created the Federal Power Commission (FPC) to coordinate the development of hydroelectric plants throughout the country.[59] The Army Corps of Engineers, an agency that traces its history to April 26, 1775, when it built the defensive earthworks at Bunker Hill, built most of the federally regulated dams. Congress then significantly amended the Act in 1935 to extend the FPC's regulatory authority to the rapidly developing electric industry.[60] This same regulatory scheme was also applied to the natural gas industry in 1938.[61]

In 1934, the newly created Federal Communications Commission (FCC),[62] replaced the prior Federal Radio Commission to regulate interstate communications by wire, radio, telegraph, telephone, and broadcast. Although the FCC had no price-setting authority, it did have licensing responsibilities that assigned frequencies, set standards, and labeled telecommunications operators as common carriers with an obligation to use radio in ways that benefited the public interest.

In 1903, Wilber Wright steadied the wings of the airplane that he had built with his brother Orville. As his brother released a restraining wire, the plane took off for a 120-feet flight on the beach at Kitty Hawk, NC. The development of an aviation industry was off and flying. In 1911, the Post Office started using airplanes to carry the mail. Earle Overton became the first pilot to carry the mail when he dropped mailbags from his biplane to the ground in Mineola, New York, which were picked up by the city's Postmaster, William McCarthy. In 1925, the Air Mail Act gave a bigger boost to the developing airline industry by authorizing the Post Office to contract with private airlines to deliver the mail.[63] The country had come a long way from the Pony Express. To protect its investment, the government was authorized to regulate the aircraft that carried the mail including licensing pilots and aircraft.[64]

By the 1920s, airline companies began to carry passengers – an experience that was nothing like today's flights. Only the richest people could afford to fly; cabins only had a few passengers, and the cabin crew served them with "fine food and drink." On the other hand, passengers usually experienced long, noisy, risky, and turbulent flights. A famous football coach at the University of Notre Dame, Knute Rockne, was killed in a 1931 crash, and a United States Senator, Bronson Cutting of New Mexico, died in another airline crash four years later.[65] Congress responded by creating the Civil Aeronautics Board (CAB) in June 1938 to ensure the safe and successful development of the industry and to protect passengers.[66] The CAB licensed both pilots and planes, and it also awarded routes to individual carriers and regulated their air fares.[67]

Note the relationship between government and markets in these industries. By licensing interstate electricity, oil, and natural gas transportation, as well as licensing radio stations and airlines, national industries were created in the energy, telecommunications, and air transportation sectors. Government support during the New Deal was not unlike the government support of water and rail transportation in the nineteenth century. Similarly, national banking and securities regulation sustained a national financial system. In short, though, these regulations stimulated the development of national industries at the cost of competition.

There was an agreement of sorts between the government and markets. In exchange for regulating some aspects of these industries, the licensed firms enjoyed a competitive advantage because market entry was restricted to qualifying firms as market competition was reduced. At the same time, government regulated prices to protect consumers or took other actions for the same purpose.

During the Depression, the economy needed economic expansion, and the New Deal believed the protection of newly developing industries was a way of returning the country to normal. In the 1970s and 1980s, as covered later when we describe deregulation during the Carter and Reagan administrations, Congress ended the experiment of government command-and-control regulation of these markets because economic conditions in them had changed.

5.9 SOCIAL SECURITY

By 1935, the crisis had deepened. The Works Project Administration (WPA) had provided jobs for millions of people, but the WPA provided jobs to only one out of every four applicants. Those millions who could not find work, along with the aged, handicapped, and orphans, turned to state and local governments for assistance. Many of the states could not handle the burden. Some cut the size of the grants so that more of the needy could receive some assistance. Others abolished all assistance. The state of New Jersey offered the indigent licenses to beg.[68]

Passed to stem the crisis of poverty, the Social Security Act of 1935 revolutionized the nation's approach to social welfare programs.[69] At the beginning, the country followed the approach of the Elizabethan Poor Laws adopted in England in the 1600s and continued that approach for nearly two hundred years. The English and Americans distinguished between the impotent poor, who were unable to work and were eligible for direct assistance, and the able-bodied poor, including children, who were legally required to work. The impotent poor were the only persons eligible for direct financial assistance. The able-bodied were expected to work because "[t]o be poor was not merely the result of social circumstances or the fate of nature; lurking in the background must be some element of slothfulness."[70]

This first break with this penurious approach to poverty occurred in the aftermath of the Civil War. In addition to hundreds of thousands of fatalities, the Civil War produced over 2 million veterans, an untold number of whom were disabled and unable to work and care for themselves and their families. In response, new pension programs were created. In the North, federal government pensions began in 1862 under which a totally disabled private would receive $8 a month. In the South, the former Confederate states created their own programs. As an historic curiosity, the last civil war pension of $73.13 was paid in May 2020 to Irene Triplett, the daughter of Moses Triplett, who was disabled after deserting the Confederates to join the Union army.[71]

Social Security became and remains one of the government's most successful efforts to reduce poverty. It replaced state and local general assistance for four categories of poor persons: the elderly, the blind, the disabled, and dependent children, more familiarly known as Aid to Families of Dependent Children (AFDC). The Act also provided benefits for the survivors of persons eligible for retirement and disability benefits.[72]

Social Security was marketed to the public as "social insurance" to maximize public support considering the public antipathy to helping the poor that had existed previously. For retirees, the program is a form of "insurance" against poverty because they were required to contribute to the insurance fund, and only those who had contributed (or whose employer had contributed) were eligible for benefits. Children and the disabled, by comparison, were eligible for assistance because of their status rather than by making contributions to the program. The monies for helping them came from general revenue funds. Nevertheless, the idea of social insurance was still appropriate since it was clear that neither children nor the disabled were able to work, and their poverty could not be said to be their fault. To the country's great misfortune, economic security was not socialized for all.

5.10 THE NEARLY FORGOTTEN AMERICANS

Racial justice was not a highly visible part of New Deal policy or programming. In fact, the record is decidedly mixed. As one author writes: "If the New Deal's efforts to assist black Americans were halting and small and always coupled with some slight or set back, they nevertheless existed."[73]

The paramount reason for failing Black Americans was political as has historically been the case. The Democratic Party could not advance the cause of racial minorities and retain power at the same time. Roosevelt knew this clearly.[74] The essential compromise he reached with Southern Democrats to pass his social legislative agenda was to transfer administrative responsibility for several programs to the states, and the states, in turn, could and did discriminate against people based on the color of their skin.

Still, Roosevelt did engage in some outreach. Several high-profile prominent New Dealers including Eleanor Roosevelt, Harold Ickes, Frances Perkins, and Harry Hopkins, actively promoted efforts to fight racial discrimination and worked to include people of color in the administration. Further, several prominent Black Americans were popularly known as FDR's Black Cabinet.[75] They included Lawrence Oxley, a high-ranking official in the Department of Labor; Mary McLeod Bethune, the director of the National Youth Administration's Office of Negro (a word in common use at the time) Affairs; and Robert Weaver, who served as an economic advisor to the president. FDR also appointed William Hastie as the country's first Black federal judge.

Additionally, FDR, through an Executive Order, required that workers were to be paid equal wages regardless of race nearly everywhere. The WPA employed hundreds of thousands of Black Americans. Women of color were hired as teachers, social workers, librarians, and in other professional and service sectors, often working on integrated teams as Black Americans participated in the administration's relief and work programs.[76]

On the other side of the racial ledger, due to pressure from southern Democrats, agricultural and domestic workers, job categories that most Black people held, were not protected by New Deal labor laws nor were they protected by Social Security laws. When the government began to insure mortgages during the Great Depression, it drew a red line around almost all black neighborhoods and denied those areas mortgage protection. The New Deal's support of homeowners was largely for white homeowners only.

5.11 FDR'S FOUR FREEDOMS

The New Deal revolutionized the nation's approach to helping the least fortunate Americans. Speaking shortly after Pearl Harbor, FDR signaled the significance of this shift in the mix of government and markets in his "Four Freedoms" speech. The speech identified the fundamental freedoms that should be guaranteed to all people: the freedom of speech and expression, the freedom to worship, the freedom from fear, and the freedom from want. While the first three freedoms related to America's entrance into World War II, the President explained his inclusion of "freedom from want": "[T]here is no time for any of us to stop thinking about the social and economic problems that are the root cause of the social revolution which is today a supreme factor in the world."[77] He went on:

> There is nothing mysterious about the foundations of a healthy and strong democracy. The basic things expected by our people of their political and economic systems are simple. They are: Equality of opportunity for youth and for others. Jobs for those who can work. Security for those who need it. The ending of special privilege for the few. The preservation of civil liberties for all. The enjoyment of the fruits of scientific progress in a wider and constantly rising standard of living.[78]

In his last State of the Union address four years later, also known as the Second Bill of Rights, FDR declared that "[w] have come to a clear realization of the fact that true individual freedom cannot exist without economic security and independence. Necessitous men are not free men...." Economic security required, the President continued, the right to "a useful and remunerative job;" a "decent home;" "adequate medical care and the opportunity to achieve and enjoy good health;" "adequate protection from the economic fears of old age, sickness, accident, and unemployment;" and the right to "a good education." "All of these rights," he concluded, "spell security."[79]

FDR's vision of America in these two speeches is less a vision of the lone, rugged individual than it is of George Bailey, supported by his neighbors.

5.12 CONCLUSION

The New Deal took on four new responsibilities for economic security that continue to this day. One was the use of monetary tools to manage the economy to prevent significant economic dislocations, or if they occurred, to moderate them. Another was to regulate areas of the economy, particularly the stock market and banking system, to prevent anti-competitive or avaricious behavior that would cause economic disruption. A direct consequence of these first two strategies was to build out the country's infrastructure in energy, telecommunications, and transportation and in the process fortify major national industries.

The third was for the government to step in with additional spending when the previous tools failed to prevent a severe economic decline. The last responsibility was to establish the Social Security system to ensure that elderly and disabled Americans would avoid desperate poverty because they could not or had a diminished capacity to work.

In essence, FDR's Four Freedoms and his Second Bill of Rights were an ambitious agenda to get the mix of government and markets on a solid footing by stabilizing the economy and safeguarding Americans from economic developments beyond their control. These efforts reflected President Lincoln's insight that the government should assist people to better themselves when they were unable to do so through no fault of their own. Lincoln's "right to rise" is a recognition that the government can expand freedom in appropriate circumstances – freedom is not only a property of private markets.

Yet, as significant as these programs were, they did not reach millions of Americans who still faced racial discrimination and millions of others who still found themselves in poverty. Since racial inequity is directly linked to economic inequality, the divide between race and wealth indicates that the relationship between government and markets is out of balance. Although some progress toward racial justice was made when Harry Truman desegregated the military and the Eisenhower administration enacted the 1957 Civil Rights Act, it would take another generation, until LBJ's Great Society, before this imbalance was addressed, as we will discuss in Chapter 7.

6

Dwight Eisenhower's America

Prosperity and Anxiety

The shift from 20 years of Democratic rule to a Republican president seems dramatic. It was not. For many years, the image of Dwight D. Eisenhower as the golf-playing Country Club Republican captured the public imagination as someone who treated the presidency quite casually. Eisenhower was certainly a golf-playing Republican, but his presidency was actively engaged both domestically and internationally. More surprising for some is that his approach to government was a continuation of the New Deal vision that our country is best served by a healthy mix of government and markets. Ike made his own contribution to economic growth and prosperity by supporting the construction of an interstate highway system and the creation of public-private partnerships to develop commercial uses of nuclear energy, a space program, and military technology that would have significant civilian uses. These were a continuation of the government making the type of infrastructure investments that date back to Alexander Hamilton.

Government investments of the New Deal and by the Eisenhower administration created a vibrant and growing post-war economic boom that created a vast middle class and reduced economic inequality. What economists call the "great compression" of the 1950s meant that economic inequality was at an historic low and social mobility was at an historic high.[1] Yet these hallmarks could not hide the social and political strains that accompanied economic good times.

There was something disquieting about living in the 1950s even while enjoying its prosperity. Fears of communism, the atomic bomb, and about the future coexisted in contrast with the placid life in America depicted on television. There were deeper, more unsettling, undercurrents in 1950s America as well – racism, unease concerning the role of women in society, the suppression of artists and the firing of government officials as communists, alienation from corporate structures that homogenized working environments, and rampant poverty amidst a growth economy. These tensions would eventually lead to another mix of government and markets in the next decades.

6.1 THE NUCLEAR AGE BEGINS

The story of Manhattan Project is the quintessential example of government harnessing cutting edge science and transforming it into a useful, albeit destructive, technology.[2] The atomic bombs dropped on Hiroshima and Nagasaki may well have ended World War II, but they haunted the psyche and imagination. Families built bomb shelters and provisioned food and water; school children were taught to shelter under their desks; the mushroom cloud was a lasting image; and geopolitics took on a doomsday meaning.

To counter the dark side of atomic energy, scientists and military leaders involved with the Manhattan Project supported the transformation of the technology into more productive uses immediately after the war. The Atomic Energy Act of 1946 transferred the authority to control the atom from the military to a five-member civilian Atomic Energy Commission that was charged with promoting the development of the technology for peaceful uses.[3] It also created an 18-member congressional Joint Committee on Atomic Energy to serve as the legislative watchdog over nuclear development. The legislation, however, restricted ownership of reactors and nuclear fuels to the government.

In 1951, the government created a small "breeder" reactor that was the first-time nuclear energy had been used to produce electricity. Then a breakthrough came in 1953 when, under the direction of Admiral Hyman Rickover, Thermal Reactor I began producing electricity to power the Navy's nuclear fleet. That reactor constituted the civilian reactor prototype for decades.

In 1953, Eisenhower delivered a speech at the United Nations General Assembly that stressed the United States had stockpiled enough atomic weapons that they exceeded "by many times the explosive equivalent of the total of all bombs and all shells that came from every plane and every gun in every theater of war in all of the years of World War II." Yes, the US had the bomb, so did the USSR, and it was time to deescalate and disarm. Because the risks of nuclear annihilation were existential, Eisenhower also announced his Atoms for Peace program to create hope for a calm nuclear future. His message was nuclear power could be used to generate electricity that was so inexpensive that a utility could charge consumers a flat fee rather than charging them by how much they used. Nuclear powered electricity would be "too cheap to meter." Walt Disney boosted Ike's peace effort with an episode, "Our Friend the Atom," on the TV program *The Magical World of Disney*.

Through commercialization, nuclear power proponents, in and out of government, hoped that the peaceful use of atomic energy might relieve anxiety over Hiroshima and Nagasaki while, at the same time, keep the United States in the forefront of the development and control of nuclear technology, and help maintain our leadership position in the increasingly threatening arms race. The desire for nuclear dominance cut two ways – energy prosperity and military superiority.

In 1954, Congress passed the Atomic Energy Act to license private utilities to construct and operate nuclear power plants.[4] The reasons for ending government control of non-military uses and substituting private ownership will sound familiar. As stated in a House of Representative Report, privatization was necessary because the legislators did "not believe that any developmental program carried out solely under government auspices, no matter how efficient it may be, can substitute for the cost-cutting and other incentives of free and competitive enterprise."[5]

Private firms, however, were unwilling to invest in nuclear power without the government shouldering some financial responsibility in the event of a catastrophic nuclear disaster. As Westinghouse chief executive Charles Weaver recalled, "When I testified before Congress, I made it perfectly clear that we could not proceed as a private company without that kind of government backing."[6] To jump start a nuclear energy industry, Congress passed the Price-Anderson Act of 1957 to limit industry liability and take over much of the compensation for the public in the event of such a nuclear incident.[7]

With contract protections, liability protections, and the promise of extremely cheap fuel, the nuclear industry was given life. Between 1965 and 1978, the commercial nuclear power industry enjoyed what is known as the "Great Bandwagon Market." In 1965, 49 plants were ordered and by the end of that era over 100 nuclear plants were in operation.[8] The Eisenhower administration had linked big science, big military, and big industry into a partnership that fully mixed government and markets and in the process created the entire nuclear power industry.

6.2 THE SPACE AGE BEGINS

If the world changed on August 6, 1945, when the Enola Gay dropped the first atomic bomb on Hiroshima, it turned again on October 4, 1957, when the USSR launched Sputnik and the space race began. The public and politicians demanded an aggressive military response, but Ike reassured them that there was no necessary connection between the arms race and the space race. Instead, he launched another collaboration between the government and industry as his administration had done with commercial nuclear power.

Initially, Eisenhower recognized the need for scientific research and education, and after consulting with scientists, appointed Dr. James Killian, president of MIT, to head the President's Science Advisory Committee. Then in 1958, the administration created the Advanced Research Projects Agency in the Department of Defense (DARPA) and the National Aeronautics and Space Act (NASA).[9] DARPA and NASA brought the public and private sectors together to significantly boost the already hot economy.

On the public side, Congress, the White House, and the military set the agenda. On the private side, multiple aeronautics and technology businesses were indispensable to the success of any space mission the United States would undertake.[10]

Today NASA oversees 20 research centers and programs that engage government, U.S. contractors, universities, and commercial partners in a wide variety of activities from the Hubble Space Telescope to the Curiosity Mars Land Rover and from commercial space travel to the International Space Station. In short, Silicon Valley's information technology explosion is the progeny of Eisenhower's public-private science partnership.

The government also built on its collaboration with universities. Initially, these research efforts were driven by military purposes, but much of the military mission was transferred after the war into civilian hands. The Department of Energy now oversees a group of 17 national laboratories that were once virtually all dedicated to military defense and now have mixed missions including developing clean energy technologies. These labs work closely with the academy and private businesses in these development efforts.

These infrastructure investments in scientific and technological research and development have had a remarkable series of positive spillover effects. DARPA has given us virtually all the technologies we currently enjoy on our cell phones including touch screens, GPS, voice recognition, and the Internet.[11] NASA gave the Kennedy administration a base for its project Apollo, which brought us to the moon, back, and beyond, and yielded technologies that are indispensable today. Camera phones, CAT scans, LEDs, athletic shoes, wireless communications, and freeze-dried foods are only some of the products that came out of the space race.[12]

The idea that the government can help build the country by making infrastructure investments dates to Alexander Hamilton, but the nature and type of investment has changed depending on economic and political developments. The New Deal adopted Keynesian deficit financing as an economic tool that has been used ever since. The Eisenhower administration demonstrated that public-private partnerships can contribute to economic progress by advancing and commercializing science and technology, that government leadership is essential but not sufficient, and that these partnerships help to build a vibrant economy.

6.3 THE GREATEST GENERATION

While Eisenhower's leadership in science and technology contributed to building a stronger economy, the end of the New Deal made another significant contribution to that effort when Congress passed the GI Bill in 1944.[13] The deficit spending before and during World War II had wiped out the Great Depression and pushed the country into full employment, but this economic progress faced a looming threat at the end of the war. After WW I, unemployment quickly rose to 20 percent of the workforce as the troops came home from abroad pushing the country into a recession.[14] To avoid a similar result, the GI Bill laid out an investment plan to absorb the 13 million returning veterans without massive unemployment. The legislation guaranteed veterans a $20-dollar weekly readjustment allowance for up to fifty-two weeks, and provided funding for vocational training or higher education, subsidies for housing mortgages, and low interest business loans.

The plan succeeded. Unemployment only climbed to 4% by 1948, instead of the 20% or more unemployment predicted by the Labor Department if nothing was done to accommodate the veterans.[15] Even more significantly, a historian labeled the GI bill as a "turning point" because it "contributed enormously to the release of economic and intellectual energy that carried America to the summit of the world."[16] Another historian found, "Quite literally, the G.I. Bill changed the way we live, the way we house ourselves, the way we are educated, how we work and at what, even how we eat and transport ourselves."[17]

Prior to the GI bill, only a reasonably small percent of Americans enrolled in college. After the bill, nearly 8 million veterans, more than 50 percent of those eligible, took advantage of the educational provisions. The legislation provided full tuition, books, and supplies and a monthly stipend that varied by family size. As of September 1947, seven out of every ten college students were veterans, and most were the first in their family to go to college.[18]

On their return from the war, it was easier for veterans to find a spot in a university or vocational school than it was to find housing. The father of one of the authors was one of those veterans. After the war, his family lived with his mother's grandparents for most of the author's early life because his parents could not find nor afford a house. The GI bill not only made it possible for first-time homeowners to get a mortgage, the increased demand by vets for houses created a robust housing industry to meet that demand. By 1952, there were 2.4 million veterans who had received government-backed loans.

William Levitt was one of the first developers to respond to the growing demand for new housing by inventing the suburbs. He purchased large scale acreage on the edge of cities, and then subdivided the land into lots for the purpose of offering affordable housing to veterans and their families. The initial homes were priced at $6,990 and in the next four years Levitt built over 17,000 homes finishing 12 houses per day. The tract house and suburbia became part of America. Some 25 to 30 million single family homes – most of them like the ranch style home of the authors' families – were constructed between 1945 and 1965, mostly in the suburbs.[19] By 1960, over 30% of the population resided in the suburbs and over 80% of the population growth occurred there instead of cities. Similarly, homeownership rates rose to nearly 2/3 of the population.

Post war initiatives, including the GI bill, together with a growing economy put money into middle class pockets – money for cars, housing, schooling, and a better life for America's families. With its infrastructure investments, the GI bill "transformed the nation from a steeply hierarchical society divided by wealth and class to one in which citizens aspired to and achieved middle class status."[20] Median income of nonfarm families rose between 1947 and 1957 by 66 percent, the greatest decadal increase in the country's history.[21] Whereas the richest five percent of income earners accounted for 38 percent of the national income in the 1920s, their share fell to 17 percent by 1950.[22] The government classified one-half of the country's families as middle class in 1951 as compared to 25 percent in 1900. As the National Bureau of Economic Research has summed up, this was "one of the greatest social revolutions in history."[23]

There was an additional benefit. Those who came of age during the Great Depression and World War II were far more involved in civic life and politics than have been later generations. The veterans responded to how the government had been a positive force in their lives by giving back to their communities and creating a more robust democracy. The GI bill, it turns out, reinforced the commitment of Americans to their country, a goal for education that dated back to the founders.[24]

6.4 TWO AMERICAS

As rosy as this picture may be, it did not include Black Americans. At the end of WWII, the Swedish economist and sociologist Gunner Myrdal published a path-breaking study of racism that found there were two Americas – one Black and one White.[25] The government's efforts to build a middle perpetuated the two Americas.

The agencies responsible for guaranteeing housing refused loans to Black home buyers, which effectively denied them the same opportunity as whites to own a home in the suburbs.[26] Developers like Levitt refused to sell homes to people of color,[27] and often, suburbs had racially restrictive covenants in their deeds. A typical housing covenant of the time said: "That no part of said property hereby conveyed shall ever be used or occupied by the Hebrew, Ethiopian, Malay, or any Asiatic race." Another covenant was blunter: "No person of other than the Caucasian race shall use or occupy any building or lot except as servants domesticated with any owner or tenant."[28] More often, suburbs had zoning and building codes that were discriminatory. As a result, Black Americans occupied only two percent of the houses built with government-subsidized mortgages in the 1950s.[29]

The migration from cities to suburbs was largely a White flight. As families looked for neighborhoods with "good schools" for their children, what is perhaps the longest living insult of suburbanization was increased school segregation along racial lines particularly in the north.[30]

Eisenhower himself was not immune to the racism of the time. Before *Brown v. Board of Education* was decided, the president met with Chief Justice Earl Warren and asked that he consider the concerns of the White parents in the South who did not wish to have their daughters sit alongside Black school children. According to an account of this conversation, Eisenhower told Warren, "These are not bad people. All they are concerned about is to see that their sweet little girls are not required to sit in school alongside some big Black bucks." After the decision, Eisenhower said that the Warren appointment was the worst appointment he had made in his administration.[31]

The impact of this racial segregation has been long lasting. Much of the difference in wealth between White and Black Americans can be traced back to these practices. Each generation of the children of White homeowners in the 1950s have benefitted from the increase in housing prices that has occurred over time because each generation has inherited the wealth built up by their parents through home ownership. Since Black families have not shared in this development, they have less accumulated wealth than their White counterparts. As of 2019, the average wealth of White Americans was 12 times that of Black Americans.[32] Additionally, there is a significant racial disparity in home ownership. In 2020, for example, over 70% of White Americans owned homes while slightly over 40% of Black Americans did.[33] This pattern contributes to the wealth gap because homeowners enjoy a mortgage deduction and renters do not.

Notably, residential segregation simply compounded the problem of school segregation because public schools were funded in part by property taxes. Consequently, inner city schools could not compete with their wealthier suburban neighbors in terms of resources and quality of education.[34]

6.5 THE INTERSTATE HIGHWAY SYSTEM

The New Deal launched a large middle class in America, and the Eisenhower administration expanded that effort and made its own significant contribution to the economy. FDR had begun to investigate the construction of the interstate highway system, but it was under Eisenhower that Congress passed the Federal-Aid Highway Act of 1956, which authorized the construction of 41,000 miles of interstate highways, which became America's largest public works program at the time.[35] The act created the Highway Trust Fund with the federal government paying 90% of the construction costs and the states picking up the reminder. The costs were mostly paid through gas taxes. Unsurprisingly, Eisenhower's interest in effective transportation grew out of his military experience with convoys in the United States and with troop and munitions transport during the war.

The development of the highway system transformed America in multiple ways for good and bad. Most notably, the growth and expansion of the highway system was directly linked to residential housing patterns and suburban development. The interstate highway system facilitated the suburban housing development started by William Levitt and was a boon to many Americans. Family vacations became routine and moving to the suburbs and purchasing single family homes constituted the American Dream.

The development of the suburbs had a variety of effects particularly when coupled with better highway travel. To start, the automobile industry and the oil industry, which was needed to fuel those cars, grew significantly, and became indispensable. Similarly, as the suburbs expanded, so did the need for electric appliances. In the 1950s, the *Live Better Electrically* campaign designed by General Electric and

Westinghouse aimed to create and satisfy that demand. In tandem with the growing sales of time-saving appliances, electric utilities built additional capacity, which led to a decline in the price of electricity that increased demand even more. The 1950s was truly a boom economy for ordinary families and more so for the energy, construction, consumer appliances, and automobile corporations that were serving that economy.

As with housing, there was a downside to this development. Highways gave new mobility to Americans and helped to create sprawling suburbs, but highways also resulted in the destruction of Black communities. Federal and state agencies chose to construct urban highways through Black neighborhoods destroying homes, churches, schools, and businesses, and cutting off those communities from the rest of the city where White people lived. The practice was justified as "slum removal," because the acquisition costs of obtaining land in Black neighbors was lower than in White neighborhoods, or because Black citizens had less political power to oppose the location of highways than their White counterparts.[36] The construction of Interstate 94 in St. Paul, Minnesota, for example, removed one seventh of the city's Black residents. This caused one commentator to observe: "Very few blacks lived in Minnesota, but the road builders found them."[37] This pattern of race-based residential segregation was practiced by many American cities.[38]

6.6 CROSSCURRENTS

For many, but not all, the postwar 1950s America was an economic and social miracle. New products and new technologies comforted the middle class. Educational opportunities abounded. People moved from the cities to the suburbs. Jobs proliferated, incomes increased, and the American Dream seemed to be a reality as advertised on that most remarkable invention – television.

Clearly, the Eisenhower years were years of economic prosperity. During Ike's presidency, a biographer notes, "many terrible things that could have happened, didn't. Dwight Eisenhower's presidency gave America eight good years – I believe the best in memory. There were no wars, no riots, no inflation – just peace and prosperity."[39] The celebration of the success of the American Dream and the rise of America's Greatest Generation, however, glossed over the many crosscurrents that were percolating. To fully appreciate the anxiety that came with the 50s, it is necessary to peek behind the curtain of prosperity.

Soon after the Korean War ended, Joe McCarthy's war on godless communism reached into every department of the government and every segment of society. McCarthyism not only created a climate of fear in the country, but it also discouraged political dissent and made it unthinkable to defend the Americans who were the innocent victims of this red baiting.[40] The country was also locked in a deadly arms race with an increasingly aggressive USSR that brought the Cold War to Cuba 90 miles off the Florida coast. And despite the Supreme Court having outlawed school segregation in *Brown v. Board of Education*,[41] the cancer of racial segregation continued to spread.

There was also growing unease with the status of women. While men and women were serving in the armed forces during WWII, millions of women entered the workplace to power war industries and produce the armament that fueled the eventual victory over Germany and Japan. Rosie the Riveter became the iconic image of these working women. The picture, created in 1942 by Howard Miller, a Pittsburgh artist, pictured a woman in a bandana flexing a muscle in her arm saying "We Can Do It."[42] It quickly became a recruiting poster used by the government to encourage women to go to work for the war effort.

In the 1950s, however, mom returned to managing the house in her house dress while Dad, in his suit and tie, came home from the office to a single-family home with a manicured lawn on a tree-lined street inhabited by 2.3 adorable children. The TV screen was a snapshot of domestic tranquility as told by shows like *The Adventures of Ozzie and Harriet*, *The Donna Reed Show*, *Leave It to Beaver*, *Father Knows Best*, and *My Three Sons*. On TV, America was a country where males worked, women stayed home, and people of color were nowhere to be seen.

Setting aside that there were two Americas, the picture on TV of American happiness and prosperity contrasted with the society described in books such as *The Organization Man*, *One-Dimensional Man*, *The Lonely Crowd*, *White Collar*, and *The Man in the Gray Flannel Suit*, the latter with its genteel anti-Semitism. These books revealed a growing discomfort in America.

Richard Yate's novel *Revolutionary Road* captured the unease that went along with postwar America. In the book, a young couple, Frank and April Wheeler, living comfortably in suburban Connecticut, confront their personal distress – her dashed dreams of becoming an actress and his frustration working in a demeaning cubicle. Frank's anxiety revealed that the routinization on nineteenth century factory floors simply moved into corporate workspaces in the 20th. April's anxiety revealed her discomfort being the suburban housewife.

Later in the decade, Harvard economist John Kenneth Galbreath began a study of poverty in America and ended up publishing a book about the wealthy. His 1958 study, *The Affluent Society*, also discovered another two Americas – one rich and one poor. He writes:

> The family which takes its mauve and cerise, air-conditioned, powered-steered and powered-braked automobile out for a tour passes through cities that are badly paved, made hideous by litter, blighted buildings, posts for wires that should long since have been put under ground. They pass on into a countryside that has been rendered largely invisible by commercial art (The goods which the latter advertise have an absolute priority in our value system.)[43]

Beyond the colorful prose, Galbraith highlighted the difference between the rich and the poor and laid the cleavage between them at the feet of government spending. Gone were the Keynesian days of the New Deal when spending on public works and spending for the lower classes was a priority. Instead, if any spending was to be done, it would be for "economic growth." Additionally, according to Galbreath, the new "conventional wisdom" was that a "balanced budget" was necessary for economic growth and success.

Amid plenty, Galbraith found a society that was enjoying its prosperity less than might be anticipated. In fact, even with a wealth of choices in front of them, Americans were disconcerted. The choices were false choices as Frank and April Wheeler found out. They were not choices that individuals would necessarily have made. The new discontent was based on alienation: alienation from work, from family, from community, and from self. For Galbraith the economist, the alienation uncovered some truths about economics that too often went unquestioned.

6.7 THE PORT HURON STATEMENT

As the Eisenhower administration ended and Kennedy's New Frontier captured the nation's attention, the conflict between 1950's prosperity and anxiety found new voices. In June 1962, a small group of political activists including the late Columbia University professor Todd Gitlin and former California Assemblyman and State Senator, Tom Hayden, met at a United Auto Workers' camp in Port Huron, Michigan to draft a statement of political purpose. By June 15, their drafting was completed, and the *Port Huron Statement* became the central document for the Students for a Democratic Society (SDS).[44]

The *Port Huron Statement* began: "We are people of this generation, bred in at least modest comfort, housed now in universities, looking uncomfortably to the world we inherit.... Not only did tarnish appear on our image of American virtue, ... but we began to sense that what we had originally seen as the American Golden Age was actually the decline of an era."[45] The decline, the statement declared, was related to alienation from work, fear of nuclear annihilation, and repulsion to racial discrimination, among other discontents.

The statement therefore called for a "search for truly democratic alternatives to the present, and a commitment to social experimentation with them." To find these alternatives, SDS endorsed the "search for orienting theories and the creation of human values" by using public, communal, and democratic participation in universities, communities, and government.[46] The message was the direction of the country should not be left to existing social institutions and political arrangements. The statement also made economic participation central to their idea of America, which meant workers would have the ability to participate in workplace decision-making to contribute to their own self-determination. And, finally, economic participation meant that the economy should not go unexamined; the impacts of economic growth and prosperity could and should be criticized.

6.8 THE CHICAGO SCHOOL

The SDS *Statement* was a manifesto for a new form of politics and of the economy; one in which there was greater citizen participation in government to correct manifest market failures and social injustices. At the same time, another blueprint for the future of America was being developed, The Chicago School of economics had a different idea about the mix of government and markets – a much different idea.

Since the end of World War II, some economists had been hard at work rebutting the Keynesian government spending policies of the Roosevelt administration. Starting in the 1940s, they began to challenge and then transform the relationship between government and markets to the point at which a new free market thinking dominated American politics. Instead of focusing on government spending for the public's welfare, these economists shifted the focus to private gain. This idea can be summarized as "a rising tide lifts all boats" or a prosperous economy will benefit everyone in the country and more so than the government can do.

Friedrich Hayek[47] and Milton Friedman[48] were the vanguard of the argument that the country would be better off if there were less government and more freedom for markets. At the end of the decade, Ronald Coase, a Nobel Laureate economist, published two widely read papers that argued legal doctrines should be shaped by economics and, more notably, markets could solve social and economic problems better than government.

In his first 1959 paper, *The Nature of the Firm*,[49] Coase contended the structure of corporations was the result of market competition, which suggested government efforts to regulate corporations, such as by limiting their size or whether they could merge with other corporations, would be counterproductive and harmful to economic prosperity. *The Problem of Social Cost*,[50] his second 1960 paper, led to the conclusion that if the government did regulate a corporation, such as to limit its pollution, it should only do so until the costs of complying with the regulation exceeded the benefits of the regulation to the public. Coase argued this formula would replicate the solution that markets would impose on companies regarding such harms as pollution. Regulating any more would reduce market freedom and harm the country. Note, though, under this cost-benefit calculation, people must still live with pollution if the costs of additional pollution abatement exceed the benefits of protecting people.

Coase's papers became the foundation stones for what was to become the Law & Economics (L&E) movement. Housed in the University of Chicago under the leadership of Aaron Director and others, the movement advocated for understanding the mix of government and markets as supporting the economic concepts originated by Hayek, Friedman, and Coase. Gary Becker (another Nobel prize winner) and law professors Richard Posner and Richard Epstein became prominent University of Chicago professors who advocated for this understanding of the purpose of law. Those concepts tilted the government/market mix decidedly in favor of markets.

6.9 SHAPING THE FUTURE

As the country debated the mix of government and markets, there were two clashing ideas about the future of the country. The aim of the first idea, personified by the Port Huron Statement was to find ways for the government to restore freedom for people of color, low-income Americans, women, employees, and others through the type of democratic conversation envisioned by John Dewey. The drafters recognized the tensions that were floating beneath the surface of the economic prosperity of the 1950s, and they called on Americans to use their political power to address these festering problems. The statement became the basis of the public interest and civil rights movements of the 1960s. Government responded, and Lyndon Johnson's Great Society was the result.

The second idea – the Chicago School approach to the mix of government and markets – was a reaction to the New Deal and Eisenhower's willingness to continue and extend the government's activities to build the country. It promised that, if the government got out of the way, markets would not only maximize individual freedom, but they would also do a better job of building the country. Markets were a better vehicle for building the country because, unlike the government, they did not depend on government officials to decide what policies would best serve the country. Markets, the Chicago School argued, did this automatically. This argument was taken up by Ronald Reagan, and it has influenced the country ever since.

Nevertheless, there has been only a limited retrenchment of government, and few programs in government were eliminated, although many have been downsized. While the Chicago School approach to public policy has been influential in debates over the mix of government and markets, there has always been a recognition that it is insufficient in and of itself to build a country true to American values. As the future chapters will relate, the reason for this reluctance recognizes two fundamental limitations of markets when it comes to fulfilling American values.

First, economics looks to markets to maximize the total wealth of the country, but it does not have anything to say about how that wealth is distributed except to claim that as wealth increases everyone will benefit. Common experience belies this claim, however. The Industrial Age, discussed earlier, grew the economy, and greatly increased the overall wealth of the country, but it also produced substantial misery for millions of workers and their families. The 1950s, by comparison, reduced economic inequality, but that was the result of government policies in the New Deal. Our historical experience indicates there is no guarantee that without government intervention markets will reduce poverty or provide people with the basic goods and services that they need to live such as health care and education. The historical record is clear that maximizing wealth favors the wealthy more than the rest of Americans.[51] The influence of the Chicago School after 1980 has produced more, not less, economic inequality.[52]

Second, there remains a commitment that how best to achieve America's fundamental values should be made by democratic decision-making rather than economic theory. While economics would limit government intervention to a comparison of costs and benefits, citizens have decided that more regulation may be necessary to achieve freedom and equality. The issue of government intervention, in other words, relates to what best achieves our values rather than to an economic formula.

6.10 CONCLUSION

The Eisenhower years were prolific. He presided over a red-hot boom economy. He moved two dangerous defense technologies – the bomb and the rocket – into peaceful as well as commercial and civilian uses. He continued the build out of America and the development of the suburbs, both of which fortified a growing middle class. All in all, Eisenhower was committed to using the mix of government and markets to increase economic opportunity and prosperity.

The result in the words of a historian was a "great leveling."[53] A variety of government investments contributed to building a middle class and greater economic equality. Another historian noted: "In the quarter-century after World War II, the country established collective structures, not individual monuments, that channeled the aspirations of ordinary people: state universities, progressive taxation, interstate highways, collective bargaining, health insurance for the elderly, credible news organizations."[54]

While the government created the opportunity, it was the people who took advantage of the government's investment to better themselves. The Eisenhower years can be seen as a time when the greatest generation received an education, embarked on careers, purchased their own homes, traveled, and raised families that placed them solidly in an economically healthy middle class.

Yet, there was something disquieting about living in the 1950's while enjoying its prosperity as Eisenhower well knew. In Ike's famous farewell address delivered on January 17, 1961, he issued a warning about the military-industrial complex that had the capacity to use its "economic, political, even spiritual influence … in every city, every statehouse, every office of the federal government." This combination should never be allowed to "endanger our liberties or democratic processes," he cautioned. Moreover, the power of the federal government was being felt by universities growing increasingly dependent on the government dollar. Eisenhower worried that "a government contract [could become] virtually a substitute for intellectual curiosity" on our nation's campuses.[55] University of California president Clark Kerr echoed Eisenhower's concerns in his still relevant and penetrating book *The Uses of the University*, published in 1963.

These tensions impacted the country and the country's views about the mix of government and markets. As the next two chapters take up, the political movements of the 1960s – anti-war, civil rights, environmental, consumer, and war on poverty – led the country into a new mix of government and markets – one that sought to address much of what troubled many Americans. The country's later history put a brake on using the government for such purposes.

7

Rachel Carson's America

Saving the Environment

The 1950s were a time of growing prosperity for many Americans. The New Deal started the country on the road to recovery, and the massive government spending needed to fight World War II had restored the economy. Dwight Eisenhower added public-private partnerships in science and technology and the interstate highway system to New Deal infrastructure. Many Americans were content with the way that things were going. The United States was the most powerful country in the world; there were expanded economic opportunities at home, new cars and houses, and abundant consumer goods were advertised and available. The GI bill created a large college-educated middle class and made it possible to start new small businesses.

By the 1960s, cracks began to appear in this picture as writers, activists, and politicians pointed to the regulatory and social issues that were troubling the country. None of these activities had a bigger impact than Rachel Carson's 1962 book, *Silent Spring*.[1] Carson jump-started today's environmental movement by questioning "humanity's faith in technological progress"[2] and warning that economic prosperity was not the unalloyed good thing that it was generally presumed to be.[3] Carson's caution echoed John Kenneth Galbraith's admonition, covered in the last chapter, that low-income Americans had been left behind by booming markets. Their concerns harkened back to 1899 when Thorstein Veblen's book, *The Theory of the Leisure Class*,[4] warned that a market economy that encouraged the consumption of goods and services may be good for producers and, in the short run, for the general economy, but it was not necessarily good for the human or natural environments.

Citizen activists joined the writers' call for a reassessment of the mix of government and markets. The civil rights movement challenged the lack of progress in creating true equality for Black Americans; El Movimiento, or the Chicano movement as the activists also called it, sought to extend civil rights to Latinos of mixed Mexican and American heritage; the women's movement supported gender equality and greater control of sexual and reproductive rights; and the student democracy movement injected the student voice into the policies and practices of university life and governance. A consumer movement battled to protect consumers from harmful products that killed and injured thousands of people annually. Labor unions and other worker advocates contested employment conditions that endangered and too often killed workers. The antiwar movement engaged thousands in protesting against American involvement in the Vietnam war. As a music critic pointed out, it is a cliché to call Bob Dylan's 1965 song, *The Times They Are A-Changin'*, "an anthem of change…, but it is exactly that."[5]

Led by President Lyndon Johnson Congress heeded the call in Dylan's song that members of Congress should respond to the political movements' demands for social and economic change. The 89th Congress (1965–1966) enacted one hundred major new programs, and the 90th Congress (1967–1968) passed a total of more than 500 more.[6] Congress also passed 25 laws to regulate business behavior between 1967 and 1973 according to one account, and 42 such laws according to another account.[7] Many familiar regulatory agencies, including the Environmental Protection Agency (EPA) and the Occupational Safety and Health Administration (OSHA), were in place by the end of the decade. By the time that LBJ was done, his legislative output exceeded that of even the New Deal. Once again, the country had changed, and the government was changed to live up to American political values.

The significant additions to government drew a counterreaction starting in the 1970s and led to the election of Ronald Reagan. The counterreaction vigorously attacked the government and favored relying on markets to organize and build the country. The activists of this time – the ones who favored the expansion of government – ironically planted the seeds of this distrust in government. The government's lack of honesty about the war in Vietnam fueled an increasing anti-war movement. Its complacency about the social, political, racial, and cultural problems just beneath the surface of the 1950s prosperity further increased the criticism of the government along several fronts. Then the Watergate fiasco underscored the widespread distrust on left and right and culminated in President Nixon's resignation.

7.1 RACHEL CARSON

Rachel Carson, with her master's degree in Zoology, joined the U.S. Fish and Wildlife Service after achieving the highest score on the 1936 Civil Service examination. While serving as editor-in-chief of all the agency's publications, she wrote several best-selling books about the natural world prior to *Silent Spring*. In *Silent Spring*, Carson argued that the government needed to attend to the interrelated consequences of production and manufacturing to protect people and guard the irreplaceable beauty of the natural wilderness. She explained how the widespread use of chemical pesticides, particularly DDT, had harmed the reproductive capacities of eagles, peregrine falcons, and other predatory birds, and she warned that people may be subject to the same harms. She discussed as an example how pregnant mothers in the Cree Tribe of Canada, which lives in a forest area that was sprayed with DDT, had higher than normal rates of premature births because of gestational diabetes.

Chemical companies attempted to discredit Carson as a Communist or hysterical woman after *Silent Spring* was published, but the book was validated by a series of awards. Carson received a National Book Award, a National Science Writing Prize, and a Guggenheim Grant. A White House Science Advisory Committee endorsed the book. Then the book was the subject of a CBS special report, *The Silent Spring of Rachel Carson*, watched by 15 million viewers.[8]

Like her predecessor, Ida Tarbell, Carson's work came to the attention of a president. After the publication of *Silent Spring*, a reporter asked President John Kennedy: "Mr. President, there appears to be a growing concern among scientists as to the possibility of dangerous long-range side effects from the widespread use of DDT and other pesticides. Have you considered asking the Department of Agriculture or the Public Health Service to take a closer look at this?" Kennedy replied, "Yes, and I know that they already are. I think particularly, of course, since Miss Carson's book, but they are examining the issue."[9]

"Through the strength and vitality of her voice," a historian has noted, "Carson altered the political landscape of America forever."[10] Carson's books joined a library of writing that made the degradation of the environment and natural resources "parts of the national conversation."[11] Earlier, Wallace Stegner's 1943 semi-autobiographical novel, *The Big Rock Candy Mountain*, described life in the West and in Canada, emphasizing its natural beauty and western lifestyle. Aldo Leopold's 1949 book, *A Sand County Almanac*, became a staple of the American land ethic that emphasized the country's respect for conservation, and it became a primer on natural history and environmental philosophy. Edward Abbey's 1968 *Desert Solitaire* described his experience as a park ranger at Arches National Park in the 1950s. Reminiscent of Henry David Thoreau's *Walden*, *Desert Solitaire* was an iconic, romantic homage to the West and to the significance of the natural environment. Abbey, along with other well-known authors, such as Thomas McGuane, Ken Kesey, and Larry McMurtry, was a student in Stegner's creative writing program at Stanford.

Carson, her fellow authors, and the scientists, lawyers, and policymakers that followed them offered Americans another perspective: human life is part of the ecology of the earth and, as such, it deserves people's respect and protection, not only as a matter of survival, but as a moral imperative. Clearly, the "horrors Carson detailed about pesticides allowed readers to understand their position as part of, rather than aloft from, nature's web."[12]

7.2 THE ENVIRONMENTAL MOVEMENT

On Wednesday, April 22, 1970, one of the authors joined the 30,000 people who attended an Earth Day "teach-in" in Fairmont Park in Philadelphia.[13] Earth Day was really an "Earth Spring" since all Spring there had been teach-ins at 1,500 colleges and universities, 10,000 schools, thousands of churches, temples, city parks, and in front of corporate and government offices. All in all, 20 million Americans participated in the events – ten percent of the total U.S. population at the time.[14] Besides Senator Edmund Muskie who spoke in Philadelphia,[15] there were tens of thousands of speakers from a diverse group of professions, including anthropologists, zoologists, professors, students, bureaucrats, architects, doctors, engineers, a "handful of Fortune 500 executives," religious leaders, union members, artists, writers, musicians, celebrities, and activists from many national organizations, such as the Sierra Club and the National Wildlife Federation.[16] The message became "man is an epidemic ... destroying the environment upon which he depends."[17]

New public-interest organizations were formed to advocate on behalf of citizens for government action. The Conservation Law Foundation was established in 1966, the Environmental Defense Fund started in 1967, and the Natural Resources Defense Council was founded in 1970. These organizations had ties to older environmental groups such as the Audubon Society, the Sierra Club, and the John Muir Society. They were created and staffed by young lawyers, had close ties to first-class scientists, establishment lawyers, and "legendary families in natural conservation politics, such as Pinchot, Rockefeller, and Roosevelt," and even more importantly, they had connections to philanthropies like the Rockefeller and Ford Foundations.[18]

The activists were able to point to several well-known environmental disasters to amplify their campaign for government regulation.[19] The 1969 Santa Barbara Oil Spill dumped about three million gallons of crude oil into the ocean after a Union Oil drilling platform exploded off the coast of Santa Barbara. The episode received massive local and national media coverage after oil washed up on the beaches, covering more than 35 miles of Southern California coastline. The government confirmed that the spill killed an estimated 3,700 birds, particularly gulls and grebes, and caused tremendous ecological damages along the shoreline. At the time, it was the worst oil spill in the history of the country, and it is still one of our worst environmental disasters.[20]

News reports also revealed the Hooker Chemical Company had dumped 21,000 tons of toxic chemicals including known carcinogens into the Love Canal in New York. Investigators found afterward that there were unusually high rates of birth defects and miscarriages in a neighborhood near the canal. There were also reports of inexplicable illnesses including asthma, epilepsy, migraines, and nephrosis.[21]

The most headline-grabbing incident was when the Cuyahoga River caught fire in Cleveland in 1969 after sparks from a passing train likely ignited oil-soaked debris floating on the river's surface. The idea of a river catching fire was so out of the ordinary that it made Cleveland the symbol of the deeper problems the country was facing. On late-night TV, the comedian Johnny Carson joked, "What's the difference between Cleveland and the Titanic? Cleveland has a better orchestra."[22] And Randy Newman was inspired to write his satirical song about the city, "Burn On."[23]

As it turned out, this was not as unusual an event as it might have appeared to be. It was relatively common for rivers in the Great Lakes region to catch fire, including rivers in Chicago and Buffalo as well as Cleveland, because they were so polluted with chemicals. There were so many frequent fires on the Chicago River that they became a spectator sport when residents gathered on bridges to watch the conflagrations.[24]

7.3 CARSON'S LEGACY

The Love Canal, Santa Barbara, and the Cuyahoga River demonstrate the reason why markets on their own will fail to protect people from toxic substances, air and water pollution, pesticides, and other hazards. Simply put, it costs polluters money to abate the pollution that they create, which decreases profits. By comparison, disposal into the ground, water, and air costs little to nothing for the polluter. The country, however, does not escape the costs of pollution because they are shifted onto those who live near environmental disaster sites, drink polluted water, or are exposed to toxic substances. Instead, these costs are paid by the people who are harmed. The victim pays, not the harm doer. Moreover, as Carson warned, pollution and other environmental injuries change the world in which we live in ways that are noticeable and in ways that will come to haunt us. The existential challenge to life and the planet presented by global climate change is the latest result of the failure of markets voluntarily to abate pollution.

There is also an unfortunate racial dimension to environmental disasters. Unsurprisingly, industrial firms will purchase the cheapest land they can find for their polluting plants. Too often because that land is found in poor communities of color, people living in those communities bear a disproportionate share of the costs of pollution and the emission of toxic substances. Since the early 1980s, and continuing, the environmental justice movement has identified those past disparities and, going forward, focused on the fair and equitable distribution of economic benefits and burdens, and especially the reduction of the harms visited on the most vulnerable Americans and their most vulnerable communities.[25]

Congress passed seven laws in response to the public agitation, which form the heart of the government's efforts to protect people's health from environmental risks. The Clean Water Act, passed in 1965[26] and amended in 1972,[27] regulates the discharge of pollutants into rivers, lakes, and the ocean and establishes water quality standards for those water bodies. The 1966 Clean Air Act regulates air pollution from stationary sources such as coal-fired electric power plants and from mobile sources such as cars and trucks.[28]

In 1972, Congress passed a third law, the Federal Environmental Pesticide Act, to address the regulation of pesticides, which Carson had warned about.[29] With the passage of the 1974 Safe Drinking Water Act, Congress established another regulatory regime to protect the quality of the water we drink,[30] while a fifth law, the Toxic Substances Control Act of 1976,[31] authorized the Environmental Protection Agency to regulate the production and use of dangerous chemicals such as asbestos and lead-based paint. The sixth law, the 1976 Resource Conservation and Recovery

Act,[32] regulates the disposal of solid and hazardous waste. Finally, Congress passed the 1980 Comprehensive Environmental Response, Compensation, and Liability Act,[33] widely known as the Superfund law, after news reports about the Love Canal. Among other provisions, the law made companies that dump toxic chemicals financially responsible for cleaning up the soil or water bodies that they contaminated.

There was bipartisan support for environmental legislation reflecting the broad and deep public concerns about smog in the cities, rivers that caught fire, oil spills, and other environmental incidents. In his 1970 State of the Union Message, President Nixon called on the Congress to make "the 1970s a historic period when, by conscious choice, [we] transform our land into what we want it to become."[34] He then used his authority to reorganize the government to establish the Environmental Protection Agency in that year by consolidating functions scattered among some forty-four government offices. He explained that EPA would treat "air pollution, water pollution, and solid wastes as different forms of a single problem."[35]

Other new laws were aimed at protecting the environment itself. The 1964 Wilderness Act, for example, created a regulatory system to protect unspoiled wilderness areas across the country and keep them in their pristine states.[36] The 1970 National Environmental Policy Act required agencies to provide a detailed study of adverse environmental impacts before taking any actions that could significantly adversely affect human and natural environments.[37] It also established the Council on Environmental Quality in the White House to monitor and advise the government on environmental protection.

The animal kingdom was also protected by law. The Marine Mammal Protection Act, passed in 1972, as its name implies, protects marine mammals by regulating when they can be harvested or used.[38] Similarly, the Marine Protection, Research, and Sanctuaries Act, passed the same year, regulates the dumping of waste and other materials into the ocean to protect marine ecosystems.[39] Congress passed the Endangered Species Act in 1973 to establish a regulatory system to conserve and protect animals and other species as well as their habitats that are in danger of extinction.[40]

Prior to this legislation, states had developed common law doctrines that allowed some of the people who were harmed by pollution or exposed to toxic substances to sue the polluter, but as the environmental catastrophes in the 1960s and 1970s revealed to the public and Congress, the system of state common law was not up to the task. While there were many reasons why this was so, such as the cost of hiring lawyers and the difficulty of demonstrating a link between the pollution and a person's illness, the main reason was that state common law was not preventative. While the common law works once the harm is suffered, regulation works to reduce or prevent harm before it occurs. When the environmental statutes have been successful in protecting people, those who are protected have greater liberty to pursue their lives as they see fit. They are freer to pursue their livelihoods and interests.

7.4 RALPH NADER

Harm to the people and environment from industrial pollution and toxic releases was not the only market harm recognized as problems. In 1966, the Government Operations Subcommittee, chaired by Abraham Ribicoff (D. Conn.), held a series of sensational hearings about automobile safety. The star witness was a young consumer activist, Ralph Nader, who had published a book entitled, *Unsafe at Any Speed: The Designed-In Dangers of the American Automobile*.[41] The hearings revealed that General Motors had hired private detectives to dig up embarrassing evidence about him. This plan not only failed, but it also backfired. The story about the "country's paradigmatic giant business corporation" attempting to dig up dirt on a "penniless, idealistic reformer" gave Nader national recognition and a platform to support new government regulations.[42]

Nader's study of people injured in auto accidents led him to conclude that the design of the cars, rather than the driver's behavior, caused many accidents. The book opened with Nader's evidence that a GM car, the 1960–63 Chevrolet Corvair, had a suspension defect that caused drivers to lose control and sometimes roll their cars over. The remaining chapters similarly identified numerous safety issues, including issues with brakes, poor crash protection, and the failure of steering wheels to collapse in an accident. Nader claimed that the auto industry knew about and ignored the gaps between "existing designs and attainable safety." Car manufacturers, he charged, ignored a "moral imperative" to build safer cars.[43] His book then led to regulatory changes.

Nader filed a lawsuit against GM for spying on him and used the money from settling the case to finance a series of organizations known as Public Interest Research Groups.[44] According to a 1971 *New York Times* profile,

> Nader, now 37 years old, is no longer a lonely figure bravely fighting off the excesses of governmental and corporate bureaucracy and standing up all by himself for consumers. With him now are Nader's Raiders—hundreds of students, housewives, lawyers, professors, engineers, and scientists throughout the country who are working or have worked for him part-time and a handful of lawyers, a teacher or two and a few other professionals who have enlisted full-time and who operate from his several redoubts in Washington.

This team of advocates produced "an avalanche of reports, books, television programs, testimony at Congressional and administrative hearings, lawsuits, petitions, letters to government and corporate administrators and campaigns to organize college students in a nationwide consumers' crusade."[45] There were, among others, reports on chemicals and food safety, water pollution, consumer protection, unsafe food, and transportation costs.[46]

As in the environmental movement, current events highlighted the demands by consumer and worker advocates for greater government protections. The public, for example, learned about how modern medicines could injure, as well as heal, after it was revealed that Frances Kelsey, an employee of the Food and Drug Administration (FDA), almost single-handedly kept thalidomide from being sold in the United States. The drug, which had been approved for treating morning sickness in pregnant women in Europe, Britain, Canada, and the Middle East, had produced thousands of babies born with flipper-like arms and legs and other defects.[47] The public's attention was also drawn to the safety and health of workers by frequent mining catastrophes, such as the death of eighty-eight miners in Farmington, West Virginia, and the discovery of new occupational diseases, such as "brown lung."[48] Workers in textile mills, who developed the condition after breathing cotton dust during work hours, suffered from impaired lung capacity and shortened lives.

7.5 CONSUMER AND WORKER LEGISLATION

What Nader and other advocates recognized was that automobile and other consumer product manufacturers, in efforts to reduce costs, had failed to offer safer products for sale, and that resulting injuries and fatalities were preventable by building and selling safer products. Since the cost of injuries was paid by consumers, product sellers lacked strong incentives to build safer products, and consumers often lacked information about the dangers of the products that they purchased. It was unlikely people who bought the Corvair knew about the risk that they could lose control of their car through no fault of their own. Injured consumers could sue sellers, but this opportunity arose only after people were injured or killed. Moreover, as Nader's Raiders and news reports verified, scattered lawsuits were not sufficient to avoid the preventable deaths and injuries that were occurring because not all injured persons sued.

Workers faced a similar situation. They lacked information about the dangers they faced in going to work, particularly concerning occupational diseases like brown lung, and even if they were aware of some of these risks, many workers lacked the bargaining power to demand that employers make safety and health improvements. Injured or sick workers could try to claim compensation from workers compensation systems run by the states, but the historical experience indicated this option did not produce strong incentives for employers to make safety and health improvements. Further, the compensation offered by these systems was miserly at best.[49]

Acting on this information, Congress created four new federal agencies to protect consumers and workers and it added to the regulatory authority of existing agencies. Congress formed the National Highway Traffic Safety Administration (NTSA) in 1966 to reduce the number of deaths and injuries on our nation's roadways,[50] the Occupational Safety and Health Administration in 1971 to protect the health and safety of workers,[51] the Consumer Product Safety Commission in 1972 to protect consumers from dangerous products,[52] and the Mine Safety and Health Administration in 1977 to protect miners from being injured or becoming ill.[53] In addition, the Food and Drug Act Amendments of 1962 updated the authority of the Food and Drug Administration, founded in 1906, to protect consumers from unreasonably dangerous pharmaceutical drugs, such as thalidomide.[54]

7.6 THE INVISIBLE POOR

In the 1960s, Americans discovered that consumer markets and workplaces could be unsafe to the point that their lives were at stake. Americans made another discovery about their country. Despite the Social Security Act and the economic prosperity of the country, millions of low-income Americans struggled to pay for housing, food, medical care, and the other necessities of life.

Michael Harrington's book *The Other America* documented that close to fifty million people got by on less than the government's early 1960s' poverty-line benchmark of a $3,000 income for a family of four. He highlighted the general unawareness in the country about the extent of poverty by referring to low-income Americans as the "invisible" poor. As Harrington wrote, "the millions who are poor in the United States become increasingly invisible. Here is a great mass of people, yet it takes an effort of the intellect and will even to see them."[55] He pointed out, "Nearly one-third of the population lived 'below those standards that we have been taught to regard as the decent minimums for food, housing, and clothing.'"[56]

Senator Robert Kennedy's Subcommittee on Poverty held hearings on the poor in America, and he then visited the Appalachian region of eastern Kentucky and western Pennsylvania, California's Central Valley, and the Mississippi Delta. This "poverty tour," as it has come to be known, "found a nation within our nation in need of aid and wrongs that needed righting."[57] Kennedy's committee then sent physicians and psychologists to these areas who confirmed there was widespread hunger and malnutrition with attendant physical and psychological damages.

Lyndon Johnson responded to Harrington's call for action by proposing a Great Society in a 1964 speech at the University of Michigan.[58] In such a society, he explained, there were government programs that had the "purpose of protecting the life and liberty of our people." The country's "success in that pursuit," the President observed, "is the test of our success as a nation." Harkening back to Abraham Lincoln's definition of equality as "a fair chance in the race of life," LBJ challenged the country to move "upward to the Great Society," a place where there is "an end to poverty and racial injustice" and where "every child can find knowledge to enrich his mind and to enlarge his talents." The intent was to provide "an equal start and an equal opportunity to all Americans, regardless of race or background."[59]

The Economic Opportunity Act passed in 1964,[60] also known as the "War on Poverty," contained initiatives intended to provide people with the tools they needed to build and sustain a good life. Head Start operated summer programs to help prepare low-income children to start elementary school. It was expanded in 1981 to become a more comprehensive program focused on early childhood education, health, and nutrition. The Job Core, modeled on aspects of the Civilian Conservation Corps of the 1930s, provided food, shelter, work clothes, health care, and job training to teenagers and young adults. Neighborhood Health Centers brought medical care to low-income neighborhoods. The Volunteers in Service in America (VISTA) program organized volunteers to work with community groups in reducing poverty, and the Foster Grandparents program organized retired people to help tutor students struggling in school in poverty-ridden school districts.

The administration also created the Legal Services Program to provide legal assistance to low-income Americans who could not otherwise afford a lawyer. Tenants, for example, now had access to legal relief against landlords who failed to provide safe and sanitary housing. In 1974, when President Richard Nixon signed legislation to strengthen the program, he called it "a workhorse" in the effort to secure equal rights in America because "each day the old, the unemployed, the underprivileged, and the largely forgotten people of our Nation may seek help.... These are small claims in the Nation's eye, but they loom large in the hearts and lives of poor Americans."[61]

Congress was not done. In 1965, it created Medicare to finance hospital and related services for retired and other Social Security beneficiaries and Medicaid to help low-income families and individuals.[62] The same year, Congress also passed the Elementary and Secondary Education Act that provided funding to help poor children with their reading and other basic skills to give them a better chance at educational success and decent jobs.[63]

These many new laws were a continuation of the past. The country had assisted the poor in some form or another since colonial America. This aid was limited and begrudging, however, because it was believed that helping individuals who could work would discourage them from doing so and from developing self-independence. State programs were focused and run locally, but poverty was a national problem. The New Deal broke with this orthodoxy because it was obvious that many were suffering from no fault of their own – they were out of work, hungry, and ill-housed because there was no work to be had. Similarly, the millions of Americans who lived in deep poverty in the 1960s indicated to policymakers that poverty was the result of factors, particularly racism and economic conditions, that made it difficult for people, no matter how hard they worked, to achieve self-independence. There was additional help for people who could not work – the retired, children, and the disabled – but there was also help for those who could and did work.

7.7 EQUAL RIGHTS

The Roosevelt administration refused to address the Jim Crow laws that permeated the South and established a caste system that meant the country's black residents were second-class citizens. FDR did so because he needed the support of Southern senators to pass the New Deal, who, because of their longevity in the Senate, chaired key committees. While in the Senate and as majority leader, Lyndon Johnson had been a member of that club, resisting efforts to expand civil rights. As president, though, Johnson was free to pursue "full equality" as a key part of his Great Society. His political fate did not depend only on the voters in Texas; he could respond to the growing sentiment outside of the South that the time had come to act on the civil rights agenda just begun by his predecessor.

While he was majority leader in the Senate, Johnson was famous for his ability to cajole, negotiate, intimidate, and drag reluctant Senators to support legislation he wanted to pass. Robert Caro entitled his biography of Johnson's years in the Senate, *Master of the Senate*,[64] to reflect his political leadership skills. The President set about passing civil rights legislation over the opposition of long-time southern senators, using every one of the talents he employed as majority leader. The resulting success was a tribute to the president's perseverance and dedication to the cause.

The Civil Rights Act of 1964 outlawed discrimination based on race, color, or nationality by hotels, motels, restaurants, theaters, and other public accommodations engaged in interstate commerce, by state or local governments in public facilities, by federally funded state and local programs, and by employers and unions.[65] The same law also prohibited gender discrimination in hiring, firing, pay, and other conditions of employment. The 1965 Higher Education Act prohibited discrimination based on race, color, or nationality as a condition of receiving federal aid to local school districts with significant numbers of low-income children.[66] This law became the tool that the federal government wielded to speed up school integration. Additionally, the Voting Rights Act of 1965 established remedies to ensure that Black Americans had unfettered access to the ballot box.[67]

Race has been a defining issue for the country, and its impact can be seen from the signing of the Constitution until now.[68] Any history of how the country has been defined by the nation's values must confront the role of slavery, Jim Crow laws, and the civil rights revolution that took place in the 1960s. The next chapter will consider the impact of racial attitudes on the mix of markets and government that previous generations of Americans have chosen.

7.8 THE GREENING OF AMERICA

Closing the decade with his 1970 book, *The Greeting of America*,[69] Yale Law professor Charles Alan Reich indicted American society for a variety of political and economic sins, not the least of which was a corporation-dominated society that was tone-deaf to the individual need for self-expression and self-definition, resulting in a loss in the "degree of independent sovereignty enjoyed by the individual."[70] Following Galbraith, an individual consumer's choice was not her own. Instead, "producers largely create their own demand for products,"[71] and often those products involve the destruction of the environment, the buildup of a trillion-dollar defense state, and simply generate unneeded goods.[72]

Reich argued for a new public consciousness that would empower individuals to fashion new and more fulfilling lives. Once the public understood that government and corporations were in bed together, voters would reject "a society that is unjust to its poor and its minorities, is run for the benefit of a privileged few, is lacking in its proclaimed democracy and liberty, is ugly and artificial, that destroys the environment and self, and is, like the wars it spawns, 'unhealthy for children and other living things.'"[73]

Corporate leaders could have dismissed this jeremiad as an airy headed, left-leaning academic's idea of an unachievable utopia, or they could have ignored it altogether. Instead, big business seized on critics like Reich as radicals, Marxists, and revolutionaries. Reich was in fact nothing of the sort. He was arguing that the government had not done enough to eradicate poverty, ensure civil rights, regulate harmful market behavior, and so on because the close ties between government and corporate America were preventing a more full-on effort to achieve fundamental American values.

Reich was advocating for the government to do what it has always done although more of it. The regulation of markets existed in colonial America, and the federal government's involvement in a significant way started in the Progressive era. Support for low-income Americans likewise dates to the colonies, but it took the New Deal to recognize that poverty was the result of economic conditions beyond the control of individuals, and it took the Great Society to operationalize support for the poor. The national government had to take the lead because the economy, through technological innovation and modernization, was a national and international, not local, economy. Individual states were ill equipped to either manage or monitor it.

7.9 FAITH IN GOVERNMENT

Even as the country looked to the government to make needed changes in markets, attitudes about government began to shift. Faith in government was shaken by the revelations that the Vietnam War was not going as well as the government continually claimed, and academics and public interest advocates were not willing to trust the government to deliver on the new programs. By drawing doubts about whether the government could be trusted, these left-leaning critics of the government unintentionally opened the door for its opponents to argue that the country should primarily depend on markets, not government, to build the future.

7.10 THE VIETNAM WAR

While the Great Society was making a substantial adjustment in the mix of markets and government, protests about the Vietnam War grew to the point that LBJ chose not to run for re-election despite the popularity of the economic and social reforms that he had driven through the Congress. The war had another impact. It weakened the government's credibility. This loss of faith in government would spill over to regulatory and social programs.

The U.S. had been involved in Vietnam since the middle of the 1950s when it started providing military aid to fight a communist insurgency. John Kennedy sent more military advisors to head off what foreign policy experts were calling the "domino theory" – the claim that once one Southeast Asian country became communist may others would follow suit.[74] In August 1964, following an announcement of an attack on two U.S. ships by North Vietnamese torpedo boats off the coast of Viet Nam, Congress passed a resolution authorizing Johnson to take all necessary measures to retaliate and secure peace and security in southeast Asia.[75] By March 1965, Johnson had committed thousands of combat troops to expand the fight being carried out by the South Vietnamese army.[76]

Back home, demonstrations against the war were growing. In November 1969, as many as half a million people attended an anti-war protest in Washington, D.C., on the mall, and there were smaller protests in several additional cities.[77]

Pete Seeger captured the growing sentiment in his song, *Waist Deep in the Big Muddy*.[78] When the Smothers Brothers invited Seeger to sing the song on their popular TV variety show on CBS, the network cut the performance before the program could air, which resulted in even greater attention being paid to the antiwar movement.[79]

The anti-war movement, and the reactions to it, accelerated beyond society's capacity to control it. On April 28, 1970, President Nixon ordered the invasion of Cambodia and protests followed. On May 4, Ohio Governor Jim Rhodes directed the National Guard onto the Kent State campus where they fired on demonstrators, killing four students and wounding nine others. Widespread protests, not all peaceful, followed as campuses across the country shut down. The country's violent political polarization had already been televised by the news coverage of the 1968 Democratic National Convention in Chicago.

That violence was again on full display in New York City on May 8.[80] Following the Cambodian invasion and the Kent State killings, student anti-war protests multiplied, and, on that day, what started with 1,000 peaceful protesters evolved into a full-blown melee. Hundreds of construction workers confronted the protesters with each side trading taunts with the other. "Peace Now" versus "America, love it or leave it" being the more polite chants hurled between the groups. As construction workers confronted the protesters, the demonstrations spread throughout lower Manhattan. Eventually, there were at least 20,000 demonstrators and onlookers as 1,000 construction workers joined the fray.[81] The police, ostensibly there to preserve order, sat aside and let the hard hats beat students and onlookers. They stood by "laughing and smiling and … amiably chatting together and with the construction workers because as one policeman said, 'We're with them.'"[82] One week later, police opened fire on a student protest at Jackson State College, killing two students and injuring a dozen more.

7.11 THE CIVIC SKEPTICS

The flood of civil rights, consumer, environmental, and social welfare legislation appeared to address the problems underlying the economic success of the 1950s. Yet, the same activists who campaigned for the new legislation were not sure that they could trust the government to implement the new regulatory and social programs. Their distrust was related to the perception that the business community had dispro-portionate influence regarding government regulation just as Reich argued. Critics were concerned that the legislation that had been won in the halls of Congress could easily be lost in the halls of regulatory agencies responsible for implementing it.[83]

Yet, the same activists knew they needed the government to address those problems. They therefore became "civic skeptics."[84] They relied on the government to address the many problems facing the nation, but they supported legal procedures that would facilitate them in making sure that the government did its job. They advocated for the rights to intervene in agency decision-making, present their own evidence and argu-ments, and sue agencies that failed to take this evidence and arguments into account.[85]

The unofficial battle cry of the activists was "civil balance."[86] A Public Citizen report emphasized the need to "strive for a reawakening of the democratic impulse — the promise that people can shape the decisions which affect their lives."[87] Ralph Nader aimed "to build countervailing forces on behalf of the citizen."[88] William Reilly, who later would become the EPA administrator, called for a "much more equal balance of power."[89] And the *Environmental Handbook* claimed, "only a return to large scale citizen involvement in all levels can turn us from our destructive path."[90]

Social welfare advocates had a different, but related, concern. Large-scale bureau-cracies made decisions about low-income Americans without ever hearing from them or considering how they were forced to live their lives.[91] The problem again was a lack of participation in decision-making by the recipients of the social welfare benefits. In a series of earlier influential articles, Charles Reich argued that welfare beneficiaries should have the same constitutional due process rights as someone who is deprived of his or her private property by the government.[92]

The courts were responsive to these claims. They changed legal doctrines to rec-ognize the right of public interest groups and individuals to influence decisions that impacted them and the environment in which they lived. This participation sometimes held the government's feet to fire when it came to implementing the new laws.[93] But it also had an unintended impact that would be amplified in the 1980s – that the government could not be trusted to do the right thing.

7.12 CONCLUSION

In the 1960s and 1970s, the federal government took on the job of providing more assistance to the millions in poverty, securing equal rights for racial minorities and women, protecting people from environmental hazards as well as protecting the environment itself, and reducing the safety and health risks of consumer products and workplaces. As in previous adjustments, the new mix was responsive to changes in the economy that persuaded Americans that government action was necessary to rebalance America's fundamental values.

Markets promote individual liberty by allowing people to make their choices concerning the products they buy, the places they live, and where they work, among other advantages of a market economy. Yet, as the country came to realize during this time, people do not have this choice if, through no fault of their own, they lack the money to participate in that market economy or if they are the victims of discrimination. A person's liberty is also reduced if she or he is injured or killed because of environmental hazards, dangerous workplaces, and products that threaten them.

Yet the very people who supported the dramatic expansion of government ended up undercutting the faith in government to carry out its new missions. Conservative critics of the Great Society skipped over the nuances of the left's critique of government saying that the problem was corporate influence over government. Instead, they painted the left's criticism as a government that could not be trusted to intervene in markets. They argued the new procedural rights gave the left too much influence over government to pursue their radical agenda of changing the country. The fact that the government was doing pretty much what it had always done was lost in a wave of conservative criticism.

Despite what was to come, the history of government and markets was altered by the 1960s in ways that improved the country and its allegiance to fundamental American values. People who are free from being harmed by market behavior have more freedom. People who no longer live in dire poverty have more freedom. And people who are free from being discriminated against based on their skin color have more freedom. LBJ's courage to fight for civil rights at a time when many in the country were not ready for that campaign maybe his greatest legacy, but he could not have done it but for John Lewis and a remarkable group of Americans who, as discussed in Chapter 8, picked up the cause of civil rights and helped to make it happen.

8

John Lewis's America

Equal Justice for All

The yearning for the proper mix of government and market is essential for achieving the American Dream, but it is partial. The American Dream is also a yearning for a society of liberty, equality, and fairness. This book is the story of obtaining those aspirations, and this history establishes that finding the proper balance between government and markets is necessary but difficult to achieve. As markets denied freedom and equality, the country eventually made the needed changes with one glaring exception: the 250 years of the perpetuation of slavery from its inception to the Civil War, and then the widespread racial discrimination that followed for another 100 years. Freedom and equality for Black Americans remained out of reach for too much of the country's history. The effort to overcome this history is the story of this chapter. It also the story of John Lewis' life.

Lewis believed in the promises of America; he believed in the American Dream. As related earlier, James Truslow Adams defined the American Dream in 1931 as a society in which "each man and each woman shall be able to attain the fullest stature of which they are innately capable."[1] In the New Deal and again in the Great Society, the country realized that this requires individuals to have such basic securities as income, food, shelter, health care, and education.[2] Something more is needed from the government, however. As Truslow recognized, the American Dream requires that individuals must be "unrepressed by social orders which had been developed for the benefit of classes rather than for the simple human beings of any and every class."[3]

What is most remarkable about the American Dream is its staying power even in a racially polarized society. The Dream appears in colonial America in a poem written by Phyllis Wheatly, an enslaved woman, and in a poem by Amanda Gorman, the nation's first Young Poet Laureate, who recited it at Joe Biden's inaugural 250 years later. And it appears as the guiding light of John Lewis' life. Lewis knew that the realization of the American Dream for many required the assistance of government.

94

8.1 JOHN LEWIS

A 20-year-old named John Lewis started his lifelong engagement with civil rights when he organized sit-in demonstrations at Nashville lunch counters. Later that year, the Student Nonviolent Coordinating Committee (SNCC) was formed, and Lewis later became its chair. On May 4, 1961, he was one of the original thirteen Freedom Riders who boarded a bus from Washington, D.C. to New Orleans to test Supreme Court decisions that outlawed racial segregation in interstate bus travel. As SNCC Chair, at age 23, Lewis became one of six organizers of the 1963 civil rights march on Washington where Reverend Martin Luther King gave his "I Have a Dream" speech. Two years later, Lewis and Hosea Williams, a colleague of Rev. King, led the March on Montgomery in response to the death of a 26-year-old church deacon from Marion, Alabama, Jimmie Lee Jackson, who died from being shot by an Alabama state trooper.

The Montgomery March began on May 7, in Selma Alabama, 54 miles away as 600 civil rights protestors tried to walk across the Edmund Pettus Bridge, where Alabama state troopers blocked one end of the bridge. After the marchers refused an order to disperse, the troopers and horse-mounted police attacked the nonviolent demonstration with clubs and tear gas. As white onlookers cheered, Lewis at the head of the protesters was the first demonstrator attacked by the police, and he nearly died from the skull fracture that resulted. Television pictures of the attack, which became known as "Bloody Sunday," spurred passage of the 1965 Voters Rights Act two months later.[4]

Lewis represented Georgia for 33 years in the U.S. House of Representatives until his death on July 17, 2020. He led an annual march across the same bridge to "kindle hope in the ongoing struggle for racial justice" for the twenty years before he died. On the 50th anniversary of Bloody Sunday, Lewis was joined by President Obama. When Lewis died, Obama delivered a eulogy for him in the Ebenezer Baptist Church in Atlanta, Georgia, which is the same church in which Martin Luther King, Jr. and his father preached. The president recognized that Lewis had a faith in our Founding; he believed that his faith could be redeemed, and he never wavered despite being severely beaten. In speaking about Lewis and other civil rights leaders, the president said that "America was built by people like them" and that their efforts "as much as anyone in our history brought this country a little bit closer to our highest ideals."

Just before he died, Lewis wrote an editorial directed to the country's youth that was published posthumously in the *New York Times* on July 30, 2020. Lewis wrote how he was inspired by the efforts to combat police violence and continue the search for racial justice after George Floyd's death and the rise of the Black Lives Matter movement. He wrote that he had been there before. "Emmett Till was my George Floyd." Till was 14 years old in 1955 when he was abducted, tortured, and lynched in Mississippi after being accused of offending a white woman.

Lewis then noted that Martin Luther King had said that "we are all complicit when we tolerate injustice. He said it is not enough to say it will get better by and by. He said each of us has a moral obligation to stand up, speak up and speak out."[5] For all his life, Lewis stood up, spoke up, and spoke out. He liked to advocate getting into "good trouble," relying on nonviolence, fighting for racial justice, struggling together, and reaching for America. "Good trouble" changed the laws of America. It also changed American hearts and minds. He ends his last editorial: "So I say to you, walk with the wind, brothers and sisters, and let the spirit of peace and the power of everlasting love be your guide."

8.2 A LONG HERITAGE

The winds of Lewis' fight for racial justice have blown continuously and longer than the history of the country. In 1761, a seven-year-old girl endured the ship voyage to this country after being seized in West Africa. Upon her arrival in Boston, she was sold to the Wheatley family. Like all those who were enslaved, the young girl was given the family name, and in a cruel twist, she was also named after the slave ship, *The Phillis*, that transported her to the colonies. Phillis Wheatley soon learned English and published her first poem in 1770. Shortly thereafter, her first book, *Poems on Various Subjects, Religious and Moral*, was printed in England because she could not find a publisher in colonial America. Well received in England, she returned to Boston to care for her failing mistress and was given her freedom.[6]

In *On Being Brought from Africa to America*, Wheatley captures one of the recurring themes and the deep contradictions of slavery:

> 'Twas mercy brought me from my *Pagan* land,
> Taught my benighted soul to understand
> that there's a God, there's a *Saviour* too:
> Once I redemption neither sought nor knew.
> Some view our sable race with scornful eye,
> "Their color is a diabolical die."
> Remember, *Christians*, *Negroes*, Black as *Cain*,
> May be refin'd, and join th' angelic train.[7]

After the Continental Congress appointed George Washington general of the North American armies in 1775, Wheatley sent him a poem to commemorate that honor. The poem ends in praise and hope for freedom from British rule:

> Proceed, great chief, with virtue on by side,
> Thy every action let the goddess guide.
> A Crown, a mansion, and a throne that shine,
> With gold unfading, WASHINGTON! be thine.[8]

Wheatley's poetry exhibits America's deepest and unresolved paradox – the commitment to liberty and equality in the presence of America's original sin of slavery.

For Wheatley, Christianity was an answer. But, despite her hopes and prayers, Washington and America's other leaders did not resolve that paradox nor did their successors.

To the contrary, the country relied on slavery to build the South's economy and its plantations,[9] to enrich the Wall Street institutions that financed the slave trade and the cotton and other goods that enslaved people produced,[10] and the manufacturing firms of the North who bought those goods and used them to make money.[11] Money made in the slave trade was instrumental in starting many of the nation's universities, including those in the Ivy League, and the same schools benefitted from the work done by enslaved people.[12] More disturbingly, slavery was embedded in the very constitutional fabric of the country.

8.3 OUR SACRED DOCUMENTS

On July 4, 1776, the colonists declared their freedom from Great Britain. In brief, the Declaration of Independence had one principal objective – self-government. Issuing the Declaration against the King was not an easy decision for many Americans. Many still hoped that Britain would grant them a role in its government. Such was not to be. Consequently, if the colonists could not have a voice in Parliament, then they would go it on their own.

To make their case, the colonists needed a persuasive argument not only for themselves and the King but, as the Declaration itself states, for the world. The Declaration first asserts that there comes a time when the political bonds between ruler and ruled can be severed. For the colonists, the time had come. King George had overreached his legitimate authority, and in twenty-seven paragraphs, the Declaration lists with particularity the grievances against him. More importantly, they grounded the declaration of their independence in a natural right to human equality.[13]

Human beings have a natural right to determine their own destiny; they cannot be controlled by another power, otherwise they are enslaved. Ironies aside, and aspirations unfulfilled, the desire for liberty and self-government was grounded in equality even if unrealized and even if American slavery directly contradicted those values.

Often unnoted, Thomas Jefferson drafted a remonstrance against the King, alleging that it was the King who perpetuated slavery. The King, Jefferson wrote, "waged cruel war against human nature itself, violating its most sacred rights of life & Liberty in the persons of a distant people who never offended him, captivating & carrying them into slavery in another hemisphere, or to incur miserable death in their transportation thither."[14] Jefferson intended to blame the King for slavery and to use slavery as a justification for seeking American liberty, but delegates from Georgia and South Carolina would not tolerate any mention of slavery in the draft and threatened to withdraw from the Continental Congress if that remonstrance was not removed. The drafting committee removed the slavery complaints against the King in their entirety.

The perpetuation of slavery was the necessary condition for the colonies to reach an agreement to declare their independence from Britain, and it was necessary to adopt the Constitution. As is too well known, the three-fifths clause, the fugitive slave provisions, and several other portions embedded slavery in the soon-to-be United States of America without ever mentioning the word.[15] Whether the Constitution is regarded as a "Faustian bargain or as a political compromise," there is no getting around the fact that it legitimized racial injustice.[16] William Lloyd Garrison, a newspaper publisher and abolitionist, characterized the Constitution as a pact with the devil. As a direct result of that compromise, the first twelve presidents were enslavers during their lifetime, and eight of them were enslavers while they were severing as president.

8.4 THE FUGITIVE LAWS OF SLAVERY

While the Constitution turned a blind eye to racial and chattel slavery, the government did far more than merely get out of the way. Government establishes the property laws that enable markets, and according to those laws, enslaved Black Americans and their children, legitimate and illegitimate, were the property of their owners. This meant that the owners or their agents had a legal right to recapture fugitive enslaved people and return them to being enslaved as a matter of law.

Article IV of the Constitution provided: "No person held to Service or Labour in one State, under the Laws thereof, escaping into another, shall, in Consequence of any Law or Regulation therein, be discharged from such Service or Labour, but shall be delivered up on Claim of the Party to whom such Service or Labour may be due."[17] Enslavers argued, however, that a stronger law was necessary because the Constitution did not specify what procedures were necessary to recapture fugitive enslaved people and because it failed to do so, it left an opening for abolitionists in non-slavery states to maneuver against slavery by, for example, granting rights such as the right to counsel or to trial by jury.

To fix that perceived loophole, Congress passed the Fugitive Slave Act of 1793 that allowed the recapture of fugitive enslaved people upon a simple affidavit by the owner claiming title.[18] Enslaved people could not offer evidence of their own, and the act provided criminal penalties for anyone obstructing or aiding fugitives. Anti-slave states reacted to this legislation by extending due process rights to enslaved people such as the right to a judicial hearing contesting their capture. Those laws were not effective. Instead, the federal laws took precedence.

Toni Morrison's *Beloved* is a fictionalized account of the story of Margaret Garner, the cruelty of chattel slavery, and of odiousness of fugitive slave laws.[19] Garner found her way to Cincinnati where she was pursued as a runaway. Rather than return South and have her children live in slavery, she murdered one child, was arrested, and brought to trial. Her defense attorney argued that she should be tried as a free person in the free state of Ohio. His argument was rejected. Instead, the federal judge ruled that as property she must be returned to her owner. Garner, as chattel, had no voice and could not even argue for her own life in a court of law.

The Supreme Court ensured that the Constitution and the Fugitive Slave Act was enforced in a case involving a Pennsylvania statute that made it a felony to take a runaway slave from the state. Edward Prigg forcibly captured Margaret Moran and one of her children, who was born in Pennsylvania, and returned her and her children to her owner in Maryland. After Prigg was indicted in Pennsylvania, he contested the indictment and challenged the law. In an opinion by Justice Joseph Story, Prigg's indictment was overturned, and the Pennsylvania law was declared unconstitutional as a violation of the Constitution and of the 1793 federal legislation.

Story wrote that without the fugitive slave clause, "the Union could not have been formed,"[20] and not only was it necessary for the formation of the Union, it remained necessary for its preservation. According to Story, the clause was intended to give slave holders the "positive, unqualified right"[21] to recapture their enslaved people because the "true design ... was to guard against non-slaveholding states from inter-meddling with, or obstructing, or abolishing the rights of the owners of slaves."[22] Since owners had more rights to the bodies of the people that they owned than people themselves had in their own bodies, the opinion strips away a state's authority to impose procedural safeguards in favor of runaway enslaved people.

In reaction, some Northern states passed personal liberty laws in another attempt to prevent the capture of enslaved persons and the disruption of their families. In response to this round of abolitionist protections, slave owners again argued for the legal protection of their property, and again Congress responded with the Fugitive Slave Act of 1850.[23] Under that law, federal officials had a duty to arrest runaways, and any official who failed to capture a runaway was liable for a $1,000 fine. Also, any person aiding and abetting a runaway was also subject to a $1,000 fine. Adding insult to injury, if a magistrate held in favor of the slave owner, their compensation was $10. If they held in favor of the runaway, then they were compensated $5. The act worked as intended. During the decade of the 1850s, 332 slaves were returned, and only 11 were declared free.[24]

In the 1857 *Dred Scott Case*, the Supreme Court went even further to deny rights to enslaved people. Scott, an enslaved Black man, was taken from Missouri, a slave state, to Illinois, a "free" state that did not have slavery. When he was returned to Missouri, he sued and argued that he had been freed from slavery because of being in Illinois for a time. The Court responded that "People of African ancestry were not citizens, held no rights or privileges of citizenry." Instead, "They [have] ... been regarded as beings of an inferior order, and altogether unfit to associate with the white race, either in social or political relations; and so far inferior, that they had no rights which the white man was bound to respect."[25]

The Declaration of Independence, the Constitution, federal legislation, and Supreme Court precedents deeply enshrined slavery throughout the laws of the country. And it would take both the Civil War and three constitutional amendments to end it. Or, at least, attempt to end slavery and its effects.

8.5 A DIFFERENT AMERICAN DREAM

Frederick Douglass was born in 1818 to enslaved parents. After making his escape to Philadelphia in 1838, his career as an orator, thinker, and writer began. Douglas was not unfamiliar with the yet to be named American Dream. When he was often called on to speechify on noted occasions, he unleashed his view of that dream.

At a Fourth of July celebration in Rochester, New York, in 1852, he had much to tell the crowd. Although Douglas was invited to give the day's oration, he told the celebrants that he did not stand on the same stage with them. July 4th was a national celebration for his listeners. It was a recognition of their freedom and independence. But the "Fourth of July is yours, not mine" Douglas told them.

Douglas reminded his audience the fight for independence was about contesting an unjust government that imposed unreasonable and oppressive laws; laws that threatened to make the colonists slaves. It was more than ironic that Douglas was asked to speak while the multitude of his race was denied the freedoms that his listeners were celebrating. Still, Douglas noted the power contained in the Declaration. He called it "the ringbolt to the chain of your nation's destiny; so, indeed, I regard it. The principles contained in that instrument are saving principles."[26]

Noting the great divide between a speaker and the audience, Douglas turned his attention to American slavery, noting that it exposes the falseness of America, its inhumanity, and its violation of the virtues of the Constitution and of the Bible. Everyone he reminds the crowd knows that slavery is wrong as a matter of the country's founding aspirations and, echoing the opening paragraph of the Declaration of Independence, as a matter of God's law. Slavery is the great sin and shame of America, and there is no way to soften that indictment. The founding laws of the country stole the labor of enslaved people, broke their families apart, prevented their education, and, at bottom, undermined their humanity. Worse, the fugitive slave laws simply and cruelly legitimized the hunting down and murder of escaped enslaved people. There is no amount of logic or argumentation in the courts or Congress to justify the institution.

As for Phillis Wheatley's faith that Christianity would lead the nation to end slavery, Douglas told his audience that American Christianity is "a religion for oppressors, tyrants, man-stealers, and thugs." Simply, the American church is guilty of tolerating slavery, for perpetuating it, and for its refusal to take the steps necessary to abolish it.

After the Civil War began, Douglas reminded Americans of the role that black soldiers played in their fight for freedom. Then, literally days before Lincoln's assassination in a speech before the Massachusetts Antislavery Society, Douglas delivered a speech on "What the Black Man Wants."[27] His answer is as simple as it is direct: "Do nothing with us!" If the people of the country were true to the aspirations contained in their sacred documents of ensuring liberty and equality, then the country owed Black Americans nothing other than what was already theirs. Simply, "Let us have slavery abolished, … let us have labor organized, and then, in the natural course of events, the right of suffrage will be extended." In this way, Douglas insists freedom for enslaved Americans is not a gift; it is the repayment of a debt long overdue. It is also a right to self-government, a right that was demanded, fought for, and won in the Revolutionary War, at least for Whites.

8.6 EIGHT YEARS IN POWER

Abraham Lincoln was aware of the costs of that debt as he acknowledged at Gettysburg: "[W]e here highly resolve that these dead shall not have died in vain – that this nation, under God, shall have a new birth of freedom – and that government of the people, by the people, for the people, not shall not perish from this earth." The war continued for another deadly 18 months after that address; Lincoln won reelection; and again, the president acknowledged the terrible price of slavery. The war then still raging "would continue until all the wealth piled by the bondsman's two hundred and fifty years of unrequited toil shall be sunk, and until every drop of blood drawn with the lash shall be paid by another drawn with the sword." A month after this speech, Lincoln died in Petersen's boarding house at 7:22 am on April 15, 1865. A month later, on May 9, 1865, the war ended, and Lincoln's new birth of freedom began in the form of the Reconstruction that succeeded for a short while.

Thomas Ezekiel Miller was a Reconstruction success story. Although he was light enough to "pass as white," he chose to live as a person of color and was active in the political life of South Carolina. He was elected to three terms in the State House and one term in the State Senate. Then, in 1888, he ran for the U.S. House and won a disputed election but only served for a few weeks before being defeated in a re-election bid. In 1895, as a member of the South Carolina Constitutional Convention, he implored his fellow citizens to maintain the racial progress of Reconstruction in a speech at that state's constitutional convention:

> We were eight years in power. We had built schoolhouses, established charitable institutions, built and maintained the penitentiary system, provided for the education of the deaf and dumb, rebuilt the ferries. In short, we had reconstructed the State and placed it upon the road to prosperity.[28]

His plea went unheeded. The constitution that was adopted provided for literacy tests and property requirements instead of protecting the franchise. When "those measures proved insufficient to enforcing white supremacy, black citizens were shot, tortured, beaten, and maimed."[29]

Reconstruction, often referred to as the Second Founding, encompasses the Emancipation Proclamation of 1863, the 13th Amendment (1865) abolishing slavery, the 14th Amendment (1868) protecting citizenship, and the 15th Amendment (1870) protecting voting rights. The Reconstruction Amendments literally redrafted the Constitution by negating its slavery provisions, the fugitive slave laws, and all other impediments to full citizenship and participation in the government of the United States by enslaved peoples. By all accounts, the Reconstruction witnessed significant gains toward the achievement of racial justice. Although estimates vary, over 1,000 black men served in various public offices at the state, local, and county levels,[30] and 16 served in the United States Senate and House of Representatives.

Those gains were erased by the country's second pact with the devil – the conclusion of the 1876 presidential election.[31] After the votes were counted, the election between Democrat Samuel Tilden and Republican Rutherford B. Hayes was too close to call, and various disputes arose over who should be counted as electors in the face of claims of fraud, intimidation, and violence. To resolve the dispute, a compromise was reached, and an Electoral Commission was created composed of ten Republican and Democratic senators and congressmen and five Supreme Court justices (two Republicans, two Democrats, and one independent) to decide which votes to count and resolve the dispute. The independent justice refused to serve and was replaced by a Republican justice. And that was all it took to throw the race to Hayes, who won the presidency by one vote, and the country paid an awful price for that single vote.

Within two months after taking office, "Hayes ordered federal troops surrounding the South Carolina and Louisiana State houses ... to return to their barracks. [He] did not, as legend has it, remove the last federal troops from the South, but his action implicitly meant that the few remaining soldiers would no longer play a role in political affairs." This troop "withdrawal" "marked a major turning point in national policy." It meant the end of Reconstruction.[32]

The 1876 election was the country's centennial election to celebrate its Declaration of Independence. Sad irony, then, is that just as our sacred documents enshrined slavery, the 1876 election substituted Jim Crow laws to wipe away any gains made by the Civil War and the Reconstruction Amendments.

8.7 JIM CROW AMERICA

The name "Jim Crow" was originated by Thomas Dartmouth Rice, a white minstrel entertainer who performed a song and dance act in which he played a Black man he named Jim Crow by darkening his face, acting "like a buffoon," and speaking "with an exaggerated and distorted imitation of African American Vernacular English."[33] Due to Rice's success, other white minstrel performers adopted Jim Crow as a stage persona. The end of Reconstruction, aided and abetted by the Supreme Court, cleared the decks for most southern and border states to establish the laws, customs, and etiquette that segregated and demeaned Black Americans from the 1870s to the 1960s, and this way of life became known as the Jim Crow era.

The end of the right to vote for Black Americans in the South was a centerpiece of the Jim Crow South. Among whatever gains that were made during Reconstruction for Black Americans, the most significant was the increased participation in the political processes of the country. That participation was then severely contracted. Since the ability to vote meant the ability to participate, white Southerners understood all too clearly the importance of the franchise and the effect it had on improving Black representation. For the white South, the benefits gained from restoring the vote had to be taken away from the newly emancipated Americans, and this was done with a vengeance. Literacy tests, poll taxes, and voter intimidation to the point of lynching became methods of choice for denying the vote to Black citizens.

Racial violence was used in general to enforce the Jim Crow regime. The National Memorial for Peace and Justice, located on a six-acre site overlooking the Alabama State Capitol, is dedicated to these victims. As a visitor, you enter a walkway with 800 weathered steel columns, each one hanging from a roof. On the column is etched the name of an American county and the people who were lynched there, although many are simply listed as "unknown." Some columns report the circumstances of the hanging. Paris Banks was killed in Mississippi in 1922 for carrying a photograph of a white woman, and Caleb Gadly became a victim in Kentucky in 1894 for "walking behind the wife of his white employer."[34] Southern courts and white juries routinely acquitted the perpetrators of these crimes if they were arrested, which most were not.

None of this would have been possible without the Supreme Court. Congress had attempted to fulfill the promises of the Reconstruction amendments when it passed the 1875 Civil Rights Act that guaranteed equal treatment in public transportation, public accommodations, and jury service.[35] In The Civil Rights Cases of 1883, the Supreme Court in an 8-1 decision ruled that Congress lacked the constitutional authority to reverse state laws that allowed racial discrimination in public accommodations.[36] The consequence, as Justice Harlan noted in his dissent, was that the country entered "an era of constitutional law" in which "the rights of freedom and American citizenship cannot receive from the nation that efficient protection which heretofore was unhesitatingly accorded to slavery and the rights of the master."[37]

Thirteen years later, the Court enhanced the Jim Crow laws when it decided *Plessy v. Ferguson*, again with Justice Harlan in dissent. The majority, which upheld a Louisiana statue that prohibited integration in public transportation, rejected the argument that "the enforced separation of the two races stamps the colored race with the badge of inferiority." According to the majority, inferiority existed "solely because the colored race chooses to put that construction upon it."[38]

Harlan's dissent pointed out that the intended purpose of the law was to separate the races and treat one as inferior to the other. To Harlan, such treatment was pernicious. "The destinies of the two races, in this country, are indissolubly linked together, and the interest of both require that the common government of all shall not permit the seeds of race hate to be planted under the sanction of law." Further, he asks rhetorically: "What can more certainly arouse race hate, what more certainly create and perpetuate a feeling of distrust between these races, than state enactments which, in fact, proceed on the ground that color citizens are so inferior and degraded that they cannot be allowed to sit in public coaches occupied by white citizens?"[39]

8.8 THE LEGAL BATTLE

Black Americans, as related earlier, were by and large left out of the New Deal because Southern Senators insisted on their exclusion as the price of supporting Roosevelt's ambitious legislative agenda. The government not only continued to ignore the needs of Black citizens in the Eisenhower administration, but the administration's policies regarding housing mortgages and its highway program had lasting negative impacts on Black citizens, as covered earlier. The situation only changed after the Supreme Court outlawed the Jim Crow laws and the civil rights movement forced White Americans to confront the country's failure to live up to its fundamental values.

The NAACP began its campaign against legally sanctioned racial discrimination in 1935 when it challenged segregation in graduate and professional schools. In 1938, the Supreme Court held that Missouri had to provide Black law students with facilities and educational opportunities equal to those available to White students.[40] The NAACP's strategy was that it would be too costly for states to establish separate, but truly equal, graduate opportunities for Black students, leaving a state no choice but to integrate its graduate and professional schools.[41]

The organization changed its strategy in 1948 and began to press for the end of the Jim Crow laws. Thurgood Marshall was appointed to lead this effort. As a biographer of Marshall recognized, "Few Americans have affected our nation's legal, political, and social lives as Thurgood Marshall."[42] His successful legal campaign leading to *Brown v. Board of Education* changed the nation as the Supreme Court in a series of cases dismantled Jim Crow America.[43] When the Southern states were intransigent after *Brown* about implementing school desegregation, the Court ruled that the states were constitutionally required to integrate.[44]

In *Brown*, the Court recognized that segregation of white and black children had a detrimental impact because "the policy of separating the races is usually interpreted as denoting the inferiority" of Black children. Moreover, this impact was greater because "it has the sanction of the law." Thus, "[s]eparate educational facilities are inherently unequal."[45] In these few sentences, the Court overruled *Plessy v Ferguson* and its claim that inferiority existed "solely because the colored race chooses to put that construction upon it."[46]

8.9 THE MARCH ON WASHINGTON

With these decisions, the Supreme Court finally included Black Americans within the meaning of the equal protection clause of the Constitution, and it ruled that it had the authority to order the states to comply. But as the 1963 March on

Washington for Jobs and Freedom reminded Americans, outlawing segregation was not enough. New laws to establish these rights were necessary, not only to ensure equal legal treatment of Black citizens but also to integrate them into the economy. As Abraham Lincoln said years before, the government's job was to ensure a "fair chance in the race of life."

The title of the march – "Jobs and Freedom" was the continuation of an idea that began twenty years earlier. In 1941, A. Philip Randolph, a labor and civil rights activist who founded the Brotherhood of Sleeping Car Porters, the first predominantly Black labor union, planned a march on Washington to protest racial exclusion in defense industries. A day before the march, it was called off after FDR promised to end racial discrimination in war industries and in the federal government. By Executive Order No. 8802, the Federal Employment Practices Committee was created to expand job opportunities for Black Americans, and it succeeded until the end of World War II when Congress ordered the agency to cease operations.

Martin Luther King' closed the march attended by an estimated 250,000 with his immortal "I Have A Dream" speech. King also used another more practical metaphor:

> In a sense we have come to our nation's capital to cash a check. When the architects of our republic wrote the magnificent words of the Constitution and the Declaration of Independence, they were signing a promissory note to which every American was to fall heir. This note was a promise that all men, yes, black men as well as white men, would be guaranteed the "unalienable rights of life, liberty, and the pursuit of happiness."
>
> It is obvious today that America has defaulted on this promissory note insofar as her citizens of color are concerned…. We refuse to believe that there are insufficient funds in the great vaults of opportunity of this nation. So we have come to cash this check—a check that will give us upon demand the riches of freedom and the security of justice.[47]

Earlier that day, Lewis amplified the call for economic opportunity. Lewis' speech was not delivered as he originally wrote it because civil rights leaders and the Kennedy administration thought his prepared remarks were too incendiary, and they implored him to tone them down.[48] In a sentence that was cut out of the speech, he claimed, "The revolution is at hand, and we must free ourselves of the chains of political and economic slavery."[49] Yet he retained that message in the speech that he gave:

> We march today for jobs and freedom, but we have nothing to be proud of. For hundreds and thousands of our brothers are not here. For they are receiving starvation wages, or no wages at all. While we stand here, there are sharecroppers in the Delta of Mississippi who are out in the fields working for less than three dollars a day, twelve hours a day …
>
> I appeal to all of you to get into this great revolution that is sweeping this nation. Get in and stay in the streets of every city, every village and hamlet of this nation until true freedom comes, until the revolution of 1776 is complete.[50]

Lewis was critical of the Kennedy administration for what he correctly perceived as its foot-dragging on civil rights legislation. Throughout his life, he sought a Beloved Community but did not find it in America. His call to revolution was a call to a nonviolent revolution but that call was not made casually or without deep commitment, a commitment he carried through until his death on July 17, 2020. Lewis brought us full circle. If the American Dream is to be achieved there must be equal participation in government and in markets. Political dignity and economic dignity go hand in hand.

8.10 BLACK NATIONALISM

Another Black leader, Malcom X, also spoke about a revolution, but he was skeptical it would come about using civil disobedience. In the popular mind, Malcolm X was the antithesis of King. For one thing, he made much of white America nervous as the chief disciple and spokesperson for Elijah Muhammad, the leader of the Nation of Islam, an Islamic and Back nationalist movement. After a speech given less than two weeks after JFK's assassination,[51] Malcom was asked what he thought of the tragedy, and he said that the assassination was an example of the "chickens coming home to roost." As H. Rap Brown, who followed John Lewis as SNCC leader and later the Minister of Justice for the Black Panther Party, said in 1967, violence in this country was as "American as cherry pie."[52]

In a speech before two thousand people delivered months before the passage of the 1964 Civil Rights Act, Malcom X attacked the legislation as too weak and too much of a compromise.[53] Black Americans, he indicated, were losing their patience waiting for Congress to act after they provided decisive votes to put the Democrats in power: "They get all the Negro vote, and after it the Negro gets nothing in return."[54] Rather than wait for white Americans to recognize and act on the long national shame of racism, Malcom X advocated for a "black nationalism" that means "a Black man should control politics and the politicians in their community," and "we should control the economy of our community." And he issued a warning to white America. "If it's necessary to form a black nationalist army, we'll form a black nationalist army. It will be the ballot or the bullet. It'll be liberty or it'll be death."

8.11 THE CIVIL RIGHTS ACT OF 1964

Following in the footsteps of the civil rights leaders, Lyndon Johnson led the fight to pass civil rights legislation by reminding voters that racial discrimination was a glaring and long-neglected failure for the country to live up to its fundamental values.[55] And, as he saw it, Black Americans lived in increasingly segregated communities, suffered greater poverty, lacked decent medical care, and suffered from a "devastating heritage of long years of slavery and a century of oppression, hatred, and injustice." These infirmities reinforced each other and needed to be reversed. For Johnson, the reversal required decent jobs, homes, welfare and social protection, health care, and the chance to "move beyond opportunity to achievement."[56]

The Civil Rights Act of 1964 was and remains the most sweeping civil rights legislation since Reconstruction.[57] It makes it illegal to discriminate based on race, color, religion, sex, or national origin in voting, public accommodations, public facilities, public education, federally funded programs, and employment. When LBJ signed the legislation, he echoed Fredericks Douglas' plea that Black Americans simply wanted to be treated equally when he stressed that the law did not "give special treatment to any citizen":

> We believe that all men are created equal. Yet many are denied equal treatment. We believe that all men have certain unalienable rights. Yet many Americans do not enjoy those rights. We believe that all men are entitled to the blessings of liberty. Yet millions are being deprived of those blessing. Not because of their own failures, but because of the color of their skin.[58]

Johnson then pointed out the need for additional legislation in his 1965 commencement address at Howard University.[59] The address is memorable for its analogy to Lincoln's dedication to creating a "fair chance in the race of life." "You do not take a person who, for years, has been hobbled by chains and liberate him, bring him up to the starting line of a race and then say, 'you are free to compete with all the others,' and still justly believe that you have been completely fair."

Congress passed the Voting Rights Act of 1965 two months later.[60] The legislation outlawed the discriminatory practices, mentioned earlier, which the Southern states had adopted after Reconstruction to prevent Black southerners from voting. It gave the federal government the legal authority to enforce the 15th Amendment to the Constitution, adopted 95 years earlier, which establishes the "right citizens of the United States to vote shall not be denied or abridged by the United States or by any state on account of race, color, or previous condition of servitude."[61]

8.12 CONCLUSION

Slavery is a moral crime. In the United States, that crime was supported by legal, political, and economic institutions that did not live up to our asserted ideals. If the American Dream, its values, and aspirations are to be redeemed, government is needed to realize equal participation in the political and economic marketplaces of the country. A market system responds to the preferences of those who participate in markets. If those preferences reflect racial prejudice, then markets will support segregation and discrimination. Attitudes about race were so deeply buried in America's DNA that government was used for too long to assist and prolong slavery and then impose Jim Crow America.[62] Government was not the solution to the problem; it became part of the problem.

The obviousness of the discrepancy between America's values and its treatment of Black Americans finally led the country to put the government on the side of addressing the racial discrimination in markets and in democracy itself. The strategy of nonviolence paid off, but Malcom X was still correct that the changes did not come peacefully. It took pictures of John Lewis being badly beaten by a white policeman and similar horrific images to gain support for civil rights legislation. And the civil rights period of the 1960s ended tragically. On April 4th, 1968, Martin Luther King, age 39, was assassinated. On June 5th, 1968, Robert F. Kennedy, age 42, was assassinated. Less recognized but, perhaps no less important, on February 21, 1965, at the age of 39, Malcolm X was assassinated.

On January 20, 2021, the nation's first Young Poet Laureate, Amanda Gorman, read a poem at Joseph R. Biden's Inauguration entitled *The Hill We Climb*. The poem noted how a young black girl, the descedent of slaves, dreamed of becoming president "only to find herself reciting for one."[63] Gorman's poem can trace its roots to Phillis Wheatly, as it too walks with the winds blowing toward justice. John Lewis would approve.

9

Alfred Kahn's America

Rebalancing the Mix

The government played a central role in shaping the country during the New Deal and the Great Society. The relationship between government and markets then took a decidedly different turn from the preceding 40 years after the election of Jimmy Carter.[1] The Carter administration deregulated the transportation, energy, and financial services markets with broad bipartisan agreement. The idea of changing the mix of government and markets began with the peanut farmer from Georgia, not with the movie star from California who succeeded him.

It has been very common for the foes of government to call for an end to regulation, but the country has only rarely eliminated a regulatory program and for a good reason. Regulation is put in place, as seen, when markets have failed to protect consumers, and that threat usually remains. But markets can change over time in ways that call for a regulatory adjustment and, in rare instances, deregulation.

Regulation normally aims at making markets work better or at protecting people from unreasonable or discriminatory market behavior. The regulatory programs that Carter eliminated, by comparison, were ones where the government replaced market competition and determined prices and services, which is seldom a good idea. History shows market competition is much better at directing those choices than the government. Regulation of the delivery of natural gas and electricity, however, are two exceptions because competition is impractical in those markets.[2]

Carter was guided by two sholars of government regulation – economist Alfred Kahn, and Stephen Breyer, then a Harvard Law professor and later a Supreme Court justice. Although both were academics, they put their academic expertise into practice and worked on Carter's deregulatory initiatives on Capitol Hill. Both were strong supporters of the government, but they believed in a careful assessment of whether regulation was needed to protect people and the environment.[3] Together, these two men began to unravel the expanse of the New Deal government through selective deregulation and a return to market forces.

The Carter administration became a transition between the New Deal and Great Society expansion of government and the free-market sentiment popularized by

Ronald Reagan. The bipartisan rethink of government regulation signaled a turn to regulatory reform and a slowdown in the expansion of government. There were still significant additions to the government, but public sentiment went back to greater reliance on markets to build the country.

9.1 THE FATHER OF AIRLINE DEREGULATION

Alfred Kahn graduated from New York University first in his class at the age of 18 in 1936 and went on to earn an economics Ph.D. from Yale in 1942. After joining the Cornell faculty, he eventually served as chair of the economics department and dean of the College of Arts and Sciences. Author of 130 articles and 10 books, he was an expert in public utility regulation. In 1974, he was appointed to chair the New York Public Service Commission, the agency responsible for the regulation of the electric, gas, telephone, and water companies in New York.[4]

Kahn came to Carter's attention when he testified before a Senate committee chaired by Ted Kennedy. Kennedy – hardly a foe of government – was using the hearings to develop bipartisan support for transportation deregulation. He called on experts like Kahn to show how changes in the transportation markets meant that the existing regulatory schemes were no longer needed.[5] Kennedy also hired Breyer, who took a leave of absence from Harvard, to organize Kennedy's deregulation effort.

Kahn became known as the "architect of airline deregulation" when Carter appointed him to chair the Civil Aeronautics Board (CAB) in order to lead the effort to deregulate airline transportation.[6] As a Washington regulator, Kahn was a colorful figure. As CAB chair, he became nationally famous for a memo to his staff:

> One of my peculiarities, which I must beg you to indulge if I am to retain my sanity (possibly at the expense of yours!), is an abhorrence of the artificial and hyper-legal language that is sometimes known as 'bureaucratese' or gobbledygook.
>
> The disease is almost universal, and the fight against it endless. But it is a fight worth making, and I ask for your help in this struggle.
>
> May I ask you, please, to try very hard to write Board Orders and, even more so, drafts of letters for my signature, in straightforward quasi-conversational, humane prose – as though you were talking or communicating with real people.[7]

After the memo was leaked, the Washington Post published it in full along with an approving editorial. Across the nation and the world, other newspapers spoke of the memo with approval. A Boston Globe columnist wrote, "Alfred Kahn, I love you. I know you're in your late fifties and are married, but let's run away together."[8]

In 1978, Carter appointed Kahn to chair the White House Council on Wage and Price Stability. When he got into hot water with the administration by talking candidly about the potential for a depression, he did not stop talking candidly about the economic condition of the country, but he began using the euphemism "banana" for the word "depression." After a banana company complained to the White House, he substituted to "kumquat" to refer to a possible recession.

9.2 THE DECISION TO REGULATE

Transportation regulation began when the federal government supported railroad development to promote the expansion of the United States as the population moved westward. As part of that support, the government gave individual railroad companies a monopoly in the areas where they operated, which the railroads then used to exploit farmers and residents by charging exorbitant and discriminatory prices.

As related earlier, Congress responded in 1887 by creating the Interstate Commerce Commission (ICC) to curb these abuses,[9] and at the urging of President Teddy Roosevelt, Congress strengthened the ICC's authority in 1906 when it passed the Hepburn Act.[10] As the trucking industry developed, Congress decided in 1935 to make it subject to ICC regulation as well.[11] The ICC set the rates that railroads and trucks could charge for moving goods between the states, and the railroads and trucking companies had to secure ICC approval to start new services to the public.

The ICC also provided the model for regulation of the airline industry when Congress created the CAB in 1938.[12] For example, if Eastern Airlines wanted to fly between New York and Miami, the CAB had to approve the new route. The CAB also had to approve the price that an airline could charge for flying between those two cities. In other words, the decision was to limit competition. The bill's proponents reasoned that regulation was necessary to keep the fledgling industry profitable and to prevent airline companies from skimping on safety to gain profits.

Whether this argument about "excess competition" was valid at the time has been disputed by historians. Gabriel Kolko, for example, presents historical evidence that the airlines did not resist being regulated and in fact supported it, making the CAB a better deal for the airlines than the public even at the time the CAB was created.[13] Although Kolko was writing about the origins of transportation, the Kennedy hearings confirmed that the airlines were entirely comfortable with being regulated. As incumbents, they had a competitive leg up on possible new entrants. And regulation ensured that they were profitable even if it meant high prices for the public.

9.3 THE DECISION TO DEREGULATE

Today's airline customer would be amazed by the level of service on a flight during the time of regulation. Because airlines could not compete based on price, which was set by the CAB, they competed by offering free meals, drinks, gifts, attractive flight attendants, and extensive advertising of these services. Since many passengers, particularly those on expense accounts, were indifferent to costs and preferred frequently available flights and less crowded planes, the airlines also added more flights even though many planes were not nearly filled. As these amenities increased airline costs, the CAB would raise prices so that the airlines would continue to be profitable.

All this meant that air travel was a luxury for most families in the 1950s and 1960s because it was so expensive. Most Americans did not resort to the skies for family vacations, and when they did, it was a special occasion. Parents and their children dressed up. A majority of Americans at the time had never been on an airplane.

As Carter's principal cheerleaders for deregulation, Kahn and Breyer argued that competition was possible because the airline companies would move their planes around to undercut the prices of other companies when they got too high, and that would lead to lower prices. Southwest Airlines, formed 11 years before deregulation, became living proof of the academics' arguments. Since the airline flew only within the state of Texas, linking San Antonio, Dallas, and Houston, it largely avoided CAB regulation. It was therefore able to charge lower prices and undercut the airfares charged by its regulated, potential rivals.[14]

In March 1977, Carter sent legislation to Congress for the repeal of the regulation of prices and routes by the government. He argued the CAB, which was designed 40 years earlier "to protect a developing industry" was outdated: "Regulation, once designed to serve the interests of the public, now stifles competition.... It has discouraged new, innovative air carriers from offering their services and it has denied consumers lower fares where they are possible."[15] Congress responded by passing the Airline Deregulation Act of 1978 with overwhelming bipartisan support.[16]

Scholars are split on whether airline deregulation has been an overall success, but they agree that as compared to regulated markets, consumers are much better off.[17] Prices are lower than under regulation, and more cities and routes have been opened for consumers. In total, consumers have saved millions of dollars because of lower airlines fares as compared to regulated rates. But there has also been a reduction in the number of competitors, and American, Delta, and United shored up their positions and came to dominate the market. Passengers can find low fares, but at other times fares are much higher, particularly along some routes when one airline tends to have most of the flights in and out of a hub airport.

Deregulation of the railroads and motor carriers quickly followed. In 1980, the Staggers Rail Act[18] and the Motor Carrier Act[19] eliminated the ICC and its regulation of the railroads and motor carriers, respectively. Trucking deregulation meant that new firms could obtain licenses for interstate carriage based on the argument that increased competition was a boon to the economy.

9.4 NATURAL GAS DEREGULATION

The Carter administration was not done rethinking New Deal era regulation. It also deregulated the production of natural gas. Again, deregulation was based on the recognition that competition would be a better way of protecting consumers than having the government regulate prices.

In the 1930s, when a handful of natural gas producers and pipelines had monopolized the sale and delivery of natural gas, Congress responded by passing the Natural Gas Act of 1938 to regulate natural gas that was traded in interstate commerce. It gave the Federal Power Commission the authority to set prices that were just, reasonable, and non-discriminatory.[20]

Starting in the 1970s, there were several related developments that promoted rethinking the regulation of energy markets. In October 1973, in response to the Arab–Israeli war, Mideast oil countries reduced the flow of oil to the United States, which caused oil, natural gas, and gasoline shortages, a quadrupling of oil prices, rapid inflation, and a stagnant economy. Some readers, and likely their parents, will recall waiting in lines at service stations on alternate days of the week to fill their cars with gas.

That was not all. When the Arab countries reduced the supply of oil, the price of oil on the world market increased considerably as did the price of natural gas along with it, which led to a shortage of natural gas supplies in the United States. Because domestic natural gas producers could only charge the regulated price, which did not take into consideration the energy crisis and its impact on prices, they tried to sell as much gas as they could in the states where it was produced, which was not restricted by regulation in the same way as interstate sales. They also did what they could to slow the production of natural gas until the government allowed them to adjust prices in response to the world price of energy.

By the time Jimmy Carter reached office, the 1970s had become the decade of energy crises, and energy independence was at the top of the president's policy agenda. Congress with Carter's support passed the National Energy Act of 1978,[21] which mandated a comprehensive overhaul of the energy sector including traditional fossil fuel resources, renewable energy, and conservation. Additionally, the Natural Gas Regulatory Policy Act of 1978 deregulated price controls on natural gas production and oil price deregulation soon followed.[22]

Government regulation of prices was unnecessary because there were plenty of natural gas and oil producers who would compete with other suppliers. Not only was regulation unnecessary to protect consumers, but it discouraged oil companies from seeking new supplies of oil and gas. Both deregulation strategies worked. As oil and natural gas prices rose to competitive levels, the investment in both resources increased.

9.5 OIL DEREGULATION

The decision to eliminate price controls on the production of natural gas recognized that there would be competition among the many firms that produced natural gas. As noted, the same was true for domestic petroleum production, but the road to deregulation was complicated by Richard Nixon's decision to put the entire economy under wage and price controls.

This step was extremely radical. The government had engaged in wage and price controls during war time and during the New Deal when the government was attempting to lift the country out of the Great Recession. It was, however, generally regarded as a bad idea, except in times of extreme national emergencies.

Nevertheless, Nixon surprised the nation by announcing a 90-day freeze on all prices and wages to combat inflation on August 15, 1971. When Congress had authorized the president to impose price controls to fight inflation in 1970,[23] the Democrats, who controlled Congress, believed that a Republican president would never interfere with the economy by adopting wage and price controls. They had planned to attack Nixon during his reelection bid for failing to do so as a way of controlling inflation, but "Nixon's surprise announcement turned the tables."[24]

The initial popularity of such a bold move helped Nixon get reelected, but "the program failed spectacularly and ushered in nearly a decade of so-called stagflation—high inflation coupled with slow growth, which reduced living standards for millions of Americans."[25]

Safely reelected, Nixon ended the experiment on January 15, 1973, only to repeat it in June 1973 to redirect public attention away from the Watergate hearings and show bold leadership to address a problematic economy. As before, those controls were wildly complex and ultimately ineffective. Nixon eliminated the wage and price controls in April 1974, except for price controls over oil and natural gas.

In addition to deregulating the natural gas industry, Carter also planned to remove the price constraints put on the oil industry during the Nixon administration. He, however, lost his reelection bid. Just days after being sworn into office, President Reagan removed oil price regulations.

9.6 ELECTRICITY DEREGULATION

The historical lesson of the Nixon wage and price controls is the flip side of transportation and energy deregulation. The government can protect individuals from market excesses and support greater economic prosperity through regulation. There has been a long record of success in doing so. But historically, it also demonstrates that the government should avoid trying to set prices and determine supply because it cannot do as well as markets.

Government regulation of prices, however, cannot be avoided when it comes to the delivery of natural gas using pipelines and electricity using a grid system of wires. Because it wastes money to have multiple pipelines or electrical grids serving the same customers, it is better to have a monopolist and regulate the prices that a utility can charge for its services. The public benefits from regulation because it prevents utilities from charging excessive prices, and it also saves money for consumers by having only one owner of the grid system that delivers electricity and natural gas rather then costly and wasteful multiple grids.

When Congress deregulated price controls on the production of natural gas, it therefore retained regulation of natural gas pipelines. As compared to the production of natural gas, where there was plenty of competition, it was still necessary to protect consumers from these monopolists and the high prices that they would charge for gas transportation if they were not regulated.

A similar pattern of regulation and deregulation is possible concerning electricity. While regulation is necessary in the delivery of electricity, it turns out that competition is possible in electricity generation. You can have multiple firms make electricity and then feed it into the delivery system – the electricity grid – owned by the monopoly-price regulated utilities. Once there is sufficient competition in the generation of electricity, it is no longer necessary to set prices for that portion of the industry. Recognizing this reality, the Carter administration also passed legislation, which opened the electric industry to a wide variety of new producers and the industry became more competitive.[26]

9.7 S&L DEREGULATION AND REREGULATION

The deregulation of transportation, natural gas production, and electricity generation reflected market changes that made it possible to rely on competition to set prices and determine services. But, as Breyer and Kahn's careful analysis showed, it was necessary to retain regulation of pipelines and electricity grids because competition was not possible. In 1980, Congress, supported by the Carter administration, decided to free savings and loan banks (S&Ls), also known as thrifts, from regulatory controls that dated back to the New Deal. This decision, unlike the previous deregulations, was not a happy story.

S&Ls were local depository institutions most often used by working- and middle-class families for small loans and home mortgages. The almost 4,000 S&Ls in 1980 had total assets of $600 billion including $480 billion in mortgage loans. At the time, S&Ls provided about one-half of the approximately $960 billion in home mortgages that existed at the time.[27]

In 1980, the S&Ls lobbied Congress to get rid of many of the regulatory restrictions that Congress had put in place to prevent this type of bank from making risky investments and losing so much money that they would become insolvent. The S&Ls told Congress that they were losing depositors because commercial banks could pay higher rates of interest to get money that they could lend out. The S&Ls were not only losing depositors, but regulation also restricted the type of investments that they could make, which limited their profitability. The S&Ls argued that these restrictions were the reason for the rise in the number of insolvent thrifts.

The Carter administration supported deregulation to keep the S&L industry financially healthy and ensure families had greater access to mortgages. Congress allowed S&Ls to offer a wider variety of financial products, including credit cards, interest-bearing checking accounts, trust services, and to open statewide branches while being exempt from state usury laws.[28] Congress also expanded how much money they could lend out and allowed them to invest in a wide array of investments including commercial paper and corporate bonds.

In short, S&Ls were able to take on riskier investments to be able to compete with their commercial bank rivals.[29] And they did. But then the investments failed, the S&Ls lost large sums of money, and dozens of S&Ls again became insolvent or nearly so. In 1989, Congress passed a bailout of $124 billion and once again closely subjected that sector to regulation.[30]

The instinct to increase competition in the banking industry was consistent with the other deregulation that had occurred. Congress' mistake was to go from strict regulation to almost no regulation. While it should have been obvious that some S&Ls might make bad investment decisions, Congress did not anticipate that possibility and discontinued regulatory controls which could have prevented the S&Ls from failing. The Carter administration was all about deregulation, but it was also about a careful assessment of markets and the need to protect consumers, except this time.

9.8 CONCLUSION

Over the history of government, it has been a partner with markets in building a country truer to our national values. Government has not sought to replace markets, but to make them work better and help those who have been left behind by economic developments beyond their control. The preference for relying on market competition to set market prices recognizes the complexity of trying to set reasonable prices by government regulation and how competition can create incentives for sellers to find ways to reduce consumer prices.

This preference does not mean that markets will always work as well as they could in delivering goods and services. Some forms of regulation are still necessary. The saga of the S&Ls is a good example. Likewise, according to critics of airline deregulation, it is also an example. While the public is better off than it was under regulation, consumers are not as well off as they might be if the government had engaged in a more thoughtful, evidence-based approach to airline transportation that promoted competition and protected consumers from egregious practices.

Still, no one advocates that the government should be setting prices instead of having markets do it. That is the lesson of deregulation – a story that is continued in Chapter 10.

10

Ronald Reagan's America

Freedom for Markets

In a *West Wing* episode, "He Shall from Time to Time…," Bradley Whitford, who played Josh Limon, the Deputy Chief of Staff, informs Richard Schiff, who played the White House Communications director, Toby Zigler, about a theme for the President's State of the Union message:

JOSH
'The era of big government is over.'
TOBY
[stops] Oh, when did this happen?
JOSH
This morning, we had a meeting.[1]

The political movements in the 1960s demonstrated against the failure of markets to protect people and the environment, the widespread poverty that enveloped millions of Americans, the country's abject failure to establish the civil rights of Black Americans, and other pressing national issues. The "big government" that resulted from these movements was created to expand freedom and individual opportunity that had been restricted by market developments. Those values were the stars of the show, while other recognized political values – individualism, self-reliance, and small government – were relegated to the role of supporting characters.

Yet, critics of the government were not sleeping during the era of big government. Academics, conservative think tanks, and political leaders were laying the groundwork for emphasizing markets and reducing government. Their efforts paid off after the election of President Ronald Reagan. His famous declaration, "In the present crisis, government is not the solution to our problem; government is the problem," captures the spirit of a changing attitude.[2] For Reagan, the role of government was to get out of the way and allow individual initiative and personal responsibility to flourish.

The mix of government and markets has changed since 1980, but not to the extent that many proponents of small government favored. There have been additional legal procedures and political oversight, which has made it more difficult to regulate some markets; government services have been outsourced; and government spending on regulation and social welfare has been reduced. But nearly all the laws and programs established in the New Deal and Great Society eras remain on the books and have not been repealed. There have also been some significant expansions of government including most notably the Affordable Care Act, popularly known as Obama Care, which expanded health care insurance to 21 million people who did not have it before or who had minimal insurance.[3]

The West Wing episode was based on Bill Clinton's announcement in his 1966 State of the Union Message that "the era of big government is over."[4] But Clinton also warned that a mix of government and markets remained necessary: "But we cannot go back to the time when our citizens were left to fend for themselves.... Self-reliance and teamwork are not opposing virtues; we must have both."[5] Markets cannot do this alone because they can also reduce individual freedom and opportunity. Government cannot do this alone because markets also promote freedom and opportunity. This historical truism did not change. Americans adjusted the mix of markets and government beginning in 1980, but the country did not reject this historical lesson.

10.1 THE BLUEPRINT

The turn to markets and away from government reflected a new way of thinking that came to be known as Reaganism, Thatcherism, the Washington Consensus, or neoliberalism. As Chapter 5 related, this reconceptualization started in the 1940s with a group of economists led by Friedrich Hayek and Milton Friedman, who argued markets, unlike government, would not only expand individual freedom and choice, but once markets were less burdened with government regulation and taxation, they would produce greater prosperity that would benefit everyone. Two months before Lewis F. Powell, Jr. took his seat on the Supreme Court in 1971, he wrote a political and legal memo which took the academic ideas of Hayek, Friedman, and others from the pages of academia into the political area.

At the time, Powell was a longtime partner in the white-shoe corporate law firm Hunton & Williams in Richmond, Virginia, and his client was the United States Chamber of Commerce. The memorandum, entitled *Attack on American Free Enterprise System*, urged the business community to take the lead in overcoming the "disquieting voices located in the college campus, the pulpit, the media, the intellectual and literary journals, the arts and sciences, and from politicians.... No thoughtful person can question that the American economic system is under broad attack."[6]

Powell, having identified the enemy, proposed that the business community should aggressively support the funding of scholarly journals, books, television programming, and public appearances where pro-business leaders could generate additional arguments for small government. It also urged the support of pro-business action programs in high schools, colleges, and law schools, providing support for pro-business faculty, and the sponsorship of a legal campaign to stop government regulation.

Powell's memo became the blueprint of what subsequently happened. The business community had been unprepared to fight the Great Society expansion of government largely because the 1950s had been a period of unprecedented economic growth and relatively little expansion of government.[7] It quickly, however, took up Powell's call to arms. In the 1990s, conservative foundations and groups spent $1 billion or more to create the conservative infrastructure that Powell had proposed.[8] The American Enterprise Institute, Cato Institute, Federalist Society, and the Heritage Foundation, created during this buildup, remain important sources for arguments about freeing markets and limiting government.

10.2 RONALD REAGAN

Ronald Reagan's political career started with the 1963 presidential campaign of Arizona Senator Barry Goldwater. Goldwater, who had read Hayek and was advised by Milton Freedman, offered a stark alternative to Lyndon Johnson's support of government as a source of freedom and equality. For Goldwater, "the day's overriding political challenge" was to free markets from government interference "to preserve and extend freedom." As he warned, "any government big enough to give you everything you want is big enough to take away everything you have." He opposed social welfare programs because they created dependence on the government. Instead, helping those in need should be "a private concern ... promoted by individuals and families, by churches, private hospitals, religious service organizations, community charities."[9]

Goldwater had run for president when the tide of politics was running in the direction of expanding government, but his uncompromising support of limited government also made people nervous that the country would revert to a national government that provided for national defense and little else. He confirmed this suspicion when he told his supporters at the nominating convention: "I would remind you that extremism in the defense of liberty is no vice! And let me remind you also that moderation in the pursuit of justice is no virtue!"[10]

Johnson won in a landslide, but the Goldwater campaign ignited a popular antigovernment movement that eventually would change the mix of government and markets. He also launched Ronald Reagan as a national political leader when the campaign paid for a nationally televised speech that Reagan delivered in the last week of the campaign. The speech established Reagan as the heir to the movement to free markets that Goldwater had promoted.[11]

Reagan, who was a radio sports announcer after college, met a Hollywood agent on a trip to California to cover baseball spring training. Warner Brothers Studios immediately hired him, and he appeared in 52 movies interrupted by military service during WWII. After the war, Reagan became president of the Screen Actors Guild, a union representing actors, and served as the TV host of a very popular Sunday night program – the General Electric Theater – in the 1950s. He was also paid by GE to give inspirational speeches to its employees around the nation. As a motivational spokesman, Reagan began to speak up for individualism and small government. By the time that he became president, Reagan was a leading political voice for expanding markets and restricting government.

Reagan, while a strong advocate for freedom for markets, had been a moderate governor in California, where he compromised with Democrats in the legislature and even raised taxes by $1 billion when it was necessary to balance the state's budget. He explained that he preferred "partial victories," as opposed to "going off the cliff with all flags flying."[12] His sunny disposition and optimism reassured voters in a way that Goldwater's fierce determination did not. True to form, Reagan disappointed some conservatives by his failure to accomplish a more radical restructuring of the federal government. As he began his presidency, he sought to reassure Americans that he did not plan to "do away with government," but instead his aim was "to make it work—work with us, not over us; to stand by our side, not ride on our back."[13]

Ronald Reagan has long been known as the deregulation president. However, as we have shown in Chapter 9, Jimmy Carter began deregulation, and Reagan extended that approach even though his efforts were not as extreme as his deregulatory reputation might suggest. Nevertheless, his presidency has had lasting political and economic impacts on our mix of government and markets. Ed Meese, his campaign advisor turned Attorney General, significantly affected the legal thinking of the country and deeply influenced the character of the judiciary including today's Supreme Court. William Baxter, his chief antitrust officer, effectively eliminated antitrust enforcement of big business, giving rise to the trillion-dollar companies that now dot our financial landscape.

10.3 EDWIN MEESE III

Ed Meese came to the Reagan administration with two strong attributes. He was a long-time loyal friend and Reagan supporter, and his conservative commitments were unimpeachable. Meese, who served Reagan in the governor's office and then became his chief of staff, played a key role in cracking down on the 1969 student anti-war protests at Berkeley including sending in the National Guard after a student demonstration caused property damage and injuries. Reagan's response to those protests catapulted him into the national limelight, later setting the stage for his successful presidential run.[14] Meese served as Reagan's presidential campaign chief and then led his transition team. After the election, Meese started as Counselor to the President and then became the 75th United States Attorney General in 1985, where his tenure had two remarkably lasting consequences.

His first, and perhaps most long-lasting, impact was to embed the concept of originalism deeply into the legal structure of the United States. In October 1986, Meese delivered a speech at Tulane University entitled *The Law of the Constitution*,[15] in which he proposed "originalism" as a way of interpreting the Constitution. Meese worried, as many critics of the Warren Court did, that the Supreme Court had gone too far in finding rights in the Constitution with which he and other like-minded conservative critics disagreed. The Warren Court had followed an approach to interpreting the Constitution – "living constitutionalism" – which believed the Framers intent was that the Constitution was a set of principles that "can and should change in response to changing circumstances and values."[16] Meese argued that the Warren Court was mistaken about the Framers' intent.

According to Meese, the "Constitution, the original document of 1787 plus its amendments, is and must be understood to be the standard against which all laws, policies and interpretations must be measured. It is the consent of the governed with which the actions of the governors must be squared."[17] In other words, the Justices should approach constitutional adjudication in a way that "accords binding authority to the text of the Constitution or the intentions of its adopters."[18]

Meese was not content with merely making a speech about originalism; he campaigned for a more conservative judiciary. Founding the Pacific Legal Foundation, a conservative interest organization designed in response to the public interest organizations of the 1960s, was an early effort.[19] Once in the White House, he successfully married conservative political action and conservative legal theory as articulated by the originalists. Under his direction as Attorney General, as part of the department's lawyer training, the Department of Justice (DOJ) published *Guidelines for Constitutional Litigation* that instructed prosecutors how to incorporate originalist arguments into litigation and into public discussions about their work.

Meese also created the DOJ's Office of Legal Policy, and he established a joint White House Justice Department judicial selection committee. It was there that judicial selection moved from its traditional political base in Congress to the more partisan executive branch. The idea behind the selection committee was that "Reagan judicial nominees were compatible with the philosophical and policy orientation of the president."[20] As Meese protégé and later federal judge David Ginsburg put it: "Meese's philosophical commitment to originalism transformed judicial selection: 'There's little political reward in most judicial nominations because, in our constitutional system, a judge has to be independent of politics, but Ed was committed to persuading politicians of the value of rigorous judicial selection.'"[21]

Inside the Meese Justice Department, his political commitments came to bear when he formed an important alliance with the then-emerging Federalist Society, another organization committed to what they termed originalism. And to Meese, "We were fortunate to have the establishment of the Federalist Society at that time, as a source of young, talented conservatives for high level positions within the Department of Justice…. [T] hese sources [] brought to our attention many people who were loyal to the principles of constitutionalism and justice, rather than just a political party."

Originalism has had great staying power despite the many critiques it has spawned because Meese's game plan has been successful in recruiting like-minded people to the bench and bar.[22] The key to that success has been the allegiance of the Republican Party to embedding originalism in the law. Six justices now on the Supreme Court – Justices Thomas, Alito, Gorsuch, Kavanaugh, and Barrett, as well as Chief Justice John Roberts – are Federalist Society alums and Republican presidential appointees.

10.4 WILLIAM BAXTER

William Baxter's reputation as a free market legal thinker and scholar landed him in Reagan's Department of Justice as the Assistant Attorney General in charge of antitrust. Baxter's approach to markets was consistent with the broader program of Reaganomics, which rejected Keynesian thinking about government spending and was committed to balanced budgets, supply-side economics (tax cuts to spur economic activity), deregulation, and reduced welfare payments.[23] Like Meese, he was able to put the DOJ on a path to change antitrust law – the implementation of the statutes passed in the Progressive Era to regulate predatory business practices.[24]

Baxter believed that antitrust law, as it was then used, led the government to intervene and stop business practices that were not actually harmful. He was influenced by economic criticism of antitrust law, and he set out to align DOJ enforcement with those criticisms by emphasizing the role of economists and economics over that of law and lawyers.[25] This led to two changes in antitrust enforcement that lasted well beyond the Reagan administration.

The first change was related to an influential 1978 book, *The Antitrust Paradox*,[26] by a Yale law professor and later judge, Robert Bork. Although Bork was a lawyer, he was deeply influenced by economist Aaron Director, who, like Bork, was at the University of Chicago. Both were part of the Law and Economics movement that was dedicated to infusing the law with ideas and insights from economists.[27] Simply, Bork thought that limiting business because of its large size was illegitimate, and he sought to fix that error by stressing "consumer welfare" as the one goal for antitrust enforcement over all others.

"Consumer welfare" is basically the idea that if prices are not rising, then the size of a business firm or its activities should not be considered an antitrust problem. The fact, for example, that Amazon is the largest company in the world is not a problem because consumers have benefitted from better service and lower prices. There was a dangerous hitch in this idea, however. The fact that the behavior of a large firm has had other undesirable impacts on the country does not matter. That, for example, Amazon engages in practices that can be harmful to its employees or to smaller businesses, often mom-and-pop businesses, should not matter to public policy.[28]

Regardless of the criticisms of consumer welfare as too a narrow view of antitrust, Baxter incorporated that core idea into Department of Justice policy that indicated when Justice would sue to block corporate mergers as an antitrust violation.[29] The Department largely followed Baxter's approach until the Biden administration.

Baxter incorporated another economic concept into antitrust – the idea of shareholder value. This approach measures economic progress and success by determining whether share prices are increasing. This idea was neatly captured in the 1991 movie *Other People's Money*, starring Danny DeVito as corporate raider Lawrence Garfield. In his pitch to the shareholders for board control of his takeover target, Garfield responds to skeptics of his intended buyout that no one cares about whether the employees lose their jobs. His point was that it was time for the shareholders to cash in and maximize their "shareholder value" – the fate of workers was of no concern.

10.5 DEREGULATION AFTER REAGAN

Baxter's antitrust division, the L&E movement, and the Chicago School of Antitrust Economics tilted antitrust law and practice decidedly in favor of markets and away from government intervention to curb market concentration. Despite the preference for greater reliance on markets after 1980, however, there have been only limited changes in the mix of government and markets. Although the Reagan presidency largely kept the administrative state as it found it, its pro-market, deregulatory orientation continued to be influential particularly with William Jefferson Clinton. Under Clinton, telecommunications, banking, and welfare all came under the deregulation knife, but not without profound consequences.

10.6 TELECOMMUNICATIONS

As related earlier, the Federal Communications Commission (FCC) was established during the New Deal to regulate the expanding radio industry. Regulation was necessary to assign frequencies to broadcasters or otherwise they would end up broadcasting on the same wavelength and their signals would cancel each other out. As telecommunications technologies changed, the FCC exercised regulatory authority over radio and television frequencies of various strengths. Once commercial television came online, it too was regulated as was cable television.[30]

Beginning in the Carter administration, followed by the Reagan and Clinton years, telecommunications regulation came under scrutiny. During that time, cable television was largely deregulated; broadcast satellites delivered high-quality broadcast television throughout America; high-definition television improved broadcast quality even more; and digital television delivered more options than previously imagined. These innovations expanded the quality of the broadcast signal, improved picture quality, and multiplied the number of broadcast outlets substantially.

As part of its authority to regulate in the "public interest," the FCC had established programing requirements for radio and television broadcasters, running the gamut from giving "equal time" to competing political candidates to limitations on the number of radio or television stations that one company could own. The Commission also made sure that adult programming was not easily available to children and was confined to the late hours.

The Reagan administration abolished most of these requirements on the grounds that changes in the marketplace, particularly cable broadcasting, meant that consumers had so many choices of radio and television programming that competition would ensure the diversity that the FCC has attempted to establish with its regulations. If you do not like MSNBC, for example, you can turn to Fox News.

President Clinton furthered Reagan's push for deregulation with the Telecommunications Reform Act of 1996,[31] which allowed a single company to own multiple radio and television stations as well as newspapers within a market. The direct consequences were not hard to predict – concentration of ownership with fewer broadcasters. And with fewer broadcasters, there was less diversity of ownership and less diversity of programming in radio broadcast television.[32]

The Telecommunications Act also required the monopoly grid telephone companies, which connected consumers using wires, to hook consumers up to new long-distance carriers that used microwave dishes to send signals; as a result, consumers could choose from competing long-distance companies. The development of cell phones then made local regulation of telephone service unnecessary as consumers could bypass landlines. Remember those?

10.7 BANKING REGULATION

The Clinton administration's flirtation with regulatory reform in banking also had a large impact on the country, but not a good one. In 1999, Congress repealed the New Deal's Glass-Steagall Act, which had prohibited one type of bank – commercial banks – from engaging in investment banking – a second type of banking.[33] Commercial banks made money from banking services such as car loans, mortgages, and checking accounts. Investment banks were in the business of buying and selling various types of financial instruments to fund big businesses, such as financing complex mergers and acquisitions. The idea behind the Glass-Steagall Act was to protect the financial well-being of commercial banks and their depositors by prohibiting them from making risky investments.

In 1999, though, Congress determined that market competition would prevent commercial banks from getting into trouble because their stockholders, who were the investors that owned the bank, would sell their stocks to invest in banks that had not put themselves in a risky situation. Congress was wrong, and the repeal became a disaster for the economy.

In September 2008, the banking industry imploded – an event dubbed the "The Weekend Wall Street Died."[34] The crash happened because banks purchased securities that were based on the obligations of homeowners to make payments on their home mortgages. The banks had assumed that homeowners would have no difficulty paying off their mortgages, and if not, the banks could repossess the houses and resell them to get their money back. But after thousands of homeowners defaulted on their mortgage payments, housing prices fell drastically, and commercial and investment banks were stuck with worthless securities because repossession would not get them their money back. What happened was that mortgage lenders lent money to many individuals who could not afford to keep up their mortgage payments because they did not earn enough money to afford the houses that they bought.[35]

Federal regulators had contributed to this disaster. The Federal Reserve made cheap credit available and continued to push home sales as part of the American Dream. State usury laws on mortgages were removed; state efforts to regulate lending practices were blocked by the federal government; and federal regulators, who could have substituted effective regulation of the buying and selling practices of the commercial and investment banks, instead facilitated the very financial practices that resulted in the bank failures.[36] After the crash, Alan Greenspan, the chairman of the Federal Reserve Board, one of the regulators that failed to regulate, testified before Congress that he was in a "state of shock disbelief" that the "whole intellectual edifice" that markets were self-correcting "collapsed."[37]

The banking collapse set off the Great Recession, the steepest economic decline since the Great Depression. In the immediate wake of the crash, the federal government spent about $3.1 trillion to keep the banks open and stimulate economic recovery.[38] Despite this investment, domestic output fell by 4.3 percent, the unemployment rate increased to 9.5 percent (from 5.0 percent), home prices fell 30 percent, the stock market declined by 57 percent, and the crash resulted in more than $20 trillion in lost Gross Domestic Product (GDP), which totals more than $70,000 per man, woman, and child living in this country.[39]

As in the 1930s, the Obama administrations stepped in to speed up a return to prosperity. Using Keynesian economic theory, the government used massive deficit spending that ended up costing taxpayers about $498 billion to promote economic recovery.[40] The Federal Reserve Board also stepped up to the plate by lowering the interest rate it charged banks to borrow money to 0.25 percent. The Board also purchased securities and bonds from banks and companies to give them cash that they could spend while the economy recovered. The bottom line is that the economy had stopped shrinking by June 2009 because of the government's investments. Another Great Depression was avoided.

Congress then re-regulated the banks by passing the 2,300-page Dodd-Frank Act to reform every aspect of financial markets including banking. The legislation also created a new agency, the Consumer Finance Protection Board (CFPB), for more effective regulation of consumer credit markets, which has been the target of litigation by the financial community ever since.[41]

10.8 WELFARE REFORM

Two prominent conservative analysts, George Gilder and Charles Murray, set the table for reform of the country's social welfare programs. They blamed these programs for perpetuating poverty because they removed the incentive of the poor to work hard and better themselves. As Gilder explained, "In order to succeed, the poor need most of all the spur of poverty."[42] Murray argued "with the advantage of powerful collateral evidence" that if the country reduced or even eliminated social welfare support, "the lives of large numbers of poor people" would be "radically changed for the better."[43]

In a 1987 radio address on welfare reform, Ronald Reagan echoed that message when he told the audience, "Now the question I ask about any welfare reform proposal is: Will it help people become self-sufficient and lead a full life, or will it keep them down in a state of dependency?"[44] Reagan had popularized the idea that welfare programs made people less independent by portraying the poor as freeloaders who lived off government welfare paid for by hard-working Americans.

These appeals by Reagan and other reform advocates often contained code words that suggested the hardworking people were white and the freeloaders were racial minorities. Reagan's favorite story was about a Black "welfare queen" who received welfare benefits but also who drove a Cadillac, had a fur coat, and ate T-bone steaks with food stamps. While the story was based on a real person, Linda Taylor, who had defrauded the government, the elaboration of it by Reagan misleadingly suggested that most recipients of welfare were undeserving of the government's help.[45]

The message that welfare creates dependency nevertheless became politically popular to the point that Bill Clinton as a candidate promised to "end welfare as we know it." After being elected, he signed the Personal Responsibility and Work Opportunity Act of 1996, which replaced an earlier program that had provided cash assistance to women and children living in poverty, with a new program, Temporary Assistance for Needy Families (TANF).[46] TANF requires recipients to seek and obtain work to be eligible for benefits, and it gave the states more control over who was eligible to receive benefits and for how long.

TANF harkened back to the earlier approach to social welfare covered earlier in the book that public welfare reduces individual responsibility. The requirement in TANF that people must be working to be eligible for the government's help was addressed to that concern. Social welfare programs during the New Deal and the Great Society were substantially expanded because poverty was understood to be the result of economic conditions and other market factors beyond an individual's control. The country had returned to this more restrictive view of social welfare programs.

10.9 THE AFFORDABLE CARE ACT

Reagan's election signaled a change in how the country approached the mix of market and government. Despite skepticism about government, however, there have been important new additions to government since 1980. When George H.W. Bush was president, Congress passed the Americans with Disabilities Act of 1990,[47] which prohibited discrimination against people with disabilities in jobs, schools, transportation, and any public or private space that was open to the public. The goal was to make available to persons with disabilities the same rights and opportunities as everyone else.

After the election of Barak Obama put the Democrats in charge of all three branches of government for his first two years in office, Congress enacted equal pay legislation,[48] restructured education loans for students by having the government make the loans instead of banks,[49] and, passed the Dodd-Frank Wall Street Reform and Consumer Protection Act, referred to earlier.[50] Congress also passed the Patient Protection and Affordable Care Act, better known as Obamacare, which extended health care insurance to millions of previously uninsured Americans.[51]

President Obama's election was greeted with enthusiasm in many quarters of America. Many Americans had thought the day would never come when the country elected a person of color to be president. Obama himself conceded that "[f]ew presidents have walked a more improbable path to the White House."[52] He was born in Hawaii, the son of a mother raised in Kansas and a father who grew up in Kenya. He grew up in Hawaii and Indonesia, graduated from Columbia University, became a community organizer in Chicago, and then attended Harvard Law School, where he became the first Black American to head the prestigious Harvard Law Review. Obama returned to community organizing in Chicago and then ran successfully for and served three terms in the Illinois state senate. After being elected a U.S. Senator, he served three years before becoming the nation's 44th president.

The 900-page Affordable Care Act enacted numerous reforms, but the most significant was to extend health care insurance to 20 million Americans who previously did not have it, which meant the number of people in the country who lacked health care insurance fell to an all-time low 9 percent of the population. The law also banned insurance companies from refusing to insure anyone of the 135 million people who have a pre-existing medical condition if they applied for coverage because they had already been ill, and it included additional protections such as prohibiting insurance companies from charging people more money based on their gender or health status.[53]

In a private insurance market, only those who can afford to purchase health care insurance will be insured. Employers often split the cost of health insurance with their employees, but many employers do not do so particularly in low-wage industries. The Affordable Care Act addressed this problem by subsidizing the cost of insurance for low-income Americans, which gave them access to medical care that they could not previously afford.

The Act also expanded health insurance by extending eligibility for Medicaid – the health care insurance program for the poor – by raising the maximum amount of money someone could earn and still be eligible. While the federal and state governments share the cost of Medicaid, the federal government assumed 90 percent of the costs of making more people eligible for Medicaid anticipating that this would prompt the states to extend coverage to more poor people. They did not. Many red states – states that had Republican leadership – choose not to participate saying that they could not afford additional cost and that they distrusted that the federal government would continue to pay 90 percent of the costs. More states have since joined, but 10 states, including Southern states with large populations of poor people, still have not accepted this program.[54]

10.10 THE MIX REVISITED

None of the changes that occurred from Reagan to Obama radically changed the nature of government in the country. There were subtractions – telecommunications deregulation – but additions as well including the Dodd-Frank and the Affordable Care Act. Although the need for both was obvious – the Wall Street Crash and millions of Americans without health care insurance – neither had Republican support, which suggested the influence of the freedom for markets preference introduced by Reagan.

A more significant impact on government resulted from changes that impacted the implementation of government programs. Government jobs were outsourced to the private sector, presidents of both parties asserted more control over regulatory decision-making, and Republican-sponsored budget cuts reduced government spending to implement federal programs.

10.11 OUTSOURCING GOVERNMENT

Government has depended on private contractors from the beginning of the country, particularly in the Department of Defense. The Reagan administration, however, began the effort to replace federal employees with private employees across the government during his second term, and it became a bipartisan reform when Bill Clinton endorsed outsourcing as part of his "reinventing government" initiative.[55] The idea then spread to state and local governments. As a result, the use of private contractors in all three levels of government almost doubled from 6.2% of the government workforce in 2005 to 11.9% in 2015.[56]

The theory was that private companies could do the work "better and cheaper" because, unlike the government, they are subject to competition.[57] Companies would compete to win the government's business, and the government could replace the winner if the service was not satisfactory or someone else could perform at less expense. The government's capacity to supervise and check on outside contractors, however, did not keep up with the scale of outsourcing that occurred,[58] which makes it uncertain whether the government is getting its money's worth.

Yet political support for outsourcing has remained strong largely because privatization has allowed elected officials to claim that they have reduced government employment and costs or at least that it has not increased them.[59] For the same reason, Congress established caps on government employment and on the pay of government employees, which has hindered the government in doing its job and in taking back outsourced jobs even if it turns out to be a bad idea.

10.12 PRESIDENTIAL ADMINISTRATION

Since 1980, the White House has asserted greater control over agency decision-making.[60] The size of the White House staff was substantially increased to further oversight of the bureaucracy, and there was also a significant increase in the number of agency officials who are appointed by the President with the concurrence of the Senate.[61] This expansion allows presidents to assert more control over agency decision-making by ensuring important decisions are made by presidential appointees loyal to the president's policy preferences. When presidents have been hostile to an agency's mission or cautious about too much activism, presidential appointees have reflected these attitudes in their management of a department or agency.

To manage the oversight process, President Clinton, following Reagan's lead, issued an Executive Order that required agencies to submit "significant" proposed rules to a White House office for cost-benefit analysis (CBA). A significant rule is one that has a potential $200 million dollar impact on the economy.[62] This management tool is related to the market orientation that has influenced policy since 1980. The concept is that regulation is an investment, and it makes no sense to spend more money on some investment than the monetary benefits the investment will produce. By now, CBA review has been in place so long under presidents of both parties that it has become a normal part of the regulatory process.

The impact of White House oversight has varied. Republican presidents have generally used this presidential administration to limit regulatory output. Democrat presidents have been less skeptical about regulation, but they have also moderated regulatory output in recognition of the prevailing national mood favoring market freedom.

10.13 TAX AND BUDGET CUTS

Glider and other pro-market analysts argued that tax cuts would not only spur economic growth that benefitted everyone, but tax revenues would also increase due to the growth in the economy. Congress embraced this argument by enacting a series of tax cuts that primarily benefitted wealthy taxpayers.[63] It reduced the top rate paid by wealthy people six times, and it also significantly reduced the tax rate that investors pay when they sell assets such as stocks or real estate.[64]

The net effect of the tax cuts, however, was to increase the federal deficit when the anticipated economic growth did not materialize. Although Presidents George W. Bush and Clinton signed tax increases intended to reduce the deficit, the totality of the tax cuts, the failure of Congress to account for the costs of fighting wars in Iraq and Afghanistan in the budget, and a recession following the collapse of Wall Street in 2007, produced unprecedented budget deficits, which were then cited as a justification for cutting government spending by free market advocates.

The tax cuts and budget reductions became a type of back-door way of shrinking government without the elimination of government programs. While the budget cuts did not change the mix of government and markets, they did make it more difficult for agencies to carry out their work.

10.14 CONCLUSION

In 2004, Barack Obama gave the keynote address at the national convention that nominated John Kerry to be the Democrat's candidate for president. Obama reminded listeners why the vision of America proposed by free market advocates was inconsistent with the American historical experience: The people that he met, Obama emphasized, "don't expect government to solve all their problems. They know they have to work hard to get ahead—and they want to." But people "sense, deep in their bones, that with just a slight change in priorities, we can make sure that every child in America has a decent shot at life, and that the doors of opportunity remain open to all."[65]

In 2012, President Obama won reelection in a contest that was a referendum on the economic policies of the Reagan Revolution. The president favored raising taxes on those making more than $250,000 a year as a key element in reducing the budget deficit, a proposal opposed by Mitt Romney, who was against any tax increase. Romney also favored the repeal of the Affordable Care Act.

In his second inaugural address, President Obama returned to the lesson he talked about earlier:[66] "What makes us exceptional, what makes us America is our allegiance to an idea articulated in a declaration made more than two centuries ago. We hold these truths to be self-evident, that all men are created equal." Moreover, while "history tells us that while these truths may be self-evident, they've never been self-executing. That while freedom is a gift from God, it must be secured by his people here on earth." Obama continued:

> Together we determined that a modern economy requires railroads and highways to speed travel and commerce, schools and colleges to train our workers. Together we discovered that a free market only thrives when there are rules to ensure competition and fair play. Together we resolve that a great nation must care for the vulnerable and protect its people from life's worst hazards and misfortunes.... [W]e have always understood that when times change, so must we, that fidelity to our founding principles requires new responses to new challenges, that preserving our individual freedoms ultimately requires collective action.

11

Mitch McConnell's America

Court Packing

On May 24, 2022, an abused and troubled teen, Salvador Ramos, entered the Robb Elementary School in Uvalde, Texas, and killed nineteen children and two teachers and wounded seventeen others. One day shy of one month later, the United States Supreme Court extended the right to carry weapons in public and made no exception for the types of automatic assault weapons Ramos used on his murder spree.[1] The next day, the Supreme Court, for the first time in its history, eliminated a previously recognized constitutional right, the women's right to decide if, and when, to have children, a right relied upon for nearly 50 years.[2] Then six days later, the Court announced a new legal doctrine that hampers a government response to climate change and threatens to impair the government's authority to regulate additional new threats to people and the environment.[3]

These three cases are the direct consequence of a shift in the Court's approach to democracy engineered by Senator Mitch McConnell. The shift began when he engaged in the historically unprecedented act of denying a sitting president, Barak Obama, the constitutionally protected opportunity to have his nominee for the Supreme Court receive a Senate hearing.[4] As McConnell bragged to his Kentucky constituents, "One of my proudest moments was when I looked Barack Obama in the eye and I said, 'Mr. President, you will not fill the Supreme Court vacancy.'"[5]

McConnell did not act alone, of course. He was aided and abetted by nearly four decades of anti-government work traceable to the efforts of Ed Meese, as discussed in the last chapter, and by the continuing work of conservative activists, notably the Federalist Society,[6] to remake the mix of government and markets using the Supreme Court. Those efforts have been successful.

11.1 MARBURY V. MADISON

From the beginning, the Supreme Court has been caught in a dilemma between honoring the will of the majority and protecting individuals from its possible tyrannies. *Marbury v. Madison*, decided by the revered Chief Justice John Marshall in 1803, established judicial review of legislation. A federal court of unelected judges

can overturn legislation passed by the democratically elected branches of government. The Court can reverse Congress, and it can reverse the president.

As a result, judicial review contains an intractable conflict: Under what circumstances should democratically elected majoritarian legislation be invalidated by
unelected federal judges?[7] On the one hand, overturning Congress may very well
mean that the will of the electorate has been disregarded. On the other hand, the
Court has an obligation to protect the individual rights and liberties secured in
the Constitution. As examples, Congress cannot establish a national religion, nor
should it condone racial or gender discrimination even in the face of majoritarian
will. If Congress tries, then the Supreme Court will overturn it. Constitutionally and
historically, the Supreme Court has been assigned an essential role in preserving a
democratic America as it balances majority will against minority protection.

The Court's approach to this choice has varied over the years. The Court has honored democratic decisions made by legislators, and it has overridden them. The Court's
approach to defining rights and liberties has affected which of those choices the Court
has made. While justices deny that making that choice is influenced by the justices'
own policy views about government and markets, that denial is a supreme myth.

11.2 SUPREME MYTH

The United States Supreme Court has been celebrated as a paradigm institution for
resolving moral and political conflicts and for providing an acceptable level of justice.[8]
According to this understanding, the Supreme Court enjoys the respect of the citizenry
because of the reputation it has developed over time, and because it operates within
a set of historical and political traditions widely endorsed and accepted by Americans.
Although public approval of the Court is waning,[9] this idealization of the Court is not
far off. It widely held in the legal profession. It is the vision taught in American law
schools, and it is accepted by the American public. The problem with this characteri-
zation is that it is not historically accurate; it is based on three complementary myths.

All the women and men who sit on the High Court have expressly avowed that
they are neither Platonic Guardians who make pronouncements about the good
society, nor do they act as a super-legislature making grand policy decisions. Instead,
they seek the correct and appropriate law to apply to the cases before them; they are
not there to make the law; they are there to find it.

The mantra that Supreme Court justices find the law has been played out in
Senate confirmation hearings for decades making them a type of kabuki theater. A
senator asks a nominee if it is his or her belief that it is a justice's role to make or to
find the law. Without exception, regardless of party affiliation, political allegiance,
or even ideology, the nominee has quickly and reverently intoned that it is a justice's
job to *find* the law, not make it.

None of that script is accurate. The justices make law because that is what the
Constitution requires. If the Constitution was clear, then answers would be easy to

find. If the law is so easy to find, then we do not need a multi-member tribunal to find answers to legal questions. Nor would the justices ever disagree; there would be no split decisions because the answers were there to be found. It is a myth, then, that the justices have had no role in making law when, in fact, that is exactly what they have consciously and intentionally done.

There is a second myth – the Court has served America as neutrally and objectively as possible. Over the Court's history, it has been in the nature of the institution to be a political court.[10] The Constitution is a political document; the Federalists and the Anti-Federalists were fighting about the role of government in the United States, an unavoidably political issue. Additionally, the three branches of government, including the judiciary, are political branches as per the Constitution. Further, the justices take their seats on the High Bench after having traveled through a political process again as set out in the Constitution. It would be comforting to believe in constitutional neutrality, but the Supreme Court has always been called on to resolve political issues according to the Constitution. How it does so will affect the public's authority to choose the mix of government and markets.

A third myth is related to the others. If the Court finds and does not make law, and if it is not political, then it should be a conservative social institution that narrowly views its role as a coordinate branch of government and not a superior one. As such, the Court does not make society in its own image. Rather, it honors and relies on past decisions; overturns cases carefully; respects the other branches of government and does not privilege one branch over another; does not seek out constitutional law issues, instead it tries to avoid them; and narrowly decides the cases in front of it. In other words, judicial restraint, not activism, is the hallmark of how the Court, as a conservative social institution, should go about its work.

While that description of the Court has never been historically accurate, the Court has at times been more or less accepting of the mix of government and markets decided by Congress. Additionally, for decades, the Court has also deferred to the decisions made by administrative agencies that are guided by Congress and are under the direction of the president. In other words, the agencies are more directly accountable to the two democratic branches of government than they are to the unelected judiciary. The Court that Mitch McConnell has engineered has abandoned a conservative institutional view of itself, and its judicial activism has direct consequences on how the country achieves its fundamental values. Today, the Court has vigorously made decisions, such as those noted above, that contravene both Congress and the president and, in the case of the right to choose, its own long-standing precedents. It has not always been that way.

11.3 SHAPING THE BALANCE

The Supreme Court's early years involve a gallery of colorful characters from inventors and entrepreneurs to famous justices and advocates. The Court's first decisions tackled novel legal issues that shaped the balance between the nation's developing markets and its newly formed government, and it assigned significant roles for both.

Congress chartered the First Bank of the United States in 1791 for 20 years. As related earlier, the Federalists (Alexander Hamilton) favored the bank, and the anti-Federalists (Thomas Jefferson and James Madison) opposed it because they believed the Bank was designed to benefit merchants at the expense of the agrarian population. The state of Maryland had placed a heavy state tax on the Bank and when the Bank refused to pay the tax, Maryland sued the Bank for nonpayment.

In *McCullough v. Maryland*,[11] Daniel Webster argued the case on behalf of the Bank opposing the state's power to tax a federal institution, and, in a unanimous opinion, Chief Justice John Marshall ruled in favor of the Bank and against Maryland. *McCulloch* is a landmark case because it strengthened the government's authority under the Constitution to take actions in support of the national economy. Marshall wrote that Congress could pass laws that were "necessary and proper" to fulfill the Constitution including its economic directives. Further, regarding a law passed by Maryland that interfered with the Bank's authority, Marshall ruled that since the Constitution is the "supreme law of the Land" state laws to the contrary are invalid. Score one for Daniel Webster.

Another 1819 Marshall opinion, *Dartmouth College v. Woodward*,[12] is an example of the Supreme Court protecting markets from government's attempts to interfere with existing contracts. In 1769, King George III granted a charter to Dartmouth College as a private school. After John Wheelock, then president of Dartmouth, was removed as president by its Board of Trustees, the New Hampshire legislature attempted to overturn the Board's decision by redrafting the college's original charter and giving the power to appoint trustees to the New Hampshire governor. The law transformed a private college into a public one.

Daniel Webster argued the case on behalf of the college and won. Today, students and alumni recall his speech in which Webster said that Dartmouth was "a small college and yet there are those who love it." Marshall ruled that the original corporate charter was a contract between private parties, in this case between the King and the college trustees, and that the Contracts Clause of the Constitution[13] prohibits the government from changing the terms of contracts between private parties. Dartmouth wins. Score two for Webster.

The third and fourth cases in our quartet of early Supreme Court opinions concern the Court's interpretation of Congress' constitutional authority to regulate interstate commerce. In 1808, New York granted Robert Fulton and his financial backer, Robert Livingston, a monopoly on steamboat service between New York and New Jersey. After that grant, Aaron Ogden, a former New Jersey Governor, purchased a portion of that monopoly, and he became business partners with Thomas Gibbons. After a falling out between the Ogden and Gibbons, Gibbons began operating a steamboat between Elizabeth, New Jersey, and New York City based on a

1793 license granted by Congress. Ogden sued and a New York state court issued an injunction against Gibbons. He appealed to the Supreme Court.

Gibbons' lawyer, again the great litigator Daniel Webster, argued that a state did not have the constitutional authority to regulate interstate commerce – ferry service between New York and New Jersey. In *Gibbons v. Ogden*, the Court agreed when it ruled that Congress' authority under the Commerce Clause "is complete in itself, may be exercised to its utmost extent, and acknowledges no limitations, other than are prescribed in the Constitution."[14] Simply, federal constitutional law takes supremacy over state law. Gibbons wins. Score three for Webster.

The other case involved a Massachusetts law passed, which granted the Charles River Bridge Company a charter to build a toll bridge between Cambridge and Boston. Under that legislation, Harvard University had a right to a portion of the fees that the company collected from the people who crossed the bridge. As the population of Boston grew, as travel increased, and as the public protested the high bridge tolls, the Massachusetts legislature in 1828 granted another company the right to build the Warren Bridge 275 yards from the Charles River Bridge. The Warren charter stipulated those tolls would be collected until the cost of construction was recouped or for six years, at which time the bridge would be turned over to the state and would offer free service to the public.

The owners of the Charles River Bridge sued in state court, claiming that the new bridge violated its license from the state (its charter) to their financial detriment, but they lost and appealed. Once again, Daniel Webster stood in the well of the Supreme Court, arguing the case for Charles River. Webster argued their charter prevented competition, and, because of the competition, his client had gone broke and lost an estimated $10 million. He claimed that the Constitution did not allow the government to take private property in this manner, but the Court in a 5–2 decision ruled against him.[15] Webster's string of victories was broken, and Harvard's ferry boat fees were diminished.

Chief Justice Roger Taney, writing for the majority, said the case was simply a matter of contract interpretation, and the contract between the legislature and Charles River Bridge did not grant them exclusivity. He explained that state contracts should be read to serve the public interest, which is to discourage monopolies, or otherwise they would stultify the development of new transportation networks.

These Supreme Court decisions furthered the government's authority to intervene in markets to promote economic development and prosperity. The National Bank was constitutional; federal private corporate charters would be honored against state interference; state charters would be narrowly interpreted in favor of national competition; and state laws could not interfere with interstate commerce. By contributing to a strong central government and to a national economy, these decisions endorsed Henry Clay's three-pronged American System of government support for infrastructure, new industrial development, and central fiscal controls that were noted previously.[16] But the Court also supported the importance of markets to the country's development and prosperity by its enforcement of the Contracts Clause. Shortly, we will see the Contracts Clause used again to protect big businesses at the expense of their workers.

11.4 THE DREADED DRED SCOTT

The Court unfortunately continued its support of government efforts to promote economic expansion and development by routinely treating enslaved people as the property of the enslaver as an earlier chapter pointed out. In the most notorious of those cases, Justice Roger Taney wrote that black men "had no rights which the white man was bound to respect." Adding insult, "the negro may justly and lawfully be reduced to slavery for [the white man's] benefit."[7]

Regrettably, *Dred Scott* is an integral part of the history of government and markets. The North and the South were bound together in a symbiotic economic relationship. To the extent that the North, as well as the federal government, wanted to have a strong economic state that could compete with European powers, then tobacco and cotton from the slave South and sugar from the enslavers in the Caribbean provided the goods for transatlantic trade. Wall Street financing for these commercial activities was the economic glue that strengthened the national state. Imbued with the same racist attitudes as much of the rest of the country, the Court went along with these harsh and dreadful arrangements.

11.5 THE GILDED AGE COURT

As mentioned earlier, Mark Twain and Charles Dudley Warner in 1873 published *The Gilded Age: A Tale of Today*, a novel about American greed and corruption and the name stuck. The phrase "Gilded Age" conjures images of fancy carriages, top hats, ball gowns, and debutantes. The images stand in contrast with those of a Tocquevillian world at the beginning of the century with an "equality of conditions." The late 18th and early 19th centuries consisted of a world of small-scale merchants and farmers independently working for themselves and their families. The Gilded Age may be known for many things, but equality of conditions was not one of them.

Fifth Avenue mansions and Newport summer cottages were visible signs of that gilded wealth. Those homes contrasted dramatically with the slums and sweatshops of Manhattan, where ordinary workers suffered from unsafe workplaces, long hours, child labor, and poor living conditions. At the end of the nineteenth century, the pressing question for the country was whether laborers had any legal recourse to challenge the harsh working conditions imposed on them.

In 1905, the Court decided against workers and against democracy in *Lochner v. New York*,[18] which considered the constitutionality of a New York statute that limited bakers' hours to 60 per week. The Court had previously considered the same issue and had no trouble upholding similar protections.[19] *Lochner*, though, ruled that the

New York statute was an unconstitutional infringement of the liberty of contract. The Court reasoned that if bakers wanted to work more hours to make more money, then they had a constitutionally protected right to do so; the state legislature lacked the authority to protect workers such as bakers.

The *Lochner* majority distinguished previous cases upholding a state's authority to regulate mines and other hazardous workplaces by saying that bakeries presented no similar health dangers. In his dissent, Justice Harlan recited empirical findings that working long hours in a bakery subjected workers to numerous health risks, and there was also evidence by a muckraking journalist, as well as by a state report, which showed working conditions to be unsanitary and unhealthy.[20] Harlan also disagreed with the majority's assumption that the employer and employees were equal. He noted the state statute was based upon "the belief that employers and employees in such establishments were not on an equal footing, and that the necessities of the latter often compelled them to submit to such exactions as unduly taxed their strength."[21] The state, Harlan concluded, determined there was no bargaining equality and regulations were then necessary to protect workers.

Harlan's point was a simple one. A state legislature should determine whether an occupation was within the state's police powers to protect worker health, not a court, because the legislature was elected to make exactly such policy choices, and it had access to more expertise than the courts about the wisdom of its own legislation. Roscoe Pound, dean of the Harvard Law School, president of the American Bar Association, legal philosopher, and progressive critic, rhetorically questioned, "[w]hy do so many of [judges] force upon legislation an academic theory of equality in the face of practical conditions of inequality?"[22]

11.6 OH CAROLENE

The 1920s were a time for flappers, jazz, and illegal hooch; Jay Gatsby's tuxedo parties at East Egg; highflyer stocks; and market manipulation. The irrational exuberance of the Gilded Age through the 1920s did not affect the Supreme Court's view of a balance favoring markets over government. As *Lochner* indicates, the Supreme Court "[f]or five decades … sided with the rich and powerful against the poor and weak in virtually every area of law."[23] In the early years of the New Deal, the Court continued the *Lochner* penchant for overturning state legislation intended to protect labor and deciding in favor of business firms.[24] Franklin Roosevelt became so frustrated with the Court ruling against New Deal legislation that he threatened to restructure the Supreme Court by adding new justices. FDR's threat was a wake-up call for the old jurisprudence. The world was changing, and the Court needed to change with it.

Overruling *Lochner* presented a tricky issue for the Supreme Court to decide. If the Court always ruled in favor of legislation, then the majority could always outwit the minority even if legislation harmed the minority, which had no way to protect itself against a majority vote. However, if courts always decided who to protect and not protect, then the will of the majority could be frustrated as courts substituted their preferences for those of democratically elected legislatures.

In 1937, the New Deal Court found an ingenious way to mediate that problem in a case involving a conflict between dairy farmers and companies that sold cheaper canned milk.[25] The Filled Milk Act had prohibited sales of filled milk – skimmed milk with a fat or oil added to it – in interstate commerce. After Carolene Products sold filled milk in interstate commerce and was indicted for doing so, the company challenged the legislation in the Supreme Court as unconstitutional.[26]

The milk company offered two basic defenses. First, Congress's arguments about health and safety were bogus. Congress had justified the legislation by arguing that the new law protected public health and protected consumers by eliminating confusion between dairy milk and milk substitutes, but it was also true that it was acting at the behest of the dairy industry. And second, Congress should not "suppress trade in one article of commerce in order to eliminate competition with another."[27] In other words, Congress should not pick winners in marketplace competition.

Justice Harlan Stone's majority opinion ruled that "Congress is free to exclude from interstate commerce articles … [that] it may reasonably conceive to be injuries to public health, morals or welfare."[28] Unlike *Lochner*, he said the Court would give great deference to a legislature concerning the need for legislation. At the same time, the Court ruled in a footnote that Congress does not have an entirely free hand to fashion any legislation that it wants.

The footnote starts by presuming that legislation involving ordinary commercial transactions is constitutional when it is based "upon some rational basis within the knowledge and experience of the legislators."[29] After all, legislatures are closer to the public will than courts. Then the Court provided three escape valves from a blind acceptance of majoritarian decision-making. First, if ordinary commercial legislation conflicts with a "specific prohibition of the Constitution, such as those of the first ten amendments," then a court can invalidate the legislation. Second, if legislation "restricts those political processes," then it may be subject to "more exacting judicial scrutiny." And third, legislation that exhibits prejudice "against discreet and insular minorities," such as racial or religious minorities, and "which tends to seriously curtail the operation of those political processes is ordinarily to be relied upon protecting minorities" may call for a "correspondingly more searching judicial inquiry."[30]

In other words, courts should defer to legislatures when they decide the proper mix between government and markets. If legislators prefer markets, then so be it. However, the government will not take a backseat to even market-preferred legislation when it impairs individual rights and liberties or when it impairs democratic political processes. This balancing trick is based on fairness in the political process and on a commitment to democratic participation in government.[31]

The Court's willingness to stay out of the way of Congress is captured by *Wickard v. Filburn*,[32] a 1942 decision in which the Court upheld a federal marketing regulation that restricted a farmer's home consumption of his own wheat. The farmer had argued that since his own consumption was entirely within a state, the federal government could not regulate it because its authority to do so only extended to interstate commerce under the Constitution. However, as the opinion noted, the cumulative impact of home consumption could affect more than 20% of the total crop and directly affect national market prices. The Court therefore ruled that Congress could constitutionally exercise its Commerce Clause authority and impose this market quota.[33]

Starting with *Carolene Products*, the New Deal Court provided constitutional protection for the modern administrative state into the twenty-first century. Historians speak of a "New Deal settlement" consisting of five principles. Congressional legislation is presumed to be constitutional. Ordinary legislation will be upheld if it is reasonably related to a legitimate government objective, like health or safety. Relatedly, constitutional decision-making will be avoided when possible.[34] But stricter scrutiny is required for rules that negatively affect the political process or inhibit discrete and insular minorities from political participation. Finally, courts should defer to administrative expertise.[35] Today, those principles are more often honored in the breach than in their observance as we will shortly see.

11.7 THE GREAT SOCIETY

The Court led by Chief Justice Earl Warren continued the New Deal settlement when it approved Great Society civil rights legislation intended to deliver the promise of equality announced in the Declaration of Independence.[36] The *Heart of Atlanta Motel* case is indicative of this support. The case upheld the Civil Rights Act of 1964, which mandated that public accommodations, such as restaurants and hotels, had to be equally available without racial discrimination. The Court ruled Congress had Commerce Clause authority to enjoin a motel operator from refusing to rent rooms to Black Americans. The Court reasoned that the motel was not engaged in a purely "local" activity; instead, it was engaged in interstate commerce, and racial discrimination in accommodations was a national problem within Congress's purview.

In the South it was virtually impossible for Black Americans to travel as depicted in the 2018 movie *Green Book*. The title of the movie is a reference to a travel guide published by Victor Hugo Green from 1936 to 1966, which identified the hotels, shops, and restaurants that would serve black customers. Travelers could order the book by mail or buy it at Esso gas stations, which was the only oil company willing to sell gas to Black customers in the South. Green wrote in a forward to one edition:

> There will be a day sometime in the near future when this guide will not have to be published. That is when we as a race will have equal opportunities and privileges in the United States. It will be a great day for us to suspend this publication for then we can go wherever we please, and without embarrassment.[37]

In *Katzenbach v. McClung*,[38] the Court similarly held that Congress had the authority to regulate a local restaurant under the Civil Rights Act. The case involved Ollie McClung Sr. and his son who both owned a barbecue joint, Ollie's, in a black residential neighborhood in Birmingham, Alabama. The McClung's would sell take-out BBQ, but deny indoor dining, to Black consumers. They refused to comply with the civil rights law and were cited in violation, which the Court upheld because the restaurant purchased products in interstate commerce. Further, the Court noted that the Congressional record was "replete with testimony of the burdens placed on interstate commerce by racial discrimination in restaurants" and "there was an impressive array of testimony that discrimination in restaurants had a direct and highly restrictive effect on interstate travel by Negroes." Quite simply, "one can hardly travel without eating."

Ollie's complied the next day and allowed table service to its black customers. Later, Ollie Jr. acknowledged the value of anti-segregation laws but still believed the federal government should not be able to dig down deep to regulate his small, neighborhood restaurant. Ollie's business closed in 1999 but lives on. Today, one can find its sauce on the shelves of Birmingham supermarkets.[39]

11.8 REIGNING IN THE COMMERCE CLAUSE

The Warren Court was the last hurrah for this progressive constitutional vision. As the result of a campaign to appoint justices skeptical of government, the Court began to resist and then overturn the New Deal settlement.

William Rehnquist was appointed to the Supreme Court by President Richard Nixon in 1972, and in 1986, he was elevated to Chief Justice by Ronald Reagan where he served until his death in 2005. Rehnquist had a long record as a conservative. He was not a champion of civil rights and was suspicious of the reach of federal power, and he tried to curtail it on two fronts.

If *Wickard* decided Congress could regulate a family meal on a farmer's table, and if *McClung* held it could reach diners served at a local barbecue joint, because those activities involve interstate commerce, then regulating firearms near schools should be well within congressional purview. The Supreme Court did not see it that way. Instead, *United States v. Lopez* overturned 1990 federal legislation known as the Gun-Free School Zones Act that prohibited carrying guns within 1,000 feet of a school.[40] In the 5 to 4 decision, written by Chief Justice Rehnquist, the justices voted along partisan lines concerning whether the Commerce Clause could affect local activity. Even though school violence, particularly in urban settings, was not a new phenomenon, the Court ruled that the School Zones Act did not regulate commercial activity, nor did it contain any requirement that the possession of a handgun related in any way to interstate commerce, even though guns were traded in interstate commerce.

The Court, also for Commerce Clause reasons, struck down the 1994 Violence Against Women Act. In 1994, a Virginia Tech student alleged that a varsity football player raped her. She filed a complaint with the University and then filed a suit in federal court alleging that the attack violated the act and sought a federal civil remedy as a victim of gender-based violence. The perpetrator moved to dismiss because the remedy was an unconstitutional exercise of the Commerce Clause. In another 5–4 opinion, Chief Justice Rehnquist held that Congress lacked authority to enact the statute because it did not regulate an activity that substantially affects interstate commerce even though universities recruit students from out of state.[41]

11.9 RESTRICTING REGULATION

The Rehnquist Court also attempted to shrink "big government" starting with the Occupational Safety and Health Administration (OSHA). As related earlier, the 1970 Occupational Safety and Health Act authorized OSHA to set safety and health standards (regulations) for workplaces. After OSHA adopted a regulation that limited the exposure of workers to benzene, a carcinogenic chemical, the petroleum industry, which depended on benzene, sued.

The Supreme Court held the regulation was invalid because it ruled that OSHA had failed to prove benzene was a "substantial risk" to workers even though the Act authorizing OSHA to regulate did not contain those words as a limit of OSHA's authority. The Court, in effect, rewrote the statute. The majority justified adding that requirement to the statute because, unless it did so, the mandate would be unconstitutional under a constitutional requirement called the "non-delegation" doctrine.[42]

The non-delegation doctrine refers to Article I of the Constitution, which authorizes Congress to legislate, but it says nothing about delegating that authority to administrative agencies; hence, there is no delegation or non-delegation. Since the 1800s, however, the Court has recognized that Congress cannot accomplish much on its own and needs to rely on agencies to carry out its will. Consequently, the Court has interpreted the doctrine to permit Congress to authorize agencies to regulate if Congress establishes a clear limit on an agency's authority to do so through, for example, by providing an "intelligible principle."[43]

The majority in the benzene case said that since the OSHA statute failed to establish the necessary clear limit, it was necessary to add the limitation that regulations had to address "significant risks" to save the statute from being unconstitutional. The dissenters maintained the statute was as specific in terms of its limits on OSHA's authority as many other similar statutes approved by the Court over the years.

11.10 THE COURT TURNS RIGHT

The Court's decision literally to rewrite the OSHA statute was an indication of what was to come. The Court's turn to the right was not accidental. It was engineered by those opposed to big government and preferred free markets.

The Right's interest in using the courts to support a conservative political agenda began after LBJ fumbled an opportunity to install his friend Abe Fortas as Chief Justice. Johnson had appointed Fortas as a Supreme Court justice in 1965. He was a well-known lawyer at the time who had represented a convicted felon, Clarence Gideon, in one of the most famous cases in the Court's history. In *Gideon v. Wainwright*,[44] the Court held 9–0 that the Sixth Amendment requires states to appoint and pay for a lawyer to represent indigent people accused of a felony. Gideon had been convicted without a lawyer representing him because he could not afford one.

After Chief Justice Warren decided to retire in 1968, Johnson nominated Fortas to become Chief Justice, but Senate approval was required. Senate hearings on its nomination brought to light that Fortas, while serving as a justice, also attending meetings at the White House, was a close advisor of the president, and lobbied members of Congress on behalf of the White House. Even worse, Fortas was accused of questionable financial dealings including taking a paid teaching position at a local law school and accepting a $20,000 fee from someone then being investigated by the SEC for insider trading. Johnson withdrew the nomination, and later Fortis resigned from his seat.[45]

After that gaff, Nixon successfully maneuvered to put four reliable conservatives on the Court. Nixon nominated and the Senate confirmed Warren Burger as Chief Justice, and Harry Blackman, Lewis Powell, and William Rehnquist as Associate Justices. Then Reagan, under Ed Meese's directions, made it a political priority to put conservatives on the lower courts. After the Senate voted down Robert Bork's nomination by a 52–48 in 1987 because of his extreme anti-government views, the right's focus on courts became a Republican article of faith that McConnell turned into a dark arts form.

Obama nominated Merrick Garland for the Supreme Court on March 16, 2016, 10 months before the 2016 election. McConnell argued that the Senate should not proceed with a nomination during an election year even though there was more than enough time to hold confirmation hearings. McConnell persuaded his Republican colleagues, and the Senate refused to hold hearings on Garland's nomination. After the election, Neil Gorsuch became Trump's first Court appointment. He would get two more.

Brett Kavanaugh took his Court seat in 2018 after a controversial Senate hearing. Then in the last year of the Trump presidency, Justice Ruth Bader Ginsburg died just six weeks before the 2020 election. In complete and hypocritical disregard of his concern that a Supreme Court seat should not be filled in an election year, McConnell jumped. Within hours of the announcement and on the very night of RBG's death, McConnell pushed Trump to fill her seat with Amy Coney Barrett,[46] giving the Court its 6–3 conservative majority.[47] In the game of raw power politics, hypocrisy is not a character flaw; it is a prized virtue.

After Mitch McConnell's successful takeover of three Supreme Court seats, a Supreme Court with a 6–3 conservative majority is generating a new deconstructive jurisprudence.[48] The majority is on a path to reduce Congress' authority, block agencies' capacity to regulate, revive the *Lochner* era jurisprudence, bias elections, and eliminate constitutional rights previously established by the Court.

11.11 LOCHNER RETURNS (IN ANOTHER GUISE)

The New Deal settlement involved courts deferring to the expertise and experience of agencies. As the Supreme Court itself recognized, agencies have more expertise than the courts and, unlike judges, they are politically accountable to the president and Congress.[49] When statutory language is ambiguous, the Court would therefore defer to an agency's interpretation because the resolution of what the statute meant involved policy choices implicating that expertise and accountability.[50] But now the Court has decided it will interpret the statutory language itself when a case involves a "major question" – one of important "economic and political" significance.[51] Indeed, the current Court has ruled that it will decide policy issues unless an agency can "point to 'clear congressional authorization.'"[52] Given the reality that congressional delegations to agencies involve future, unanticipated problems, this requirement is difficult to satisfy and restrains agency actions.

The Court defended this shift by assuming that Congress would intend for the courts to decide such questions even though there is no actual evidence that this is what Congress intended. Instead, it is more likely that Congressional intent – if that could be known – was that an agency should take the lead in interpreting the language for the reasons the Court itself previously recognized: agencies have more expertise than judges, and they are more politically accountable.

As *Lochner* illustrated, the Court before *Carolene Products* would decide for itself whether a regulation was a good idea or not. There was no limit to this assumption of authority, and the Court used this doctrine to impose its anti-government ideology on the country.[53] Likewise, there is no limiting principle that would say when the interpretation of a statute is of "economic and political significance." This new doctrine opens the door for the Court not only to resolve a statutory ambiguity, but to decide for themselves what interpretation is best for the country according to a justices' view about the proper mix of government and markets rather than according to expert policy analysis.[54]

In *West Virginia v. EPA*,[55] for example, the majority struck down an EPA effort to reduce the greenhouse gas emissions that cause climate change based on statutory language that was not entirely clear but which arguably authorized EPA to adopt its regulation. Using the new doctrine, the Court also struck down OSHA's attempt to protect workers from COVID by requiring employers to mandate that their employees wear masks while at work,[56] and FDA's effort to regulate tobacco products to reduce teenage smoking.[57] And it ruled that the Biden administration did not have the authority to forgive up to $20,000 of the student loan payments owed by millions of Americans.[58] The Higher Education Relief Opportunities for Students Act of

2003 had authorized the Secretary of Education to make changes to any provision of applicable student aid program laws in the aftermath of the September 11, 2001, terrorist attacks on the country, but the Court ruled that authorization was not a sufficient basis for the agency to act.[59]

As the previous decisions indicate, the Court can block important policy decisions because Congress did not spell out an agency's authority to adopt a regulation to the Court's satisfaction. The upshot is that the Court is demanding what Congress is not very good at doing. Congress speaks generally, and agencies act particularly. Regardless, the Court is not better placed to do either. The Court is therefore deregulating through the backdoor.

11.12 BIASING THE POLITICAL PROCESS

The Warren Court exalted voting as the way to make the political process fair and democratic.[60] The Rehnquist and Roberts Courts see things differently. According to these newer decisions, unlimited campaign contributions for political favors do not constitute corruption. Corporate money deserves the same amount of political protection given to individuals.[61] States may require voter ID laws.[62] They may purge voter rolls.[63] School integration plans adopted by democratically elected school officials can be set aside.[64] Weakening, but not completely invalidating,[65] the Voting Rights Act of 1965, the Court has ruled that Congress need not regulate racial gerrymandering[66] and making it harder for racial minorities to challenge restrictive state election laws.[67] And, perhaps most troubling, the Court has declared that the Court is incapable of determining when politically partisan gerrymandering has occurred even though there have been a number of state courts that have made that determination.[68]

The Court's reluctance to expand voting showed up in Wisconsin during the COVID pandemic. Wisconsin's spring elections were scheduled for Tuesday, April 7, 2020. Absentee ballots were to be mailed and postmarked by then. Stay-at-home orders were issued on March 24 and, because of public health risks, voters requested 1 million more absentee ballots than normal. As a result, many ballots were not sent to voters in time to meet the April 7 date, and voters sought a one-week extension to April 13 that was granted by a federal district court. The Republican National Committee appealed to the Supreme Court, and Justice Kavanaugh invalidated the lower court's order. Despite the Constitution granting wide discretion to states over how elections are conducted, he ruled that state discretion does not allow for a one-week extension for even mail-in ballots during a pandemic.[69] The consequence of not extending the deadline meant that either voters would be denied the right to vote or, they would be forced to vote in person during a pandemic and risk contracting a potentially fatal illness.[70]

One theme holds these cases together: they all weaken democratic processes. It is also probably not coincidental that the cases also benefit the Republican Party. Once the Supreme Court signaled that voter suppression was allowed, many states moved aggressively with literally hundreds of bills toward restricting voters with a specific intent of favoring Republicans over Democrats and disenfranchising Black voters.[71] These restrictions, which were predictable,[72] were based on the groundless claim that they were needed to protect voting rolls when, in fact, evidence of voter fraud approaches zero.[73] In 2021, for example, the Associated Press conducted a study of the six battleground states disputed by Trump in the 2020 election. The study found fewer than 475 possible cases of voter fraud out of 25.5 million votes cast in those states. Further, Biden won those states by a combined total of 311,257 votes. In short, even if all the alleged voter fraud cases were true, they had no effect on the outcome.[74]

11.13 REVERSING CONSTITUTIONAL RIGHTS

In May 2022, there was an unprecedented leak of a copy of a draft opinion written by Justice Alito that indicated the Court had voted to overrule *Roe v. Wade*.[75] Despite the forewarning, many people were shocked when the Court issued its opinion in in *Dobbs v. Jackson Women's Health*,[76] eliminating a constitutional right that had existed for 50 years, protecting a woman's right to choose an abortion. The Court until *Dobbs* had never eliminated a constitutional right once it had been established. When the Court had not followed previous cases, it had done so to expand a constitutional right, such as in *Brown v. Board of Education*, or in some instances limit a constitutional right, but not to overrule it.

The fact that five members of the Court were willing to take this unprecedented step indicates the historically radical nature of what the Court has done.[77] Justice Alito said that *Dobbs* was not a signal that the Court would overrule other constitutional rights, but the Justices have also signaled in other opinions that they might do so.[78] Justice Thomas, in his concurring opinion, expressly writes that prior decisions regarding contraception, same-sex marriage, and sexual relations are "demonstrably erroneous" and that the Court has a duty to revisit and reverse them.[79]

11.14 WALKING BACK EQUAL OPPORTUNITY

In another case reversing previous decisions dating back nearly 50 years, the Court ended the use of race as one of multiple factors as a consideration in university admissions,[80] The prior decisions had approved race-conscious college admissions policies as a way to advance "the Constitution's guarantee of equality" and the vision of *Brown v. Board of Education* as "a Nation with more inclusive schools."[81] According to the six conservative members of the Court, "Eliminating racial discrimination means eliminating all of it."[82] The three dissenting justices accused the majority of "let-them-eat-cake obliviousness" because "deeming race irrelevant in law does not make it so in life."

As readers may recall, Abraham Lincoln defined the need for government "to clear the paths of laudable pursuit for all – to afford all, an unfettered start, and a fair chance, in the race of life."[83] Justice Jackson's dissent refers to the ways that Black Americans still do not enjoy a fair chance in the race of life, several of which were described in Chapter 8. The Court was not compelled to eliminate race as a factor in college admissions, and the Court had previously approved of race-conscious remedies chosen by Congress and state legislators in a wide variety of circumstances. While the majority did not overrule those other choices, the Court left it uncertain and unclear to what extent considerations of race could be considered in any matter of public policy in the future.

The Roberts Court has also ruled that businesses can discriminate against gay persons when they offer services relating to the marriage of two people of the same sex.[84] As noted earlier, the Civil Rights Act of 1964 mandated that public accommodations had to be equally available without racial discrimination. In similar fashion, some states and cities have mandated that businesses cannot discriminate based on sexual orientation. The Court's ruling was the first time it had ever held that there was a constitutional right to discriminate against a discrete minority of persons.

The lawsuit was filed by a web designer who said that she might sometime in the future want to offer her services to engaged couples who wanted to create a website for their wedding, and if she did, she wanted to advertise that she would not offer her services to same-sex couples because she objected on religious grounds to people of the same sex marrying.

The Constitution requires that a plaintiff be injured in some way before the person or entity can sue. For that reason, the Court normally will reject a case if there is no immediate and concrete harm or injury to the plaintiff bringing the lawsuit. The conservative majority, however, was so anxious to establish a constitutional right to discriminate against gay couples that it took up the case despite the lack of injury to the plaintiff who, after all, was only planning to offer her services to engaged couples. And even if she had offered such services, there would never be an injury if she did not have any gay clients.

11.15 CONCLUSION

The Supreme Court matters. For most of the twentieth century, Court decisions and doctrine shaped modern government; they shaped, and validated, modern government. Now, in the third decade of the twenty-first century, the Court is poised to radically change history.[85] In the current Court's eyes, it is their obligation to reverse the mix created by the New Deal and Great Society; reduce the authority of administrative agencies; and reserve for the judiciary, and especially the Supreme Court, the power to make major policy decisions as to how the country's economic policies and fundamental values should be implemented. Simultaneously, the Court is aggrandizing power for itself at the expense of Congress, the agencies, and the popular will.[86]

In short, the new Court has taken upon itself the task to reset the balance between government and markets.[87] In doing so, the Court has shown itself to be extremely aggressive. It is willing to overrule prior decisions dating back decades. In the past, because the country relies on and adjusts to the Court's decisions, it is normally reluctant to overrule past decisions even if the current justices disagree with the prior decision. Likewise, it is willing to overrule a constitutional right that it has established, which has never happened before, or establish a constitutional right to discriminate against a discrete minority, which has also never happened before.

Since federal judges have life-time tenure, neither the composition of the Supreme Court nor its radical views about the mix of government and markets are likely to change soon. But voters are not impotent. They can vote for presidents and members of Congress who will appoint justices who would respect the New Deal settlement when the time comes. And Congress has the authority to add justices to the Court, as Roosevelt threatened to do. Change may come slowly, but if history is a guide, change will come if enough voters will make it happen.

12

Donald Trump's America

Challenging Democracy

In 2013, Netflix premiered its version of a TV show, *The House of Cards*, that was based on the original BBC series. In the American version, Frank Underwood, an ambitious and amoral congressman, planned and schemed to bring down a president and gain the office for himself. He did not hesitate to use blackmail and even murder to carry out his plan. Even as compared to the public's most cynical conceptions of politicians, Underwood (and his British counterpart) went beyond anyone's idea of normal political behavior.

Viewers knew the House of Cards was fiction. Donald Trump was real. According to the *Washington Post*, he made 30,573 false or misleading claims during his presidency, deflected efforts to correct the record by telling his supporters that they should ignore this "false news" because traditional news sources were the "enemies of the people," and ignored or undermined the norms of the presidential behavior of his predecessors in twenty additional ways.[1] His actions regarding the government and markets were likewise more radical than any of his predecessors. Other presidents have favored smaller government, but as the previous history shows, they understood and respected the need for government as well as markets even as they favored an adjustment in the mix.

Trump abandoned this history. Instead of a conversation about the mix, he led an effort to make politics about the distrust and animosity of Americans toward other Americans.[2] He had no plan other than self-aggrandizement, and when the traditional institutions of government got in his way, he did what he could to diminish them across the board including the national security apparatus and judiciary. He knew almost nothing about government and what it does, and like Andrew Jackson, he did not think that competence and expertise were important or necessary to running the government. And he supported radical deregulation, tax cuts, and a trade war against China that did identifiable harm to the country. Most destructively, when Trump was not reelected in 2020, he set about overturning the result by pressing the "big lie" – the claim that he lost the election because of election fraud, although none existed – and then encouraged the invasion of the Capitol on January 6 to prevent the certification of Joe Biden as president.

When the country has experienced the type of disruptions, distortions, and violence that occurred during the Trump presidency, when the balance between
government and markets is on a tilt, then there has been a responsive renewal of
democracy as voters became reengaged with reliable public policies. Often this has
been a bumpy ride, and the recovery has taken time, but the country has adjusted
the mix of government and markets to stable conditions when voters focus on how
we can best achieve America's fundamental values. In short, a healthy government-
market mix directly implicates our democratic values, especially the freedom and
equality to participate in markets and exercise voice in government. Political polarization disturbs that balance to the detriment of the common good.[3]

12.1 US VERSUS THEM

The election of Donald Trump in 2016, despite losing the popular vote by 2.8 million votes, surprised many people in the country because he seemed to them so obviously unfit for the office. Trump himself was apparently surprised that he won.[4] He
won by amplifying the grievances of rural, working-class, and high school-educated
voters, and they in turn helped him carry the states he needed to be selected as the
winner by the Electoral College. As George Packer reported, "Trump sensed this
rage that flared from this pain and made it the fuel of his campaign."[5]

Arlie Russell Hochschild, a sociologist, found that residents in rural Louisiana
perceived themselves as standing in line, working toward the American Dream
of bettering themselves and their families, but that line for them was at a stand-
still despite their diligence and hard work. They attributed their lack of progress to
government policies that allowed other people – minorities, immigrants, refugees,
women, and people of different sexual and gender orientations – to cut in line in
front of them. In a similar way, voters blamed the concerns about the environment
for blocking their progress.[6]

A political scientist, Katherine Cramer, learned that for rural residents of
Wisconsin, the "demons are not affluent people but, rather, the government, the people who work for it, and urban areas that are home to liberals and people of color."[7]
Similarly, Robert Wuthnow, another sociologist, found people living in communities of less than 25,000 residents considered themselves under siege because the rest
of the country was unconcerned about the fracture of the social expectations, obligations, and relationships that are part and parcel of small-town life.

The "us versus them politics," amplified by ambitious politicians, not only makes
it difficult to talk across this divide, but it also prevents people from seeing how the
mix of government and markets has contributed to the loss of economic opportunity,
and how new government policies can address the lack of opportunity and other mal-
adies. Us versus them politics blocks recognition that voters in rural and urban areas
may have similar concerns. Hilary Clinton paid the price when she failed to recognize the real needs of Trump supporters and labeled them "a basket of deplorables."[8]

The novelist Barbara Kingsolver was awarded the 2023 Pulitzer Prize for her novel, *Demon Copperhead*, about poverty, opioid addiction, moral collapse, and the institutional failures in Appalachia. As one reviewer pointed out, Kingsolver's book is about what it is like to be "born into a life without choices."[9] The same can be said of children born in cities whose landscape can be equally blighted.

The us versus them politics prevents voters from making common cause with the people who would favor government policies to address the situation. Instead, voters have remained loyal to candidates who favor small government because they denigrate the educated elites, urban dwellers, and minorities they regard as their enemies. The difference between rural and urban citizens is the difference between Black and White that politicians exploited. That many Trump voters were struggling economically because of the pro-market tilt in the country since the election of Ronald Reagan did not register with them.

There was an even darker side to the us versus them politics. For many, their grievances were social and economic, but Trump and other candidates tainted these grievances with the racialization of public policy, harkening back to a dark side of American history – slavery, the Civil War, and Jim Crow laws. It has been common for candidates to blame immigrants for job losses and crime and minorities for taking the rightful place of White Americans to prosper and lead. And the anti-gay and anti-Semitic tropes in some of the conspiracy theories endorsed by Trump and other politicians have been linked to shootings at a gay nightclub, a movie theater, a military base, a Black church in Charlottesville, and a synagogue in Pittsburgh, all resulting in fatalities.

12.2 UNBUILDING THE MIDDLE CLASS

"The United States built the world's greatest middle-class economy," Jordan Weisman writes, "then unbuilt it."[10] Between the late 1940s and the 1970s, middle- and lower-income Americans increased their share of the nation's wealth, and the incomes of the least well-off households (the bottom one-fifth) grew the most of any group in the country.[11] By the time Trump and Hilary Clinton campaigned for president, the country was experiencing nearly unprecedented levels of wealth inequality.[12] The share of the national wealth of the richest families increased from 60 to 79 percent between 1983 and 2016, while the middle-class share declined from 32 to 17 percent. Low-wealth Americans' share of the national wealth fell from 7 to 4 percent.[13] By 2021, 10 percent of the wealthiest Americans owned $70 of every $100 in household wealth.[14]

Government unbuilt the middle class in three ways. The "guns and butter" policies of the Johnson administration led to rampant inflation. Then, as the globalization of trade was sweeping the world, the U.S. failed to adjust the mix of government and markets to take account of the impact on economic opportunity at home. Plus, a series of tax cuts increased inequality and hampered the government's capacity to invest in helping those who were falling behind.

12.3 GUNS AND BUTTER

The country began its long slide into unprecedented wealth inequality in the Johnson administration. Since a country only has a limited number of resources to produce all goods, it can use those resources to fight a war or invest in the domestic economy. Economists have referred to this as a choice between "guns and butter" – should the country invest in defense or social programs? But LBJ wanted both – fight the Vietnam War and invest in Great Society programs.

The runaway inflation that resulted was predictable.[15] When there is more demand to use resources than available goods and services, suppliers will raise their prices to sell what is available to those who can afford the higher costs. People who can afford the increased prices can still get what they would like, but many others are priced out of the market. The government was able to afford higher prices because Johnson decided to borrow the money to pay the higher costs. If the government had increased taxes, consumers would have curtailed their spending, which would have offset some of the inflationary pressures created by government spending.

Prices in the late 1960s had been stable with inflation running about 2 percent, but inflation increased to 12 percent by 1974, and by 1980, it hit a whopping 14.5 percent a year.[16] To make matters worse, the price of oil quadrupled when Arab countries imposed an oil embargo against the United States in retaliation for supporting Israel in the 1973 Yom Kippur War. The price doubled again when oil supplies declined as the result of the Iranian revolution that established an Islamic Republic.[17]

After the high prices and the lack of affordable goods and services slowed economic growth,[18] Johnson asked Congress to raise taxes in 1967 so that the country could continue to fight the Vietnam War and pay for the Great Society.[19] "That bitch of a war," Johnson observed near the end of his life, "killed the lady I really loved – the Great Society."[20] The word "taxation" is toxic to politicians, and Congress refused tax increases.

12.4 GLOBALIZATION

Millions of Americans who could not afford the rising prices lost even more ground as the United States supported the unprecedented expansion of globalized trade that was occurring.[21] Since countries specialize in what they do best when there is free trade, the United States became a world leader in markets that rely on the intensive use of technology and on a highly educated workforce, such as in communications, education, finance, health care, and information technology.

The economic opportunities created by globalization greatly benefitted Americans who had the opportunity to take advantage of these developments, but it left behind others who had been employed in manufacturing and other jobs lost to

other countries as corporations moved their factories to countries to employ a workforce that was paid less, and often much less, than here. Other routine and easy-to-
duplicate jobs, such as call centers, were also outsourced.

12.5 REDUCED ECONOMIC OPPORTUNITY AND MORE TAX CUTS

The loss of economic opportunity for many Americans was not an accident. It
resulted from decisions by the government not to pay for the Vietnam War by raising taxes and not to address the distributional impacts of globalization. It was also
the result of a series of tax cuts, which favored wealthy Americans and reduced the
government's capacity to invest in economic opportunity.

In December 2017, Trump signed the Tax Cuts and Jobs Act, the largest corporate
tax cut the country had known. He was unequivocally proud of the cut he deemed
the "biggest in history," when just hours after he signed them into law, he told his
friends at dinner in his private club Mar-a-Lago "You all just got a lot richer."[22]
Corporate taxes were reduced from 35 to 21 percent, a 40 percent reduction.

The promise was that corporations would take the money they had saved from
reduced taxes and use the savings to create new jobs and pay higher wages. Trump
promised the tax cuts "would be rocket fuel for the economy"[23] and he bragged that
the average American household would receive "around a $4,000 pay raise." History
tells a different story. Trump's tax strategy was another version of Reagan's supply-side
economics and trickle-down theory that failed then,[24] and failed again under Trump.

Corporations spent only about six percent of the tax savings on workers. The rest
went to stockholders when corporations bought back their own stock. The direct
consequence of stock buybacks is to raise stock prices. With these gains, corporations paid themselves and their shareholders higher dividends.[25] Since ten percent
of Americans own 84 percent of corporate stocks, most of the corporate tax savings
ended up in the pockets of the wealthiest Americans.[26] The tax cuts are not proj-
ected to come anywhere close to paying from themselves, rather they simply added
to the government deficit. Based on Congressional Budget Office data, tax experts
estimate the tax cuts will increase the government deficit by as much as $3.4 to $3.8
trillion over 10 years.[27]

This and previous tax cuts not only reduced government revenues, but taxes also
became less progressive. The result was wealthier people paid a lower tax rate on the
money that they earned from investments and other types of income than taxpayers
whose only source of income was the money they were paid at work.[28] While most
taxpayers had a lower tax bill because of the 2017 tax cuts, the top 20 percent of
Americans with the largest tax bills received more than 60 percent of the savings.[29]
The result replicated the experience with the tax cuts that have been enacted since
1980. The same tilt in favor of the wealthy exists in the states. Although the results
vary from state to state, low-income Americans are paying one and a half times as
much of their income in taxes as the wealthiest one percent of Americans.[30]

Emphasizing economic inequality, Warren Buffett, one of the five richest people in the world, once pointed out that he paid a lower tax rate on the money he earned (17.4 percent) than his secretary, Debbie (35.8 percent).[31] He added, "[W]e were told a rising tide would lift all boats, but the rising tide has lifted all yachts." When his critics accused him of "class warfare" for pitting the less well off against wealthy Americans, Buffett responded, "If this is a war, my side has the nuclear bomb" because we have lobbyists and Wall Street on our side. "Debbie," Buffett's secretary, "doesn't have anybody. I want a government that is responsive to the people who got the short straw in life."[32]

12.6 A TRADE WAR

As a candidate, Trump campaigned about being a "great deal maker" who would get China to agree to a trade deal that addressed the Chinese theft of intellectual property and the $350 billion trade deficit with China that was the result of globalization. As the Chinese took over the manufacture of goods previously made in this country, the country ended up purchasing many more goods from China than it purchased from the U.S. Trump bragged that "trade wars are easy to win," but the results show the opposite.

The trade war failed – it did not slow the purchase of Chinese goods by Americans – and it harmed significant sectors of the economy because U.S. exporters lost business selling goods to China. For example, according to the Farm Bureau, farmers lost most of the $24 billion in farm exports to China. Another is that U.S. importers responded to the $46 billion more they paid for Chinese products by cutting jobs and wages, raising prices they charged consumers, and accepting lower profit margins. While all of this was happening, the trade deficit with China increased, not decreased, despite the new trade agreement.[33]

There are problems with international trade, such as the theft of U.S. intellectual property identified by Trump. But the results of the trade war indicate that a more nuanced approach is necessary. When Alexander Hamilton imposed tariffs on foreign goods to protect American manufacturing, the world economy looked entirely different. Hamilton's trade war succeeded because the newly formed U.S. was largely agricultural and had limited trade with other countries because of the distances involved and the limited capacity to ship goods on small, wind-powered ships. In the globalized economy of today, the U.S. economy is deeply integrated with the Chinese economy and the economies of other nations.

12.7 RADICAL DEREGULATION

Soon after Trump named Steven Brannon as his chief White House strategist, he promised a daily fight to "deconstruct the administrative state."[34] For Bannon and Trump, regulation was holding back the American economy, and the path to greater growth was less, much less, regulation.

One of the president's first acts in office required agencies to revoke two regulations for everyone that the agency promulgated.[35] More specifically, the order prohibited an agency from imposing any new costs on regulated firms unless the new costs were offset by the repeal of two existing regulations. Any economist will confirm that a rule is an economic investment worth making when the benefits are greater than the costs.[36] The administration, however, focused exclusively on the costs of regulation, and it simply ignored regulatory benefits such as protecting people from financial and physical injuries, and most importantly premature death. Based on available but incomplete data, the government has found that regulatory benefits usually exceed the cost of the rules by at least 2 to 1, but often the benefits are 10 to 1 or higher as compared to the costs paid by industry to implement regulations.[37]

The administration then set out to eliminate or cut back on hundreds of regulations. No regulation was too small to escape the anti-bureaucracy scythe, particularly rules adopted during the Obama administration. The administration not only repealed President Obama's regulations protecting transgender students, but it also repealed school lunch nutritional rules promoted by Michelle Obama and issued the repeal on her birthday.[38] Environmental regulations were a favorite target; the Trump administration attempted to roll back more than 112 environmental regulations.[39]

The administration's war on regulation also stopped the country's efforts to slow climate change and adjust for the weather changes that were occurring. In 2017, Trump announced the U.S. would pull out of the Paris Climate Agreement, and the country did so in 2020.[40] Trump also stopped EPA and other agencies from taking actions to slow climate change to the extent of banning agencies from using the term "climate change" on government websites.[41] When scientists from thirteen agencies issued a National Climate Assessment in November 2018, which concluded that it was extremely likely based on extensive evidence that the dominant cause of climate change was emission of greenhouse gases and other human activities, Trump replied, "I don't believe it. No, no, I don't believe it."[42]

Market advocates are fond of the political slogan "job-killing regulation" since Ronald Reagan. The story, however, is not so simple. History shows regulation, on balance, has little impact on the number of jobs or creates new jobs in the regulated industries.[43] This is because when companies are regulated, they spend money on regulatory compliance, which adds to economic growth. Also, regulation creates new markets and new industries. Clean energy using solar and wind power is a clear example. This does not mean that every worker benefits. New jobs may be created in different industries than where the worker is employed. Trump's solution was the equivalent of throwing out the baby with the bathwater. Rather than helping those who lose their jobs because of regulation, Trump sought to get rid of regulation, and the benefits therefrom, entirely.

Trump's deregulatory zeal was largely unsuccessful because of the unreasonableness of his deregulatory policies. The courts overturned most of the environmental repeals, as well as the repeal of Michelle Obama's school nutrition rules, because the administration did not follow proper legal procedures. The Trump administration lost 84 percent of the 132 lawsuits challenging its deregulatory agenda. Historically, by comparison, agencies typically win about 70 percent of the legal challenges brought against them.[44] One reason for this unprecedented record was the failure of the administration to seek the assistance of civil service experts in the government about how to make changes that would hold up in court. The Trump administration did not want to listen to this advice because it wanted to deregulate beyond what expertise and science would justify. The deconstruction of the administrative state involved deregulation for deregulation's sake.

Although Trump largely failed in his deconstruction efforts, the experience was not a matter of no harm, no foul. The county lost four years that could have been used to address significant new regulatory problems and fine-tune existing rules. In particular, the country lost four years that it could have been doing something about climate change, cybersecurity, or healthcare, as examples. More ominously, pro-business, anti-government fervor has not left the political scene. Today, as Chapter 11 pointed out, that fervor is found in the Supreme Court in large part because of the Supreme Court justices appointed by Trump as engineered by Mitch McConnell.

12.8 ANDREW JACKSON RETURNS

The Trump years in office had an uncanny resemblance to Andrew Jackson's and his attitudes about competence and expertise. Before Trump, an incoming administration would choose persons knowledgeable about the government to read briefing books prepared by outgoing officials and to meet with them. A federal law provides funding and office space for the transition team, but the incoming president pays the salary of the full-time transition team workers using campaign funds. When Trump found out he had to pay for the transition staff, he told the chair of the transition, "Fuck the law. I don't give a fuck about the law. I want my fucking money."[45]

The president then showed little or no interest in keeping up with the details and information found in staff memos and other briefing papers. His political appointees and high-level civil servants, including from the military, struggled to produce briefings that would hold the President's interest for more than a couple of minutes. Gary Cohn, a Trump advisor, told a reporter, "Trump won't read anything—not one-page memos, not the brief policy papers, nothing. He gets up halfway through meetings with world leaders because he is bored."[46] Trump explained he was able to make good decisions "with very little knowledge other than the knowledge I [already] had…"[47] After all, he proclaimed that he was a "very stable genius."[48]

Like Jackson, his aim was to replace existing government employees with people chosen based on their loyalty to him and his policies rather than their competence. There was Tom Price as head of Health and Human Services, a Georgia congressman who favored repealing the Affordable Care Act; Betsy DeVos as education secretary, who was a committed opponent of funding public education; and Greg

Pruitt to head EPA, a former Oklahoma attorney general who had sued EPA more than a dozen times to stop it from regulating.

Trump is not the only president to appoint anti-government and unknowledgeable administrators. Ronald Reagan and George W. Bush, for example, did likewise, but the disregard of experience and expertise became a hallmark of the Trump presidency. There was Ben Carson, a retired neurosurgeon, picked as Secretary of Housing and Urban Development, and Rick Perry, the former Texas governor who Trump picked to lead the Department of Energy, who had advocated abolishing the department and later admitted he did not know what the department did when he called for its elimination.

Instead of someone with expertise and experience, Trump installed an ideological ambassador and former Fox News commentator to head the Office of the Director of National Intelligence. Similarly, Larry Kudlow, a CNBC economic commentator with no economics degree, was appointed as the president's chief economic advisor. And there was Ryan Zinke, appointed as Secretary of the Department of the Interior, who was forced to leave office because of his ethical lapses.[49] The job test for the Trump White House was simple – personal loyalty. Only Trump loyalists needed to apply for government positions; experience was not required.[50]

The president did not stop at ignoring unwanted advice; he fired those appointees who disagreed, or he pressured them to leave government.[51] His targets included FBI agents, such as Deputy Director Andrew McCabe, and every other member of the FBI leadership who investigated him as well as other Department of Justice officials who had criticized him. He engineered the firing of McCabe with the specific intent of not only humiliating him publicly but denying him most of his pension. The president also fired State Department officials, such as Ambassador Masha Yovanovitch, and distinguished career military officers, such as Alexander Vindman, when they testified about his actions attempting to persuade a foreign government to dig up dirt on Joe Biden's son. Rick Bright, who led the government's efforts to develop a coronavirus vaccine, was fired when he pushed back against Trump's endorsements of hydroxychloroquine as a cure for the coronavirus.[52]

12.9 THE SPOILS SYSTEM RETURNS

Presidents have always found it annoying to receive advice contrary to policies they favor. As two law professors have noted, "The conflicts between political appointees and the … well-insulated-from-termination" civil servants "are legion."[53] President Nixon, for example, complained to then Treasury Secretary John Connally that "I don't believe that civil service is a good thing for the country."[54] Similarly, incoming President Eisenhower was surprised when civil servants would not immediately follow the White House's instructions but instead offer advice about proposed policies. The new President, Truman observed, will "sit here and he'll say, 'Do this!

Do that!' And nothing will happen. Poor Ike—it won't be a bit like the Army."[55] But they did not try to get rid of the civil servants who they found annoying.

Trump, unlike Jackson, did not have the option of firing civil servants. As Chapter 3 covered, Congress established the civil service system in 1883 in the wake of President Garfield assassination by a disappointed job seeker, which protects government employees from being arbitrarily fired. The administration therefore looked for ways to make their jobs so unattractive that civil servants would quit.

The president repeatedly described the bureaucracy as a "swamp" that he would drain, as "'absolute scum,'" or even as Nazis, among other derogatory terms. His deputies commonly claimed civil servants were the foot soldiers of a shadowy "Deep State" that was working to subvert democracy and sabotage the president's agenda at all costs.[56] The constant harping about incompetent bureaucrats and the denigration of environmental rules caused the exit of over 1,600 scientists from government service, most notably from the National Institutes of Health and the Environmental Protection Agency.[57]

In addition to this vitriol, the administration threatened to or did bring criminal charges against individual employees. Such actions chilled civil servants from speaking out because of the expense of hiring lawyers to defend themselves, the damage to their reputations, and the likelihood of the difficulty of finding other jobs.

Beyond intimidation, the administration proposed budget cuts, rejected by Congress, that would have resulted in the layoff of thousands of federal employees, and when it moved whole offices outside of Washington, most employees quit rather than leave their homes and lives in the Washington area.[58] When the Bureau of Land Management was moved to Grand Junction, Colorado, 87 percent of the staff quit.[59] The White House additionally disbanded hundreds of groups located throughout the government that were used to obtain the advice of experts from academia and private industry. The Interior Department disbanded more than 200 such groups itself.[60]

12.10 JANUARY 6

As a last act, Trump refused to accept the judgment of voters that they would be better off if Joe Biden were president. In a desperate attempt to hold onto office, he encouraged his supporters to go to the Capital and stop the certification of Biden as president by Congress. The invasion of the building that resulted caused five fatalities, several more by suicides, and wounded or injured 140 others, many of whom were hospitalized with traumatic brain injuries, concussions, broken bones as well as suffering post traumatic syndrome and other emotional and psychological damages.[61] Congressmen Jamie Raskin, an eyewitness to the event, recalled:

> The news reports kept saying that there had been a "breach" .... But ... it was a straightforward siege, defined by pitched, violent battles thick with people all over

the Capitol complex, waves of hand-to-hand, medieval-style combat against the offi-cers who greeted us every morning and bade us good night. Everyone could see a paramilitary storming of the entrance to the Capitol, the windows being smashed, and a savage, bloody battle with thousands of combatants raging everywhere, a strug-gle that our beleaguered security forces were, from the looks of it, clearly losing.[62]

In May 2022, the John F. Kennedy Presidential Library Museum honored Liz Cheney with its Profile in Courage Award for standing up for the Constitution and for democracy.[63] As a member of the House, Cheney contested the false claims by President Trump and other Republicans that the election was stolen, and she then accepted an invitation to be the Vice Chair of the Select Committee to Investigate the January 6th attack. For her, the issue was not about whether there is too much or too little government, although she consistently favored the latter position.[64] For Cheney, democracy was linked to our nation's values because it is how we decide how to pursue them.

In the Forward to the Final Report of the January 6th Committee, Cheney wrote:

It is comforting to assume that the institutions of our Republic will always with-stand those who try to defeat our Constitution from within. But our institutions are only strong when those who hold office are faithful to our Constitution…. The task is unending because democracy can be fragile and our institutions do not defend themselves.[65]

Cheney paid for her efforts on behalf of democracy. On August 16, 2022, Cheney was not only defeated in the Wyoming Republican primary to serve in the House, she received only 37 percent of the total vote. Her margin of defeat was stag-gering given the fact that two years previously she won her seat with 73% of the vote. Still, she remained defiant in her defense of democracy: "This is a fight for all of us together. I'm a conservative Republican … [b]ut I love my country more."[66]

12.11 CONCLUSION

Historians will be assessing the Trump presidency for years to come. They have already opined that he was one of the worst presidents in American history.[67] While Trump may not have been the worst president ever, he was far outside of the mainstream of American politics and its discussion of what mix of government and markets best achieves the nation's fundamental political values. Other modern presidents have favored markets more than government, but only Trump did not understand the role of government, expertise, and the need for a mix of both. His efforts to retain the presidency even though he lost the election based on the "big lie" poisoned trust in elections that continues, and his plan to stop the election of Joe Biden discarded democracy altogether.

Despite this, Trump remained incredibly popular among millions of his sup-porters. He was able to turn their attention away from how the government had failed to build economic opportunity for them, and how it could instead be used to better their lives. Instead, he demonized those very activities. His tactics of lying, obfuscation, and racializing made it more difficult to have a national conversation about a change in the mix of government and markets that could renew economic opportunity for those left behind by economic developments and previous decisions of government.

Both political parties had a role in contributing to the lack of economic opportunity for many in the country. Government played a major role in building a middle class after WWII. The result was historical levels of economic equality. Then the government then helped to unbuild the middle class when it borrowed money to fight the Vietnam War, ignored how globalization harmed many Americans even as it benefited others, and made cut taxes in ways that mostly benefited the wealthy and robbed the government of needed resources.

The election of Joe Biden, as Chapter 14 takes up, resulted in a president who in many ways was the opposite of Trump – experienced, competent, and knowledgeable about government. It also resulted in a significant effort to address the lack of economic opportunity that had been so keenly felt by so many in the country including Trump's supporters.

13

Anthony Fauci's America

Making Government Work

In May 2021, Dr. Jill Biden accompanied Dr. Anthony Fauci on a tour of a Washington, D.C., children's vaccination clinic to publicize the availability of coronavirus vaccinations for American teenagers. When she introduced him to the waiting crowd, she asked, "'[W]ho doesn't love Dr. Fauci? I think everybody in America loves Dr. Fauci.'"[1] President Donald Trump did not share this love. According to the president, "People are tired of hearing Fauci and all those idiots…. Fauci is a disaster."[2] As the head of the National Institute for Allergy and Infectious Diseases, Fauci was one of President Trump's principal advisors concerning the coronavirus and the pandemic. His advice was not always well received. Trump made it clear that he did not appreciate this civil servant questioning what he wanted to do.

Trump's bashing of a bureaucrat is an old American political tradition. One of Abraham Lincoln's favorite stories about government was a joke with the punchline: "That's how it happened that jackasses have been holding down all the high wage government jobs ever since."[3] President Reagan would describe federal civil servants as either "loafers, incompetent buffoons, good ole boys, or tyrants."[4] President Obama regularly made the case for the importance of government, but he also did not hesitate to tell stories about unreasonable bureaucratic behavior.[5] And from 1975 through 1988, Wisconsin Senator William Proxmire bestowed his monthly Golden Fleece awards on civil servants and departments for wasteful spending as another criticism of the bureaucracy.[6]

Over the nation's history, the government has taken on an increasing and successful role in ensuring prosperity, protecting people, and promoting equality, and this success is due in no small part to the contribution of civil servants. Like all institutions, the government fails because its employees let it down, but it also fails because of incompetent political leaders who ignore the advice of knowledgeable and experienced civil servants or reject their advice because it conflicts with their ideological agenda. Andrew Jackson famously thought running the government did not require any special skills, and Donald Trump went even further in thinking that he did not need to know anything about how the government ran or what the civil service advised. The results were disastrous for both the presidents and the country. Government needs administration, especially in times of emergency, and government needs public servants like Anthony Fauci to carry out its programs.

13.1 DR. ANTHONY FAUCI

On December 24, 1940, the day before Christmas, an unofficial two-day holiday truce began in the aerial war between Britain and Germany. On this day, Mahatma Gandhi wrote a second letter to Adolf Hitler, addressing him as a "Dear Friend," and advised him to stop the war. Also on this day, Stephen A. Fauci, a pharmacist in the Dyker Heights section of Brooklyn, New York, welcomed his second child with his wife, Eugenia Lillian. They named their son Anthony, who later in his life became one of the civil servants who are the backbone of the government.

Fauci first encountered medicine in the 1950s when he was helping his family deliver prescriptions in a working-class Italian and Jewish neighborhood in Brooklyn. After attending the College of the Holy Cross, he graduated first in his class at the Cornell Medical School, completed a residency in internal medicine at the school's medical center in New York, and joined the National Institutes of Health (NIH), where he was the director of the National Institute for Allergy and Infectious Diseases for 38 years until his retirement from government in December 2022. Fauci has been celebrated for his leadership and expertise in battling HIV/AIDS, the West Nile virus, SARS, Ebola, Zika, and H1N1, and most recently the Coronavirus, all deadly diseases. He has received 51 honorary doctoral degrees from universities in the United States and abroad, and he has been the recipient of numerous honors including the Presidential Medal of Freedom, which is the highest honor given to a civilian by the President of the United States. And his research has made him the 35th most cited living medical researcher in the world.

13.2 THE SAMMIES

Fauci, a world-class scientist and leader, is clearly a rock star among civil servants, but he is representative of many others who have excelled in their departments and agencies. According to the Partnership for Public Service, the contributions of Dr. Fauci and others are not unique. The organization annually recognizes outstanding civil servants with an award unofficially known as the "Oscars of government service." The Partnership has honored more than 600 individuals and teams of government employees in the last 20 years who have demonstrated federal leadership and innovation. The awards are the Partnership's answer to bureaucratic bashing like Proxmire's Golden Fleece Awards.

The awards are also known as the "Sammies" in honor of Samuel J. Heyman, the founder of the Partnership. Heyman, a successful business entrepreneur and corporate CEO, who was inspired by President Kennedy's call to young people to serve their nation, founded and funded the Partnership for Public Service to honor outstanding government employees. Kennedy famously ended his 1961 Inaugural Address by inviting Americans to "ask not what your country can do for you — ask what you can do for your country."[7] He explained, "the future of our nation quite simply depends on the quality of our government."[8]

Victoria Brahm, the 2019 employee of the year, restored "the quality and safety of a broken health care center for veterans that had become notorious for unsafe medical practices, excessive opioid use and a toxic work environment." Venkatachalam Ramaswamy developed "a state-of-the-art modeling system to enhance understanding and prediction of global climate and provide earlier and more accurate forecasts of severe weather events, helping save lives and property." Emily Banuelos designed "and implemented enhanced surveillance technology that warns when commercial aircraft are lined up to land on a taxiway instead of the intended runway, averting the potential for catastrophic accidents." And Kristen Finne developed a system that allows "first responders to quickly locate and assist 4.3 million Medicare beneficiaries who rely on electricity-dependent medical equipment and are at risk during prolonged power outages."

Another award winner, Arthur Allen, pioneered "and perfected a modeling program that predicts where people lost at sea will be found, cutting search and rescue times and saving thousands of lives during a 35-year career." Osama El-Lissy was recognized for his "highly effective plan that led the United States to become the first and only country to eradicate the pink bollworm, saving cotton growers tens of millions of dollars annually." There was also Jamie Rhome, who was responsible for creating "a new forecasting model and warning system that more accurately predicts the deadly storm surge caused by hurricanes, saving lives by alerting residents sooner of the approaching danger."[9]

13.3 MAKING GOVERNMENT WORK

Not every government employee performs at the outstanding level of these examples. Government does not operate perfectly. Neither do most corporations. Both have had disasters. But the record of public administration in delivering the goods is a reasonable record of success – one that does not deserve the almost universal tendency of elected leaders to bash bureaucracy.

Government, as its history demonstrates, has aligned the country with its political values by contributing to economic prosperity, protecting people from financial and physical harm, addressing discrimination, and establishing a social safety net. In short, as a partner with markets, it has built a freer and more prosperous country. None of this would have been possible if most civil servants were, as Reagan alleged, "either loafers, incompetent buffoons, good ole boys, or tyrants."

The government every day does what Congress has told it to do, from predicting the weather to ensuring that the money supply is not counterfeit and to administering

Social Security payments. Agencies every day promulgate regulations, run inspection programs, and enforce statutes and regulations. All this also indicates that public administration is not chock full of ineffective bureaucrats.

The history of government is therefore a history of public administration. As Chapter 2 discussed, one of the first acts of the new government under George Washington was to create administrative capacity. The subsequent history of public administration reveals two trends. From the founders on, there has been concern about whether government employees would be responsive to their political leadership and effective in carrying out their mission. This has not been left to chance as this history indicates. The other lesson is that government has been more successful when political leaders pay attention to the experience and expertise of the civil service, even if they did not appreciate the pushback they sometimes received.

13.4 NEUTRAL COMPETENCE

As Chapter 3 related, Andrew Jackson was the first president who was not from the upper-class Americans who occupied the presidency, and he considered himself as a man of the common people. He thought that founders' hiring practices perpetuated an "aristocracy" who ran the government. He therefore fired almost one-half of the government's employees and replaced them with men from his political party.[10] Competence was unnecessary, political allegiance was.[11] Jackson's "spoils system" of political patronage did not work as government failed to satisfy its essential functions, and Jackson had to find effective employees to do the government's work.[12]

As a result of the failure of the spoils system to do the work required of it, it soon became apparent that the bureaucracy needed reform, a project taken up by the Progressives. Their solution – a civil service that practices "netural competence" – has been the engine of government's successful implementation of its statutory responsibilities ever since.

Having supported legislation to require government employees to be hired based on expertise and experience, the Progressives turned to the concern that the founders also recognized: how do you ensure that government employees will be responsive to their political leadership and effective in carrying out their mission? The founders had depended on the character of those they hired and added political supervision and reporting requirements. The Jacksonians, by comparison, had relied on party allegiance and the threat of being fired from a job to keep employees in line with the administration's directions. Since the government was now too large to be supervised personally by the president and cabinet members, the Progressives had another idea.

Woodrow Wilson, the only country's only president to have had a Ph.D., proposed, while he was an academic, that the government ensure the responsiveness of public administration to the political leadership by establishing an expectation that employees would practice "neutral competence."[13] Wilson proposed that it was possible to train public employees so that their responsibility was to carry out the policies of the president, whether or not they personally agreed with those goals. He expected that this training and the professionalism of employees, along with good management training and skills, would promote "hearty allegiance to the policy of the government."

Herbert Croly, another Progressive thinker also mentioned earlier, made a similar argument. Recognizing that presidents come and go, he warned that without an expert and experienced civil service government, it "would degenerate into a succession of meaningless and unprofitable experiments, which would not get enough continuity either to accomplish stable results or teach significant lessons."[14] The president would be responsible to the public, Croly argued, and "the role of public administration was to assist him in converting his program into well-framed and well-administered law."[15]

The idea that civil servants would be both competent and responsive to their political leadership based on training and professionalism may seem like a fanciful idea – more idealistic than practical. To the contrary, the creation of an institutional culture of responsiveness is basic to the management of corporations and is used every day by managers to ensure employees conform to the goals of a company.[16] Reliance on a corporate culture is particularly useful when it is not possible to give detailed instructions or monitor compliance with such instructions.[17] Government, like business, uses the norms that managers establish for appropriate and responsible behavior. The key expectation in government has been "neutral competence," and the government has successfully relied on this expectation since the Progressive Era.[18]

13.5 SHOOTING THE MESSENGER

Based on the historical record, there is more reason to trust the civil service to do the government's business than not. The post-WWII experience indicates the government has a remarkable success rate of getting the job done. Congress "called on the federal government to tackle a bold agenda worthy of the world's greatest democracy" when it passed a total of 500 major laws between 1944 and 1999.[19] According to a survey of 450 history and political science professors, "the federal government did more than aim high," it "often succeeded in changing the nation and the world."[20]

A sample of the historical achievements indicates the breadth and success that the government has had. The environment is cleaner and better protected, workplaces are safer, the social safety net is stronger, and there are fewer racial, sexual, and other forms of discrimination in education, housing, public accommodations, and workplaces. The government has reduced poverty, expanded health insurance, and expanded access to higher education and vocational training. More recently, it successfully backed the development of the vaccines to fight COVID in record time.

Elected leaders and appointed administrators had a hand in making this happen, but they did not have the expertise or experience to tackle the 500 laws that

Congress passed. Nor did they have the capacity to do the challenging legwork that made the successes happen. As one observer notes, "Heroes and villains get all the press coverage," but it is "the humble public servant, patiently toiling away at paperwork, tackling administrative duties, and ferociously juggling the minutiae most of us never see that keep our communities ... running smoothly."[21]

We also know, based on the record, that the civil service by and large has worked on achieving presidential policy preferences. A survey of over one hundred published empirical studies has "demonstrated that bureaucratic outputs of many agencies are responsive to the political principals that oversee their activities."[22] Marissa Golden, who studied the reaction of civil servants after President Reagan was elected, found that "[e]ven under the most extreme circumstances, with a president attempting to turn agency policy 180 degrees from its past, career civil servants were, for the most part, responsive."[23]

Not every civil servant is dedicated and effective, of course. Any government worker can tell stories of fellow workers who were not exemplars of dedicated, experienced, and expert civil servants. Yet, as the country's history reveals, the "flaws and faults" of the civil service are not only "far fewer on a proportional basis than originally thought," they are more than outweighed in frequency and importance by instances of dedicated service on behalf of the public service missions important to all Americans.[24]

The dedication and brilliance of the civil service is often a surprise to those appointed from the outside to positions in the government by the President. A Stanford University professor, who was the Ambassador to Russia, expressed his amazement that after joining the government he found out "how exceptionally talented, creative, dedicated, and patriotic most State Department officials are."[25] He admitted that he had "no chance of succeeding in my new job without these new colleagues" because "they were true experts in their fields."[26] After John McWilliams sold his hedge fund to an investment bank for $500 million, he accepted an invitation from the Secretary of Energy to take a high-level position in the Department. McWilliams was startled by the caliber of the civil servants he met. As he explained, "This idea that government is full of these bureaucrats who are overpaid and not doing anything – I'm sure in the bowels of some places you could find people like that. But the people I got to work with were so impressive."[27] Civil servants are, after all, professionals and proud of the work they do.

13.6 CONCLUSION

This historical record confirms the findings of a report from the National Academy of Public Administration that the civil service has "proved remarkably effective for a very long time, in virtually every sphere of American life: responding to economic crises like the Great Depression, fighting two world wars (and one cold one), and stimulating technological innovation."[28] The Academy and other distinguished leaders have been concerned over the last few decades, however, that this success may not continue. The complaint, in a nutshell, has been that the country has forgotten that a successful government is powered by a competent, neutral, experienced, and expert workforce.

Distinguished public administrators have warned of "work overload."[29] While the population of the United States is now more than double the size it was after World War II (334.5 million from 151.3 million), the relative size of the federal civilian workforce has not changed with it.[30] Meanwhile, the size of the federal budget – an indication of the government's responsibilities – has increased fivefold.[31] And, as noted, Congress has passed hundreds of laws that it expects the administrative agencies to implement, but Congress has at the same time cut the budgets of the very agencies expected to do the work.

Another blue-ribbon commission has explained how the retirement of experienced and expert government workers has reduced the capacity of the civil service to make government work. The federal government has five times more employees over 60 years of age than workers under the age of 30,[32] which means about one-third of the federal workforce was eligible to retire as of 2020.[33] As an example, one-third of the most experienced staff at the Social Security Administration were expected to retire by 2022.[34] At the same time, the National Academic report quoted earlier found that "the federal government's personnel service is broken,"[35] unable to hire expeditiously, pay reasonable compensation, promote deserving employees, and fire the few that do not do the work they are assigned. The National Commission on the Public Service adds that recruiting talented people to replace the retirees will be difficult since the "notion of public service, once a noble calling proudly pursued by the most talented Americans of every generation, draws an indifferent response from today's young people and repels many of the country's leading private citizens."[36]

The Trump administration accused the civil service of being a "deep state" out to subvert the country. The nation's history rebuts this accusation. It is the men and women of the civil service who make government work. They have not always done so, but the positive accomplishments are there for all to see. The government has stumbled at times, badly and disastrously so, but Trump was simply wrong. Fauci was not a disaster. His life and service, like many others who work for the government, are emblematic of JFK's words: they "served the United State government in that hour of the nation's needs."[37]

14

Joe Biden's America

Much to Restore, Much to Build

On January 20, 2021, Joe Biden was inaugurated as the 46th president of the United States. As he took office, COVID was ravaging the country, the country was in a deep virus-related recession, wealth inequality was at record levels, and climate change continued to warm the planet and pose an existential threat to all countries. After 36 years in the Senate and eight years as Vice President in the Obama White House, Biden understood the positive contribution that the government could make in addressing these problems, but he also appreciated that reaching agreement about the mix of government and markets is difficult.

Despite that challenge, Congress in Biden's first two years passed the largest economic recovery plan since Roosevelt's New Deal, made the largest investment in infrastructure since Eisenhower's interstate highway system, the most significant expansion of veterans benefits in more than 30 years, and passed the first ever legislation to address climate change. Congress also extended and improved the Affordable Care Act passed during the Obama administration.

Biden's first two years became a turning point. Since the 1980s, the turn toward markets as the better way to organize the country's social and economic affairs had allowed only episodic additions to government. Political polarization and the us versus them politics that gripped the country made it more difficult to focus on problems such as climate change, which have been building up since the 1980s. The country had reached a point where it was obvious that the mix of government and markets had tilted too much in the direction of markets. Biden galvanized the Democrats to unite around significant and bold responses and even obtained bipartisan support for three of the bills passed by Congress.

14.1 JOE BIDEN

Joe Biden was the only member of the Senate Budget Committee to vote against Ronald Reagan's 1981 effort to cut $884 million out of Amtrak's budget. Biden was a regular Amtrak rider; he commuted by train to Washington and back to Wilmington, Delaware almost every day. He did so to take care of Beau and Hunter, his two young sons. His wife, Neilia, and his daughter, Amy, had been killed in 1971 when a semi-trailer truck plowed into their car, and Beau and Hunter had been seriously injured.[1] Biden considered resigning his Senate seat because of the tragedy, but instead decided to commute. Throughout his long career in public service, Biden continued to ride the train home to Delaware nearly every evening, even after his sons had grown up. Including his years as Vice President, Biden made 8,200 round trips, earning Biden the nickname of "Amtrak Joe" in Washington.[2] He had planned to take the train to his inauguration as president, but the Secret Service decided it would not be safe considering the invasion of the Capitol that had occurred days before.[3]

After Biden took his last trip home on Amtrak as Vice President, it appeared his long career in public service was over. He had considered a presidential run in 2015, but then tragedy struck his family again. His son Beau died of cancer, and Biden indicated that he had lost his appetite for a presidential campaign. In 2017, however, he was watching TV coverage of the white supremacists who had marched through Charlottesville, Virginia, shouting racist and anti-semitic slogans. TV also reported that James Alex Farmer, Jr, a white supremacist who had driven his car into a crowd of anti-racist counter-protesters, had killed Heather Heyer, one of the protesters, and injured others. Biden reported that he was stunned when Donald Trump blamed the violence on "both sides" and referred to "very fine people on both sides." He began contacting politicians and others for advice whether he should run against Trump. When Biden announced his run for the presidency in 2019, he attacked "Trump's 'moral equivalence between those spreading hate and those with the courage to stand against it' and declared the election a 'battle for the soul of this nation.'"[4]

14.2 A CONSTANT STRUGGLE

Biden used the occasion of his inaugural address to try to return the country to a more civil and restrained conversation about what mix of government and markets best serves the country. He stressed "we have much to do in this winter of peril and possibility. Much to repair. Much to restore. Much to heal. Much to build. And much to gain."[5] He reminded his audience that it "requires more than words" to "restore the soul and secure the future of America. It requires that most elusive of things in a democracy: Unity." Biden was fully aware that the unity he sought is not easily achieved: "America has been a constant struggle between the American ideal that we are all created equal and the harsh, ugly reality that racism, nativism, fear, and demonization have long torn us apart. The battle is perennial. Victory is never assured." Biden's words echoed those of Andrew Shepard, the fictional president in the movie, *The American President*, "You gotta want [America] bad, 'cause it's gonna put up a fight."[6]

Biden called for Americans to abandon the us versus them polarization that had gripped many in the country. Biden, like John Dewey long ago, viewed democracy as how we decide to achieve historical and universal American values. Like Norman Rockwell's idealistic picture of the New England town meeting, Biden hoped

We can see each other not as adversaries but as neighbors. We can treat each other with dignity and respect. We can join forces, stop the shouting, and lower the temperature…. And together, we shall write an … American story of decency and dignity…. May this be the story that guides us. The story that inspires us. The story that tells ages yet to come that we answered the call of history.[7]

Acting on his words, "we can join forces," Biden put together the most diverse cabinet in United States history. Half of his cabinet were women, half self-identified as Black, Latino, Asian American, Native American, or multiracial,[8] and his LGBTQ appointments were also the most in history.[9] His entire administration reflects that same diversity.[10] As a matter of racial justice, Biden fulfilled a campaign promise when he nominated Ketanji Brown Jackson as the first black woman to sit on the United States Supreme Court.

Acting on his words, "Much to repair" and "Much to build," Biden proposed an ambitious program of government initiatives to meet the unaddressed problems that had arisen since 1980 including assistance for families, job creation, infrastructure investment, and education.[11] He, however, had to confront several difficult, even impossible, challenges that were blocking his agenda.

Domestically, he had the slimmest of Senate majorities, two renegade Senate Democrats, Joe Manchin and Krysten Sinema, who effectively exercised vetoes over his spending plans, and a recalcitrant Republican "party of no" that was committed to gridlock and defended the violent January 6 attack on the Capitol as "legitimate political discourse."[12] Internationally, he was called on to manage a global pandemic, increasing right-wing populism, and put together a coalition of western countries to aid Ukraine in repelling the Russian invasion that posed the biggest threat to Western Europe since the Second World War.[13] In short, Biden faced the worst domestic economy since the Great Depression, the worst global health crisis in over a century, the deepest political polarization since the Civil War, and a dramatic change in the international order.[14]

Biden nevertheless prevailed by focusing on obvious problems that could not be fixed by markets alone, by proposing solutions that had been used time and again by the government to address similar problems, and by emphasizing the link to American values. While he did not gain the "unity" that he sought, he overcame the opposition by rallying his party, compromising as necessary, and contrasting his efforts to promote fundamental American values that benefit all Americans with the efforts to divide Americans by his opponents.

14.3 KEYNES TO THE RESCUE (AGAIN)

The United States economy deflated in the Spring of 2019 as people stayed home and businesses stayed shut because of the coronavirus. The Gross National Product (GNP) fell 10 percent because of the shutdown.[15] The government's playbook for saving the country was a repeat of the New Deal Keynesian plan to engage in deficit spending and invest in renewing the economy. Congress passed stimulus investment packages in March, April, and June 2020 with strong bipartisan support. One of the laws – the $2.2 trillion CARES Act – was the largest relief package in American history.[16] Mitch McConnell, the then Senate majority leader, described the legislation as "a historical relief package" and "a wartime level of investment for our nation."[17]

When President Biden proposed additional stimulus legislation, he did not enjoy similar bipartisan support. Some congressional Republicans had engaged the White House about additional stimulus, but after those talks faltered, Congress passed the $1.9 trillion American Rescue Plan without any Republican votes.[18] Regarding Biden's rescue plan and other administration legislation, McConnell pledged that "[o]ne hundred percent of our focus is on stopping the new administration," which is the same thing he said when Obama was president.[19] That did not stop some Republicans, including McConnell, from bragging about the financial assistance going to the local communities that they represented.[20]

The government took additional actions to save the economy and protect people from the downturn that was occurring. The Federal Reserve Board engaged in financial actions to spur a recovery;[21] the Center for Disease Control and Prevention (CDC) declared a moratorium on evictions for failure to pay rent;[22] and the administration invested millions of dollars to fully vaccinate more than 185 million Americans, which saved approximately 1.1 million lives and more than 10.3 million hospitalizations as of November 2021.[23]

The Biden White House claimed credit for economic growth of 5.7 percent in 2021, the fastest rate in nearly 40 years, 6.5 million new jobs, the most our country has ever recorded in a single year, and a 3.8 percent unemployment rate although the stimulus legislation passed during the Trump presidency also contributed to this economic rebound. Together all the stimulus bills once again rescued the country from a deeper and most devastating recession or even depression.

14.4 HAMILTON'S AMERICAN PLAN (AGAIN)

In November 2021, the Senate passed a Hamiltonian-inspired $1 trillion bill to rebuild the nation's deteriorating roads and bridges, fund new climate resilience and broadband initiatives, and many other investments. All fifty democrats in the Senate voted for the bill as did ten Republicans, including Mitch McConnell despite his pledge not to give any victories to Biden.[24]

That the country needed to invest in deteriorating American roads, bridges, and other economic infrastructure had been under discussion in Washington for years. In June 2017, the Trump administration spent a week talking about its trillion-dollar plan to "help Americans suffering from crumbling infrastructure." Trump, however, did not follow up and eventually torpedoed efforts by a bipartisan group of Senators to reach agreement on an infrastructure bill. Afterward the term "infrastructure week" became "a catchall joke symbolizing any substantive — if pie-in-the-sky — policy objective destined to go nowhere."[25]

Despite the joke, the need was obvious. A bridge in Minneapolis over Interstate 35 collapsed in 2007, sending cars, trucks, and a school bus that were crossing the bridge careening into the river below. Thirteen people died and another 145 were injured, many of them seriously. Highway engineers had rated the bridge as "structurally deficient," which meant that it was old and needed repairs. More to the point, the bridge was characterized as "fracture critical," which signaled that the failure of just one vital component would cause the whole bridge to collapse. In 2016, the American Society of Engineers found that one out of ten bridges in the country likewise had structural defects.[26]

Economists estimated that poorly maintained roads, trains, and waterways cost billions of dollars in lost economic productivity and hampered the country's capacity to compete with other countries economically. In 2021, the American Society of Civil Engineers, for example, estimated that there was an infrastructure gap of $2.6 trillion that would cost the country $10 trillion in lost GNP if these needs were not met. According to some estimates, traffic congestion delays by itself cost the economy over $120 billion per year, and delays and avoided trips related to the deteriorated state of the nation's airports cost another $35 billion a year.[27]

There was additional legislation out of the Hamiltonian playbook. The 2022 Chips and Science Bill invested $280 billion to subsidize the domestic manufacture of computer chips and billions of dollars in science and technology research. Twenty-four House Republicans in the House voted for the bill, defying the Republican House leaders who demanded that they vote no, and seven Republicans in the Senate supported the legislation.[28] Like Clay's "American plan," the goal of the legislation was to make the country more self-reliant by manufacturing computer chips in this country and by investing in science and technology to make the country more competitive, especially regarding China, in world markets.

14.5 CLIMATE CHANGE

In July 2022, one of the authors was in London when Britain recorded its hottest-ever day with temperatures hitting a high of 104.5 degrees Fahrenheit. The impact was all the greater because few locations in Britain are air-conditioned since summer temperatures have historically been temperate. As the author and his wife stayed indoors for two days with the windows shut, attempting to stay hydrated and avoid heat stroke, the rest of Europe and much of the United States also experienced record-setting heat waves during this summer. Climate change hit home in ways that are impossible to ignore.

The Trump administration infamously withdrew the United States from the international climate change treaty, ramped up the production of oil and coal, stopped EPA from trying to regulate greenhouse gases, and, as noted, wiped out mentions of climate change on government websites. In addition to rejoining the Paris Agreement, the Biden administration reversed many of Trumps' anti-environment actions and put in place a climate task force across various departments to find ways to address climate change.[29] The administration, however, was limited in what it could accomplish under existing legislative authority.

Then Congress adopted the Inflation Reduction Act of 2022 that makes a \$500 billion investment to fight climate change.[30] Among the 725 pages of investments, there is a tax credit for Americans who purchase electric cars, subsidies to car manufacturers to speed up the production of climate friendly vehicles, grants, and loans to states to accelerate the transition to clean energy, more subsidies to speed up the discovery and manufacture of emission-reduction technologies, and financial assistance to help low-income Americans buy energy-efficient home appliances.

Every Republican in Congress voted against the legislation. The two Kentucky senators, Mitch McConnell and Rand Paul, voted against the bill as rescuers were searching for people killed by the climate change-related catastrophic floods that had inundated their states. Ted Cruz and John Cornyn, the two Texas Senators, opposed the legislation even though most of Texas was experiencing a climate change-related "extreme" or "exceptional" drought.[31]

The action was not only long overdue, but it also restored the credibility of the United States to lead the world to take stronger action against climate change. As an environmental advocate summed up, the legislation was the "biggest thing" that Congress has ever done to address climate change.[32] A prominent climate change scientist called it a "welcome shock," another said this "finally gets us over the 'spinning our wheels' stage," and another said the legislation was "completely historic."[33]

This was an Alexander Hamilton meets Ralph Nader moment. Hamilton urged the idea that the government could invest in the economy and produce additional opportunity and prosperity. The climate change investments should create more than 9 million clean energy and manufacturing jobs and enable the United States to compete more successfully in a \$23 trillion global clean energy market.[34] Nader and the other 1960s public interest advocates called on the government to regulate corporations that were polluting the air, selling dangerous products and drugs, and maintaining dangerous workplaces. By subsidizing individuals and companies to invest in clean energy technologies, such as electric cars, more energy-efficient housing, and carbon-trapping technologies, experts predict that the legislation will reduce greenhouse gases by 40 percent by 2030.[35]

14.6 HEALTH CARE

In late July 2017, the Republicans thought they had the votes in Congress to achieve a long-time campaign objective of repealing the Affordable Care Act (ACA) passed during the Obama administration. No Republican voted for the ACA, and the party immediately began campaigning to repeal the act, even though the legislation has made it possible for 16 million additional people to purchase health insurance who could not afford it previously.[36] As the vote to repeal the ACA was occurring, Senator John McCain walked onto the floor of the Senate one week after he had been diagnosed with terminal brain cancer. He then shocked both Democrats and Republicans by turning his thumb down and voting against the repeal. McCain joined Republicans Susan Collins of Maine and Lisa Murkowski of Alaska in foiling the Republicans attempt to repeal the ACA despite controlling both houses of Congress. Whether he intended it to be so or not, McCain's vote "was a measure of cold revenge against Mr. Trump, a man who on the campaign trail in 2015 had mocked Mr. McCain's ordeal as a prisoner of war in Vietnam."[37] Trump had made the ACA's repeal a major aim of his presidency. He failed. Obamacare is still the law even after dozens of Republican attempts to repeal it.

The next day, McCain released a statement saying the failed vote "presents the Senate with an opportunity to start fresh." He continued, "I encourage my colleagues on both sides of the aisle to trust each other, stop the political gamesmanship, and put the health care needs of the American people first. We can do this."[38]

McCain's hope came partly true. There was broad bipartisan support for the 2022 PACT Act that made it easier for more than 5 million veterans to obtain VA health care and other benefits for health problems related to their exposure to toxic substances while on duty.[39] The legislation passed 86 to 11 in the Senate and 256 to 174 in the House of Representatives. The bill's name honors Sergeant First Class Heath Robinson, a decorated combat medic who died from a rare form of lung cancer related to his service.

All Republicans, however, voted against legislation that made health insurance available to even more Americans. The 2021 American Rescue Plan, described earlier, increased health insurance subsidies to ensure that low-wealth Americans could continue to pay for their insurance despite the COVID-related recession. The Inflation Reduction Act of 2022 extended the increased funding for an additional three years to combat rising health care costs and keep the number of Americans without health insurance at record low numbers.[40]

The Inflation Reduction Act took three more steps to make healthcare more affordable. It capped the cost of prescription drugs paid by individuals enrolled in the Medicaid insurance plan, limited the cost of insulin, an expensive diabetes drug, to $35 a month for Medicare recipients, and authorized Medicare to negotiate how much pharmaceutical companies can charge Medicare recipients for the drugs that they purchase.[41] The last step will reduce the cost of drugs for people on Social Security because of the large number of pharmaceuticals for which the government pays. Although Congress limited the number of drugs that Medicare could negotiate the price, the Congressional Budget Office estimated that the program would save taxpayers $288 billion over 10 years.[42]

14.7 BUILDING THE MIDDLE CLASS

Biden took one more step to invest in the future of the country by expanding economic opportunity, but this effort was not successful. In July 2022, the Biden administration announced that the federal government would cancel billions of dollars that former college students owed the federal government for loans that they took out to pay for college,[43] but as Chapter 11 noted, the Supreme Court ruled the administration did not have the authority to take this step.[44] Although the plan ultimately failed, the Biden administration recognized that the country had stopped investing in education despite the economic and social advantages of doing so. Although stopped by the Supreme Court, the Biden administration continued its efforts to relieve student debt with the Student Debt Relief Plan issued by the Department of Education.[45]

University presidents are fond of repeating the observation of one of them: "At one time we were state supported. Then we were state assisted. Now we are state located."[46] Beginning in the 1980s, states began significantly cutting back on public support for the public colleges and universities in their states to the point now that most states supply only 10–15 percent or less of the cost of higher education.

During the nineteenth century, colleges did not charge tuition to students. The states supported higher education for the same two reasons the states had supported secondary education. By making colleges free, states continued the historical tradition that education would make good citizens as well as good workers. Of course, not everyone was eligible. Racial discrimination abounded, and women often had much less opportunity for higher education than men. But the ideal remained. There was also a recognition that the entire country benefitted from having a larger number of college graduates. And for this reason, "society was willing to pay for it—either by offering college education free of charge or by providing tuition scholarships to individual students."[47]

The defunding of public higher education reflected the emphasis on relying on private markets to organize the country's social and economic affairs. College became like other goods and services sold in markets. If you could not afford it, you would have to do without it. As public support dried up, schools raised tuition to offset the loss of public funding, which pushed higher education out of the financial reach of many students and their families. A Harvard University economist relates the change to her own family's experience:

> My older sisters went to the University of Massachusetts Boston in the mid-1970s, when tuition and fees for in-state residents were about $600 a year. To be clear, that $600 paid for an entire year of coursework, not just for a single class. In today's dollars (after accounting for inflation) that is equivalent to $3,605. Yet by 2022, in-state residents paid nearly $16,000 in tuition and fees to go to UMass Boston.[48]

Consumers, of course, do borrow money to make purchases they could not otherwise afford. Cars and homes are a good example. But it was not so easy to borrow money to go to college. Banks and other lending institutions were reluctant to lend money to young people who had no credit rating and no collateral to seize if the loan was not paid off. A bank can repossess a person's car or house if they cannot pay their loan payments, but there is no way to repossess a student's college education.

The federal government stepped in to address that problem by guaranteeing lenders would not lose their money if someone defaulted on their education loan. Since interest rates on loans are related to the lender's risk that the loan will not be paid back, the government guarantee also reduced the cost of borrowing for college or a trade school for those who could get educational loans. In 2010, the federal government took over the student loan program.[49] Since the government was non-profit, its educational loans were less expensive for borrowers than private lenders seeking to make a profit on the loans. Congress also authorized the Department of Education the authority to settle, compromise, or close claims,[50] which is the legal authority the administration tried to use to cancel the student debt.

Predictably, student debt cancellation was criticized as helping "deadbeats"[51] and as "unfair" to the people who had paid off their loans. These criticisms renewed the us versus them politics that Trump used to divide the country. All government policies have different impacts on different people. People without children are still expected to pay taxes and support public schools. When there is a disaster and the Federal Management Agency (FEMA) swoops in to aid people in distress, the rest of the country pays taxes to help their neighbors in harm's way.[52]

By defunding higher education, "[g]overnment policy did harm," an expert in education policy noted, "and it is government policy that should work to reverse it."[53] The loan forgiveness was a retroactive effort to restore some public support for higher education and to increase economic opportunity by doing so.

14.8 CONCLUSION

The successful legislative achievements by the Biden administration are one with history. His infrastructure investments reflect Hamilton's America. His job programs recall in part efforts made during the New Deal. And his dedication to social justice reflects the Great Society and dates to Abraham Lincoln. For some, the expanse of government is something to be criticized. For others, these efforts reflect a rebalancing of the relationship between government and markets, not a displacement of it.

Biden's successes are a repudiation of the country's us versus them politics. The economic recovery bills benefited the whole country. The extension of health care attempted to make the Affordable Care Act even more inclusive than it had been previously. The legislation reflected the judgment that change was necessary to realign the country with "universal" American values. About that, there can be disagreement, but the us versus them political talk side steps that debate to polarize the nation and prevent the type of improvements that Biden was able to make.

15

Conclusion

Going Forward

By 2014, it appeared America had taken a significant and notable turn away from the deregulatory agenda that began with Jimmy Carter, gained notoriety as the Reagan Revolution, and continued through Bill Clinton and both Bushes.[1] The American Recovery and Reinvestment Act (ARRA), signed into law by Barack Obama, and the Economic Stimulus Act, enacted in the Bush administration the year before, prevented the Great Recession of 2008 from turning into a global depression by injecting hundreds of billions of dollars into the economy. Other Obama additions to government included the redesign of student lending, the Dodd-Frank Wall Street reforms, joining the Paris Climate Accord, and most notably, the passage of the Affordable Care Act.

Then the 2016 election occurred. The Trump administration, dedicated as it was to "deconstructing the administrative state," was anti-government and anti-institution to its core. Even the FBI, CIA, Department of Justice, and our national security agencies were suspects of the "deep state." The administration, its supporters on Capitol Hill, and its "base" represented a growing nationalist populism that regarded the government and its supporters as their enemies. This us versus them politics hid how anti-governmental policies had contributed to the lack of economic opportunity for many in the country including Trump's supporters.

With Joe Biden's 2020 election, the country once again endorsed the government as a crucial partner with markets in building the country. His American Rescue Plan, Bipartisan Infrastructure Deal, and Inflation Reduction Act provided coronavirus relief, reduced energy costs, promoted clean energy and carbon reduction, lowered prescription drug prices, and funded an array of infrastructure improvements ranging from increasing access to high-speed Internet, providing safe drinking water, and repairing and rebuilding roads and bridges in dangerous need of attention. Biden also rejoined the Paris Accord after Trump's exit, which once again recognized climate change as an existential threat to the country and the world.

The politics that swirl around the mix of government and markets is a lot to take in and process. Understanding the government's role in achieving the nation's fundamental political values provides a roadmap for appreciating why time after time, the country has expanded its government sometimes in bunches and sometimes in smaller batches. The history of government and markets helps us understand who we are and why we are the way we are.[2]

15.1 HOW AMERICA LIVES UP TO ITS VALUES

History reveals the country has always relied on a mix of government and markets to expand liberty and pursue equality, fairness, and the common good. Those fundamental values, which date back to the Constitution and to the Declaration of Independence, have always defined the nation and bound us together, even as we have disagreed on how best to achieve them.

The perpetual issue for the country is what mix of government and markets best serves the country. But how do we know when the mix is a good one? Quite simply, and perhaps the most significant message of this history of government, is that a healthy mix of government and markets is one in which the values of liberty, equality, fairness, and the common good are recognized and honored.

The country has changed the mix of government when it has been out of sync with those values. Industrialization increased the country's overall wealth yet brought with it dangerous workplaces, products, slums, and poverty. The Reconstruction Amendments to the Constitution granted formal equality to the newly freed, but Jim Crow legalized racial segregation that needed to be dismantled. The Great Society recognized that deep and widespread poverty was a signal that the mix had failed, and the country had to correct unchecked markets.

Government has been necessary to realign the nation with its values because markets and government have different ends. Markets promote economic opportunity, generate wealth, and grow the economy. As celebrated by the myth of the self-reliant American, a market system can foster individual liberty and serve the public interest.

Government has a different function. It is charged with achieving our national values. As the Introduction pointed out, it is the central arena where Americans choose how to achieve the nation's collective values through representative democracy. At times, this requires relying on markets, as the myth prescribes, as public policy. Markets, however, have also limited and subverted the nation's values. When this happens, the role of the government is to remedy the situation. As in our other national myth, Americans gather and reason together how to "look out for the other fellow."

Americans can choose to substantially shrink government, as those most hostile to it prefer, but history establishes that the country cannot be true to its values when it does. Without government, there would be less liberty, equality, and fairness in the country. There would also be less economic opportunity, more discrimination, and more people made ill or killed by the products and services that they purchase or by the threats posed by the environment. And there would be a larger number of Americans without adequate food, shelter, and economic opportunity because of poverty not of their doing. The work remains ongoing, but it is obvious that without government, the country would be a different place and less true to its values.

15.2 WHY MARKETS FAIL

Markets fail to live up to the nation's value for three reasons seen throughout American history. Government is necessary to create, sustain, and expand markets. Without government, there would be no markets, let alone robust and successful markets. Government is also necessary to protect people from economic loss and physical injury. Without government regulation, sellers will pursue greater profits even if it harms consumers financially or physically. Finally, the government maintains a social safety net for people mired in poverty due to age, health, or market conditions not of their doing.

As Alexander Hamilton recognized, markets encourage entrepreneurship by rewarding people with greater wealth, but they do not generate all the economic activity from which the country can benefit. The problem, as related in Chapter 2, is that private individuals will not adequately fund investments that can boost the economy because there is no practical way to charge the millions of people who benefit from these types of investments. As a result, there would not even be a market system without the government establishing property and contract laws, a banking system, and management of the money supply. History also demonstrates that the government has expanded markets by investments in transportation, communication, research, and innovation that would not have otherwise occurred.

Government invests in people for the same reason. Because markets reward work and innovation, the assumption is that everyone can better themselves. Economic and social barriers, however, have always limited what people can do. By investing in westward expansion, the GI bill, and education loans, among other similar activities, the government attempted to create a "fair chance in the race of life," as Abraham Lincoln described these efforts. When the government invests in people, history demonstrates, it produces greater prosperity and national wealth.

Government regulation recognizes that, although markets support individual liberty, they also constrict liberty when working conditions are dangerous, products hurt consumers, powerful businesses illegally force out rivals thus reducing competition, or when there are racial and other forms of invidious discrimination. History is clear that business will pursue these activities, despite these and other undesirable impacts, when it is a way to make more money. When the government regulates, some Americans are told that they will have to change their behavior, but many more benefit from the protection that government provides.

Government lastly helps vulnerable Americans and Americans experiencing poverty. Markets have no way of giving people a leg-up who find themselves unable, through no fault of their own, to afford food, health care, housing, and the other necessities of life. The Affordable Care Act, Social Security, and programs to reduce poverty, among other similar activities, address that reality. When the government helps those in need, it enhances liberty and opportunity for millions of Americans.

15.3 BIG IS NOT BAD

As the government has undertaken the previous activities, it has become large and complex, which is a reason to object to the government according to its critics. The reason for the size and complexity of government, however, is straightforward. To protect the nation's fundamental values, the country has asked government to respond to new economic developments that are inconsistent with those values. As the economy has grown and changed, so has the government. Yet, the government is still engaged in the same three basic functions it has always been. Government, moreover, has achieved those goals, not by a heavy, authoritarian hand in opposition to markets but rather by respecting and acknowledging the significance of markets in serving the public interest.

Downsizing the government just to make it smaller will likely re-establish the problems that the government was set up to address. The limitations and problems that markets create by and large have not gone away. Banking deregulation in the Clinton administration, for example, was disastrous for the country. There are some exceptions, however. The deregulation that occurred in the Carter and Reagan administrations reflected changes in markets, which indicated that some forms of regulation were no longer necessary, but other forms of regulation were still needed. Changes in regulation need to be based on policy evidence rather than an ideological commitment to smaller government. Essentially, however, the judgment that both government and markets are necessary has stood the test of time.

15.4 UNSUNG AND UNSEEN HEROES

The book has highlighted the multiple ways that the government has built a country truer to its values. In telling this story, we have pointed to individuals who had an outsized influence on their times, but they are not the only ones. Many individuals –political leaders, citizen activists, and voters – have been instrumental in the country living up to its aspirations. Some are well known, many are not. The civil servants who have staffed the agencies are one such group of unsung heroes.

If America is a better place because of the government, and it is, credit must be given to the people who, like Dr. Fauci, made it happen behind the scenes. Yet, it has always been more common to bash bureaucrats than to treasure them. We reject the continual complaints that "the swamp," or "those bureaucrats," or "the bureaucracy" are to blame for the country's ills and challenges. Of course, not every public worker is dedicated and effective. Yet, experience teaches the men and women of the civil service have made it possible to align the country with its national values. These are the workers who carry out the policies passed by the Congresses that we elect.

15.5 THE MIX IS LESS PARTISAN THAN ONE MIGHT THINK

Naturally, politics enters the debate about whether the country is out of sync with its values. It could not be otherwise. Political leaders and voters will each assess that question differently. Still, mixing government and markets has been less partisan than one might think by viewing today's considerable levels of polarization. Political partisanship has not always gotten in the way of trying to balance the mix.

Thomas Jefferson and James Madison continued the "American system" of government action to build the economy started by Alexander Hamilton despite their strong reservations about "big government" because they recognized the merits of what was being done. Andrew Jackson kicked off a long period of laissez-fairism in the country, interrupted only by the Lincoln years, that lasted until the 1880s. Yet Jackson and his presidential successors continued investment in the economy, giving rise to the "hidden government" that spawned western expansion and more. The Industrial Revolution and the Great Depression led to increases in government during the Progressive Era and the New Deal, then President Eisenhower, a solid Republican, carried these policies forward and made new investments in space, science, and technology. Despite the pro-market rhetoric and policies associated with Reagan and adopted by Carter, Clinton, and Obama, there were new additions to government throughout those years in all those administrations.

Even in today's polarized political world, Biden's infrastructure legislation passed with bipartisan support. And, while red state Republicans are happy to tell their constituents about the benefits of the legislation even if they voted against it, they still criticize Biden for being an overspending Democrat. Such is political life.

15.6 CHANGE IS POSSIBLE

Liz Cheney's brave defense of democracy reminds us that while any one of us can disagree about how the mix favors government over markets or vice versa, we must realize the necessity of the debate. Yet, as we write, the us versus them politics has made that conversation more difficult and fraught. The politics that powered Donald Trump to the White House paints choices about government and markets as zero sum – if the other side wins, your side loses – instead of focusing on what mix best serves the country's values and the common good. The political violence visited on the country on January 6 is a far cry from a civil New England town meeting.

The country has previously overcome the efforts of those who take advantage of the political process to derail the ongoing debate about the mix or stubbornly refuse to act in the face of clear evidence that a change is required. The key to recovery is finding once again the democratic conversation envisioned by Dewey, pictured by Rockwell, and defended by Cheney.

The key to recovery is for enough Americans, not everyone, to focus on how we are to achieve the nation's values. When enough of us are focused on the pressing issues of our day – climate change, rebuilding the industrial heartland to create more economic opportunity, continuing to address racial and other forms of discrimination, and more – the country once again can make more progress in achieving a "more perfect union."[3]

15.7 GOING FORWARD

History establishes that the defenders of government have a good story to tell. But they must tell it. We hope that this book can be read as part of that story, as part of our civic education. The future of the country depends on appreciating what the government does and why it does it because the government remains essential to achieving our nation and its values. Attacks on government qua government are misplaced. Government criticism is a necessity in a democracy, but it is not an end in and of itself because it ignores the reality of the long-standing partnership between public and private, between government and markets.

History does not provide a crystal ball regarding what crises will next challenge us. Nor does it point to silver-bullet solutions to the multiple problems the nation will necessarily face. Armed with knowledge about the limitations of markets, however, readers can see why the government continues to be important to the life of the country. When we confront the pressing issues of our day – climate change, rebuilding the industrial heartland to create more economic opportunity, continuing to address racial and other forms of discrimination, and more – the country can once again look to the government to achieve a "more perfect union."[4]

In today's political climate, as many times in the past, the effort to better align the nation with its values will not be easy. But the country has succeeded in the past, and it can do so again. As the historian Jill Lepore has observed, "The nation, as ever, is the fight."[5]

Notes

1 INTRODUCTION

1 Kathleen Moore, Cuomo: Wear a Mask or Get a Ticket, The Post Star, September 30, 2020, available at https://poststar.com/news/local/cuomo-wear-a-mask-or-get-a-ticket/article_a9c0bd97-7f2a-59eb-ab51-14f97a9bbb32.html.

2 Chris Cillizza, How Kristi Noam Turned Her Sate's Failing Coronavirus Strategy into a National Platform, CNN, December 9, 2020, available at www.cnn.com/2020/12/09/politics/kristi-noem-south-dakota-2024/index.html.

3 Sarah Mervosh, Florida Withholds Money from School Districts over Mask Mandates, The New York Times, September 10, 2021, available at www.nytimes.com/2021/08/30/us/florida-schools-mask-mandates.html.

4 Andrew Jeong, Texas Gov, Greg Abbott Bans Coronavirus Vaccine Mandates, Including for Private Businesses, Washington Post, October 21, 2021, available at www.washingtonpost.com/nation/2021/10/12/greg-abbott-bans-vaccine-mandate/.

5 Cinema Blend, 7 Movies That Make Us Proud of Democracy, November 6, 2012, available at www.cinemablend.com/new/7-Movies-Make-Us-Proud-Democracy-33955.html.

6 James A. Morone, The Democratic Wish: Popular Participation and the Limits of American Government 5 (1998).

7 American Rhetoric: Movie Speech, Mr. Smith Goes to Washington (1939), available at www.americanrhetoric.com/MovieSpeeches/moviespeechmrsmithgoestowashingtonfilibuster2.html.

8 Patrick Perry, Norman Rockwell's Four Freedoms, Saturday Evening Post, January 1, 2009, available at www.saturdayeveningpost.com/2009/01/rockwells-four-freedoms/; Rockwell's Four Freedoms, Norman Rockwell Museum, available at https://rockwellfourfreedoms.org/about-the-exhibit/rockwells-four-freedoms/.

9 West Wing Transcripts, Hartsfield Landing, available at www.westwingtranscripts.com/wwscripts/3-14.php.

10 John Dewey, Creative Democracy, in The Later Works (Vol. 14) 226–28 (Jo Ann Boydston ed., 1988).

11 Richard Andrews, Cost-Benefit Analysis as Regulatory Reform, in Cost-Benefit Analysis and Environmental Regulation, Politics, Ethics, and Methods, 1–7, 110 (Davis Schwartzman, Richard A. Liroff & Kevin Croke eds., 1982).

12 Benedict Anderson, Imagined Communities: Reflections on the Origin and Spread of Nationalism (1983).

13 Interview of Tony Kushner, Sway, The New York Times, April 18, 2022, available at www.nytimes.com/2022/04/18/opinion/sway-kara-swisher-tony-kushner.html?showTranscript=1.

14 Samuel P. Huntington, American Politics: The Problem of Disharmony (1983).
15 National Public Radio, Ben Franklin's Famous "Liberty, Safety" Quote Lost Its Context in 21st Century, March 2, 2015, available at www.npr.org/2015/03/02/390245038/ben-franklins-famous-liberty-safety-quote-lost-its-context-in-21st-century.
16 *Compania General de Tabacos v. Collector*, 275 U.S. 87, 100 (1927) (Holmes, J. dissenting).
17 Richard Hofstadter, The American Political Tradition (1948); Louis Hartz, The Liberal Tradition in America (1955).
18 The Woke Burnout Is Real – and Politics Is Catching Up, September 7, 2024 (transcript), available at www.nytimes.com/2023/09/07/opinion/woke-culture-wars-schools.html.
19 Jill Lepore, This America: The Case for the Nation 137 (2019).

2 THE FOUNDERS' AMERICA

1   Ritchie Robertson, The Enlightenment: The Pursuit of Happiness (1680–1790) 12 (2021) (quoting The Wealth of Nations).
2   Lyrics Aaron Burr, Sir, https://genius.com/Lin-manuel-miranda-leslie-odom-jr-anthony-ramos-daveed-diggs-and-okieriete-onaodowan-aaron-burr-sir-lyrics.
3   Lawrence Friedman, History of American Law 77 (2d ed. 1985).
4   The Federalist Papers: No. 1, The Avalon Project, Yale Law School, https://avalon.law.yale.edu/18th_century/fed01.asp.
5   Kermit L. Hall, The Magic Mirror: Law in American History, chs. 2–3 (1989).
6   Thomas Greenleaf, Laws of the State of New-York, Comprising the Constitution, and the Acts of the Legislature, since the Revolution, from the First to the Fifteenth Session, Inclusive (1792).
7   Id.
8   Brian Balogh, A Government Out of Sights: The Mystery of National Authority in Nineteenth Century America 34 (2009).
9   Id.
10 Gary Gerstle, Liberty and Coercion: The Paradox of American Government 64 (2015).
11 William J. Novak, The People's Welfare: Law and Regulation in Nineteenth Century America (1996).
12 Id. at 1.
13 Danielle Allen, Our Declaration: A Reading of the Declaration of Independence in Defense of Equality (2014).
14 Pauline Maier, American Scripture: Making the Declaration of Independence 41–46 (1997).
15 John Locke, Two Treatises of Government (Peter Laslett ed., 1988) (1690).
16 David Prindle, The Paradox of Democratic Capitalism, Politics, and Economics in American Thought 19 (2006).
17 Maurizio Viroli, Republicanism 6 (1999).
18 Harvey C. Mansfield & Nathan Tarcov (eds. and trans.), Niccolo Machiavelli: Discourses on Livy (1998).
19 Bernard Bailyn, The Ideological Origins of the American Revolution (1967); J.G.A. Pocock, The Machiavelian Moment: Florentine Political Thought and the Atlantic Republican Tradition (1975); Gordon S. Wood, The Creation of the American Republic 1776–1787 (1998).
20 Barry Alan Shain, The Myth of American Individualism: The Protestant Origins of American Political Thought 33 (1994).

21 Joseph Fishkin & William E. Forbath, The Anti-Oligarchy Constitution: Reconstructing the Economic Foundations of American Democracy 42–45 (2022); Maier, supra note 14, at 134–36; Allen, supra note 13, at 163–66.

22 Cal Jillson, Pursuing the American Dream: Opportunity and Exclusion Over Four Centuries 59 (2004).

23 Chas. D. Turner, Magna Charta, 4 Tex. L. Rev. 46, 50 (1925).

24 Marci C. Hamilton, Direct Democracy, and the Protestant Ethic, 13 J. Contemp. Legal Issues 411, 415 (2004).

25 Transcript of the Articles of Confederation (1777), www.ourdocuments.gov/doc.php?flash=false&doc=3&page=transcript.

26 Ganesh Sitaraman, The Crisis of the Middle-Class Constitution 74–75 (2017); Claire Priest, Colonial Courts and Secured Credit: Early American Commercial Litigation and Shays' Rebellion, 108 Yale L. Rev. 2413, 2414 (1999).

27 Robert A. Freer, Shays' Rebellion and the Constitution: A Study in Causation, 42 The New England Quarterly 388, 396 (1969) (quoting Washington).

28 Id. at 422–25; Richard E. Levy, Federalism and Collective Action, 45 U. Kan. L. Rev. 1241, 1248 (1997).

29 Richard Hofstadter, The American Political Tradition and the Men Who Made It 9 (1948); see also Morton White, Philosophy, the Federalist, and the Constitution 162 (1987).

30 Federalist Paper No. 51.

31 Federalist Paper No. 10; Barry Alan Shain, The Myth of American Individualism: The Protestant Origins of American Political Thought 33 (1994).

32 Wood, supra note 19, at 505.

33 Calvin H. Johnson, Book Review, Madison's Denial: The Three Lives of James Madison: Genius, Partisan President, 34 Const. Comment 193, 196 (2019).

34 Hugo L. Black, The Bill of Rights, 35 N.Y.U. L. Rev. 865, 869 (1960).

35 Akhil Reed Amar, The Words that Made Us: America's Constitutional Conversation 1760–1840 312–22 (2021).

36 Kermit Roosevelt III, The Nation That Never Was, ch. 1 (2022).

37 Peter Nabokov, The Intent Was Genocide, The New York Review Books, July 2, 2020 (reviewing Jeffrey Ostler, Surviving Genocide: Native Nations and the United States from the American Revolution to Bleeding Kansas (2020)).

38 Isabel Wilkerson, Caste: The Origins of Our Discontents (2020); Thomas D. Morris, Southern Slavery and the Law 1619–1860 (1996).

39 Colman Andrews, These are the 56 People Who Signed the Declarations of Independence, USA Today: Money, July 3, 2019.

40 Tigerlilly Theo Hopson, The Ivy League's Ties to Slavery Raise Questions for Prospective Students, TeenVogue, April 30, 2021; Stephen Smith & Kate Ellis, Shackled Legacy: History Shows Slavery Helped Build Many U.S. Colleges and Universities, APM Reports, September 4, 2017; Anemona Hartocollis, Harvard Details Its Ties to Slavery and Its Plans for Redress, The New York Times, April 26, 2022.

41 Jill Lapore, These Truths: A History of the United States 99, 127 (2018).

42 Id. at 126.

43 Nikole Hannah-Jones, The Idea of America, The New York Times Magazine, August 14, 2019.

44 Sarah Ellison, How the 1619 Project Took Over 2020, Washington Post, October 13, 2020.

45 The President's Advisory 1776 Commission, The 1776 Report (January 2021); Matthew Nelsen, Serious Historians are Criticizing Trump's 1776 Report. It's How Most U.S.

History is Already Taught, Washington Post, January 28, 2021; Michael Crowley & Jennifer Schuessler, Trump's 1776 Commission Critiques Liberalism in Report Derided by Historians, The New York Times, January 18, 2021.

46 Woodrow Wilson, The Study of Administration. 2 Political Science Quarterly 197, 200 (1887).

47 Lapore, supra note 41, at xiv.

48 U.S. Const., Art. II. §2.

49 Elizabeth Fisher & Sidney A. Shapiro, Administrative Competence: Reimagining Administrative Law 119–20 (2020).

50 Leonard White, Public Administration Under the Federalists, 24 Boston U. L. Rev. 144, 180 (1944).

51 Federalist Papers No. 70 (1788), Bill of Rights Institute, https://billofrightsinstitute.org/primary-sources/federalist-no-70.

52 An Act Providing for the Payment of the Invalid Pensioners of the United States, ch. 24, 1 Stat. 95 (1789); see Johnathan Hall, The Gorsuch Test: Gundy v. United States, Limiting the Administrative State, and the Future of Nondelegation, 70 Duke L.J. 175, 180–82 (2020).

53 An Act for Regulating the Military Establishment of the United States, ch. 10, 1 Stat. 119, 121 (1790).

54 Id.

55 White, supra note 50, at 123–24.

56 Brian Cook, Bureaucracy and Self-Government: Reconsidering the Role of Public Administration in American Politics 121 (1996).

57 Fisher & Shapiro, supra note 49, at 121.

58 Paul C. Light, A Government Ill-Executed: The Decline of the Federal Service and How to Reverse It 10 (2008).

59 Id. at 221–22 (quoting Jefferson).

60 Michael W. McConnell, What Would Hamilton Do?, 35 Harv. J. L. & Pub. Pol'y. 259, 274 (2012).

61 Lyrics, Hamilton, The Room Where It Happens, https://genius.com/Leslie-odom-jr-lin-manuel-miranda-daveed-diggs-okieriete-onaodowan-and-original-broadway-cast-of-hamilton-the-room-where-it-happens-lyrics.

62 Brian Balough, A Government Out of Sight: The Mystery of National Authority in Nineteenth Century America 98–99 (2009).

63 David Jack Cowen, The Origins and Economic Impact of the First Bank of the United States 11 (2000).

64 Alexander Hamilton's Final Version of the Report on the Subject of Manufacture, December 5, 1791, Founders Documents, https://founders.archives.gov/documents/Hamilton/01-10-02-0001-0007.

65 Michael Lind, Land of Promise: An Economic History of the United States 106–109 (2012); Arthur M. Schlesinger, Jr., The Cycles of American History 219 (1999).

66 Schlesinger, supra note 65, at 221; Prindle, supra note 16, at 37.

67 John J. Janssen, Dualist Constitutional Theory and the Republican Revolution of 1800, 12 Const. Comment. 381, 395–96 (1995).

68 U.S. Const. Art. I, §8; U.S. Postal Service, The Constitution and the Post Office, Publication 100 – The United States Postal Service: An American History 1775–2006, available at https://about.usps.com/publications/pub100/pub100_005.htm.

69 Balough, supra note 62, at 226.

70 James Willard Hurst, Alexander Hamilton, Law Maker, 78 Colum. L. Rev. 483, 506 (1978).

71 Lyrics, Who Lives, Who Dies, Who Tells Your Story, https://genius.com/Original-broadway-cast-of-hamilton-who-lives-who-dies-who-tells-your-story-lyrics.

72 Id.

3 ABRAHAM LINCOLN'S AMERICA

1 NPR, Forget Lincoln Logs: A Tower of Books to Honor Abe, February 20, 2012, www.npr.org/2012/02/20/147062501/forget-lincoln-logs-a-tower-of-books-to-honor-abe.

2 Matt McCall, In Music, Abraham's Image Evolves for Each New Generation, Chicago Tribune, February 15, 2016, www.chicagotribune.com/news/breaking/ct-abraham-lincoln-music-thesis-award-met-20160214-story.html.

3 James Truslow Adams, The Epic of America 404 (1931).

4 Harold Holzer & Norton Garfinkle, A Just and Generous Nation: Abraham Lincoln and the Fight for American Opportunity 5 (2015).

5 Id. at 65 (quoting Emerson).

6 Message to Special Session of Congress, July 4, 1861, 4 Collected Works of Abraham Lincoln 438 (Roy P. Basler, ed. 1953).

7 History Channel, Battle of New Orleans, September 26, 2019, www.history.com/topics/war-of-1812/battle-of-new-orleans.

8 Genius, Battle of New Orleans, Lyrics, https://genius.com/Johnny-horton-the-battle-of-new-orleans-lyrics.

9 Colin Woodard, American Character: A History of the Epic Struggle between Individual Liberty and the Common Good 102 (2016); Daniel Feller, Andrew Jackson: American Franchise, UVA Miller Center, https://millercenter.org/president/jackson/the-american-franchise.

10 Feller, supra note 9, at 9.

11 Cal Jillson, Pursuing the American Dream: Opportunity and Exclusion over Four Centuries 104 (2004).

12 Jill Lepore, These Truths: A History of the United. States 220 (2018).

13 Sidney A. Shapiro & Joseph P. Tomain, Achieving Democracy: The Future of Progressive Regulation 22 (2014); Phil Davis, The Rise and Fall of Nicolas Biddle, Federal Reserve Board of Minneapolis, September 1, 2008, www.minneapolisfed.org/article/2008/the-rise-and-fall-of-nicholas-biddle.

14 Shapiro & Tomain, supra note 13, at 26.

15 Brian Balogh, A Government Out of Sight: The Mystery of National Authority in Nineteenth Century America (2009).

16 Id.

17 Erie Canal National Heritage Corridor, A National Treasure, https://eriecanalway.org/learn/history-culture.

18 David McCullough, The Pioneers: The Heroic Story of the Settlers Who Brought the American Ideal West ch. 1 (2019).

19 Id. at 154.

20 Id. at 178.

21 Id. at 13 (quoting Richard John, Spreading the News: The American Postal System from Franklin to Morse 4 (1995)).

22 Nancy Pope, The Story of the Pony Express, Smithsonian National Postal Museum, available at https://postalmuseum.si.edu/research/articles-from-enroute/the-story-of-the-pony-express.html.

23 Virginia Museum of Fine Arts, Native American Indian and the Western Expansion of the United States, www.vmfa.museum/learn-archive/microsites/george-catlin/native-american-indian-and-western-expansion-of-the-united-states/#:~:text=It%20is%20estimated%20that%20between,as%20the%20Trail%20of%20Tears.

24 Joseph Fishkin & William E. Forbath, The Anti-Oligarchy Constitution: Reconstructing the Economic Foundations of American Democracy 216–20 (2022).

25 Adolf A. Berle, Jr., & Gardiner C. Means, The Modern Corporation and Private Property 1 (1937).

26 Morton J. Horowitz, The Transformation of American Law 1780–1860 109–11 (1977).

27 Herbert Hovenkamp, The Classical Corporation in American Legal Thought, 76 Geo. L.J. 1593, 1651 (1988); Incorporating the Republic: The Corporation in Antebellum Political Culture, 102 Harv. L. Rev. 1883, 1884–87 (1989).

28 Thomas Piketty, Capital and Ideology (2020).

29 Katharina Pistor, The Code of Capital: How the Law Creates Wealth and Inequality (2019).

30 Elizabeth Fisher and Sidney A. Shapiro, Administrative Competence: Reimagining Administrative Law 130–132 (2020).

31 Patricia Wallace Ingraham, The Foundation of Merit: Public Service in American Democracy 20 (1995) (quoting Jackson).

32 Id.

33 Jerry L. Mashaw, Administration and "The Democracy": Administrative Law from Jackson to Lincoln, 1829–1861, 117 Yale L. J. 1568, 1615–16 (2008).

34 Sean M. Theriault, Party Polarization in Congress 80 (2008).

35 Ingraham, supra note 31, at 21.

36 Carl Russel Fish, The Civil Service and Patronage 158 (1905).

37 The National Bank Act, 18 Stat. 123 (1863).

38 Morrill Tariff Act, 12 State. 178 (1861).

39 Holzer & Garfinkle, supra note 4, at 78.

40 Homestead Act, 12 Stat. 392 (1862).

41 Lepore, supra note 12, at 333.

42 Caroline Fraser, Prairie Fires: The American Dreams of Laura Ingalls Wilder (2017).

43 Lepore, supra note 12, at 333.

44 Morrill Land Grant College Act, 12 Stat. 503 (1862).

45 Morrill Land Grant College Act, 26 Stat. 417 (1890).

46 North East Sustainable Agricultural Working Group, Map of Land Grant Universities, https://nesawg.org/resources/map-land-grant-universities; Colleges of Agriculture at the Land Grant Universities: A Profile, Chapter 2, History and Overview of the Land Grant College System, National Academies Press, www.nap.edu/read/4980/chapter/2.

47 Id. (quoting Lincoln).

48 Id. at 75.

49 Jillson, supra note 11, at 99.

50 Holzer & Garfinkle, supra note 4, at 2.

51 Message to Special Session of Congress, July 4, 1861, 4 Collected Works of Abraham Lincoln 438 (Roy P. Basler, ed. 1953).

52 Abraham Lincoln, Gettysburg Address, November 19, 1863, Transcript of Cornell University Copy, https://rmc.library.cornell.edu/gettysburg/good_cause/transcript.htm.

53 Lepore, supra note 12, at 275.

54 Id. at 277–78 (quoting Lincoln).

55 Holzer & Garfinkle, supra note 4, at 2.

56 Digital Public Library of America, A 1876 Speech Given by Frederick Douglass at the Unveiling of the Freedmen's Monument in Lincoln Park, Washington, DC, https://dp.la/primary-source-sets/frederick-douglass-and-abraham-lincoln/sources/104.

57 Gabor S. Borrit, Lincoln and the Economics of the American Dream 1 (1978).

58 Leonard P. Curry, Blueprint for Modern America: Nonmilitary Legislation of the First Civil War Congress (1968).

59 Shapiro & Tomain, supra note 13, at 24.

60 Jennifer Hochschild & Nathan Scovronick, The American Dream and the Public Schools 1 (2003).

61 Id. at 10.

62 Id. at 14; James Rapp, 1 Education Law Ch. 1 § 1.01[4][a]-[b] (2018).

63 Gerald Gulek, Education and Schooling in America 9 (2nd ed. 1988).

64 Rapp, supra note 62, at §1.01[4][d]; see also Gulek, supra note 63, at 12.

65 Claudia Goldin & Lawrence F. Katz, The Race between Education and Technology 135 (2008).

66 Kern Alexander & M. David Alexander, American Public School Law 22 (2nd ed. 1985).

67 Goldin & Katz, supra note 65, at 136.

68 Id. at 23.

69 Id. at 136.

70 Brian W. Dotts, The Democratic-Republican Societies: An Educational Dream Deferred, 88 Educational Horizons 179, 190 (2010).

71 Lawrence A. Baines, Does Horace Mann Still Matter? 84 Educational Horizons 269, 269 (2006).

72 Joseph Persky, American Political Economy and the Common School Movement: 1820–1850, 37 J. History of Econ. Thought 255 (2015) (quoting Mann's report).

73 Id. at 247, 256.

74 Golden & Katz, supra note 65, at 12.

75 Id.

76 Id.

77 Id. at 130.

78 Holzer & Garfinkle, supra note 4, at 256.

4 IDA TARBELL'S AMERICA

1 Michael Lind, Land of Promise: An Economic History of the United States ch. 1 (2012).

2 What Caused the American Industrial Revolution? Investopedia, June 5, 2020, www.investopedia.com/ask/answers/042015/what-caused-american-industrial-revolution.asp.

3 John Rees, Industrialization and Urbanization in the United States, 1880–1929, Oxford Research Encyclopedia, American History, July 7, 2016, https://doi.org/10.1093/acrefore/9780199329175.013.327.

4 David F. Prindle, Democratic Capitalism: Politics and Economics in American Thought 100 (2006).

5 Sean Wilentz, The Rise of American Democracy: Jefferson to Lincoln 723 (2005).

6 Id. at 179.

7 Jill Lapore, These Truths: A History of the United States 274–75 (2018); Tomas Nonnenmacher, History of the U.S. Telegraph Industry, Economic History Association, EH.Net, https://eh.net/encyclopedia/history-of-the-u-s-telegraph-industry/.

8 Robert J. Gordon, The Rise and Fall of American Growth: The U.S. Standard of Living Since the Civil War 178 (2016).

9   Lind, supra note 1, at 159.

10   Alan Greenspan & Adrian Woolridge, Capitalism in America: A History 56 (2018).

11   Id. at 180.

12   Id. at 164.

13   Claudia Goldin & Lawrence F. Katz, The Race between Education and Technology 197 (2008).

14   Isabel Wilkerson, The Warmth of Other Suns: The Epic Story of America's Great Migration (2010).

15   Harold Holtzer & Norton Garfinkle, A Just and Generous Nation: Abraham Lincoln and the Fight for American Opportunity 171 (2015).

16   Michael Elliot, The Day Before Yesterday, Reconsidering America's Past, Rediscovering the Present 39–40 (1996).

17   Prindle, supra note 4, at 100–101; Elliot, supra note 16, at 84.

18   Prindle, supra note 4, at 100.

19   Holtzer & Garfinkle, supra note 15, at 174.

20   U.S. Department of Labor, OSHA, The Triangle Shirtwaist Fire, www.osha.gov/aboutosha/40-years/trianglefactoryfireaccount.

21   U.S Department of Labor, Bureau of Labor Statistics, History of Child Labor in the United States: Part 1 – Little Children Working (January 2017), www.bls.gov/opub/mlr/2017/article/history-of-child-labor-in-the-united-states-part-1.htm.

22   Eastern Illinois University, Childhood Lost: Child Labor during the Industrial Revolution, www.eiu.edu/eiutps/childhood.php.

23   Smithsonian, National Museum of American History, Balm of America: Patent Medicine Collection, https://americanhistory.si.edu/collections/object-groups/balm-of-america-patent-medicine-collection/history.

24   Hagley Museum, History of Patent Medicine, www.hagley.org/research/digital-exhibits/history-patent-medicine.

25   Irving Fang, A History of Mass Communication: Six Information Revolutions 56 (1997).

26   Id.

27   Ganesh Sitaraman, The Crisis of the Middle-Class Constitution: Why Economic Inequality Threatens Our Republic 143 (2017).

28   Id.

29   Booms and Busts, An Encyclopedia of Economic History from Tulip Mania of the 1630s to the Global Financial Crisis of the Twenty-First Century (James Climent ed. 2015) (3 vols.)

30   Kevin P. Phillips, Wealth and Democracy: A Political History of the American Rich 307 (2003).

31   Id. at 43, 49.

32   Harold U. Faulkner, Politics, Reform and Expansion (1890–1900) 91 (1959).

33   Dave Itzkoff, "The Gilded Age" Finally Arrives on HBO, The New York Times, January 20, 2022, www.nytimes.com/2022/01/20/arts/television/gilded-age-julian-fellowes.html.

34   Jacob Viner, Adam Smith and Laissez-faire, 35 J. Pol. Econ. 198, 199–200 (1927).

35   Prindle, supra note 4 at 105, quoting Arthur Latham Perry, Elements of Political Economy 129, 134–135 (1873).

36   Id. at 109–110.

37   Id. at 110.

38   Holtzer & Garfinkle, supra note 15, at 177.

39   Id.

40   Id. at 53; Library of Congress, Railroad Maps 1828–1900, Land Grants, www.loc.gov/collections/railroad-maps-1828-to-1900/articles-and-essays/history-of-railroads-and-maps/land-grants/.

41 Lapore, supra note 7, at 333; Jürgen Osterhammel, The Transformation of the World: A Global History of the Nineteenth Century 331–45(2014).

42 Arthur M. Schlesinger, Jr., The Cycles of History 234 (1986).

43 Lawrence Friedman, History of American Law 177 (2005).

44 *Munn* v. *Illinois*, 94 U.S. 113 (1877).

45 Robert Rabin, Federal Regulation in Historical Perspective, 38 Stan. L. Rev. 1189, 1199 (1986).

46 Id. at 1203.

47 *Wabash, St. Louis & Pacific Railroad* v. *Illinois*, 118 U.S. 557 (1886).

48 Interstate Commerce Act, Pub. L. 49–41 (1887).

49 Kermit Hall, The Magic Mirror: Law in American History 205 (1989).

50 Hepburn Act, Pub. L. 59–337 (1906).

51 Id. at 205–06.

52 Doris Kerns Goodwin, The Bully Pulpit: Theodore Roosevelt, William Howard Taft, and the Golden Age of Journalism (2013).

53 Gilbert King, The Woman Who Took On the Tycoon, Smithsonian Magazine, July 5, 2012, www.smithsonianmag.com/history/the-woman-who-took-on-the-tycoon-651396/.

54 Goodwin, supra note 52, at 171.

55 Id.

56 Id.

57 Rabin, supra note 45, at 1226.

58 Obituary, Not Forgotten: Upton Sinclair, Whose Muckraking Changed the Meat Industry, The New York Times, June 30, 2016.

59 Theodore Roosevelt Center, Dickinson University, Muckraker, www.theodoreroosevelt center.org/Learn-About-TR/TR-Encyclopedia/Culture%20and%20Society/Muckraker.

60 Muckraker, Theodore Roosevelt Center, www.theodorerooseveltcenter.org/Learn-About-TR/TR-Encyclopedia/Culture%20and%20Society/Muckraker (last visited March 5, 2021).

61 Herbert Croly, The Promise of American Life (2014 ed.) (1909).

62 Id. at 131.

63 Id. at 143.

64 Id. at 152.

65 Melvin I. Urofsky, Louis D. Brandeis: A Life 300 (2009).

66 Louis D. Brandeis, Other People's Money and How Bankers Use It (1914).

67 Id. at 319.

68 Id. at 319.

69 Urofsky, supra note 65, at 326.

70 Sherman Act, 26 Stat. 209 (1890).

71 Federal Food and Drug Act, 59–384 (1906).

72 Federal Meat Inspection Act, 59–242 (1906).

73 Federal Trade Commission Act, 38 Stat. 717 (1917).

74 Sidney A. Shapiro & Joseph P. Tomain, Achieving Democracy: The Future of Progressive Regulation 26 (2014).

75 Cal Jillson, Pursuing the American Dream: Opportunity and Exclusion Over Four Centuries 167 (2004) (quoting Teddy Roosevelt).

76 Tim Wu, The Curse of Bigness, Antitrust in the New Gilded Age 49 (2018).

77 Id. at 171 (quoting Woodrow Wilson).

78 *Northern Securities Co.* v. *United States*, 193 U.S. 197 (1904).

79 Goodwin, supra note 52, at 343.

80 Id. at 441–42.

81 *Standard Oil Co of New Jersey* v. *United States*, 221 U. S. 1 (1911).
82 Danial Yergin, The Prize: The Epic Quest for Oil, Money and Power (1991).
83 Prindle, supra note 4, at 75 quoting Smith.
84 Woodrow Wilson, The Study of Administration, 2 Pol. Sci. Q. 197, 209–210 (1887).
85 Id. at 210, 212.
86 David Rosenbloom, The Politics and Administration Dichotomy in U.S. Historical Context, 68 Pub. Admin. Rev. 57, 57–60 (2008).
87 Elizabeth Fisher & Sidney A. Shapiro, Administrative Competence: Reimagining Administrative Law 136 (2020).
88 Mike Maciag, Federal Employment State by State, Governing: The Future of States and Localities, April 20, 2017, www.governing.com/gov-data/federal-employees-workforce-numbers-by-state.html; Jessie Bur, Is Anyone Actually Tracking Political Appointee Data, Federal Times, March 18, 2019, www.federaltimes.com/management/2019/03/18/is-anyone-actually-tracking-political-appointee-data/.
89 Anne Joseph O'Connell, Vacant Offices: Delays in Staffing Top Agency Positions, 82 S. Cal. L. Rev. 913, 926 (2009).
90 B. Guy Peters, Institutional Theory in Political Science: The New Institutionalism 30 (3d ed. 2012); James March & Johan P. Olsen, Rediscovering Institutions 23–24 (1989); Sidney A. Shapiro, Why Administrative Law Misunderstands How Government Works: The Missing Institutional Analysis, 53 Washburn L. J. 1, 5–8 (2013).
91 Sidney A. Shapiro & Ronald F. Wright, The Future of the Administrative Presidency: Turning Administrative Law Inside-Out, 65 U. Miami L. Rev. 577, 586–589 (2011).
92 Hebert Kaufman, The Forest Ranger: A Study in Administrative Behavior (1960).

5 FRANKLIN DELANO ROOSEVELT'S AMERICA

1 Eric Rauchway, The Great Depression and the New Deal: A Very Short Introduction 28 (2008).
2 Library of Congress, President Franklin Delano Roosevelt and the New Deal (quoting Roosevelt); www.loc.gov/classroom-materials/united-states-history-primary-source-timeline/great-depression-and-world-war-ii-1929-1945/franklin-delano-roosevelt-and-the-new-deal/.
3 Rauchway, supra note 1, at 137–42.
4 H.W. Brands, Traitor to His Class: The Privileged Life and Radical Presidency of Franklin Delano Roosevelt (2009).
5 Peter Arno Cartoon, of Congress, Prints and Photographs On Line, www.loc.gov/pictures/item/2004679096/.
6 Patrick J. Maney, The Roosevelt Presence: The Life and Legacy of FDR xii (1992).
7 Photography and the Great Depression, Margaret Bourke White, https://lis471.wordpress.com/margaret-bourke-white/.
8 James Agee & Walker Evan, Let Us Now Praise Famous Men (1988) (1939).
9 Rauchway, supra note 1 at 40; David F. Prindle, The Paradox of American Capitalism: Politics and Economics in American Thought 75 (2006).
10 VCU Libraries, Social Welfare History Project, Brother Can You Spare a Dime – 1932, https://socialwelfare.library.vcu.edu/eras/great-depression/brother-can-you-spare-a-dime-1932/.
11 Kennedy Center, Brother Can You Spare a Dime?: The Story behind the Song, www.kennedy-center.org/education/resources-for-educators/classroom-resources/media-and-interactives/media/music/story-behind-the-song/the-story-behind-the-song/brother-can-you-spare-a-dime/.

12 Id.
13 The American Presidency Project, Franklin D. Roosevelt Address at Oglethorpe University in Atlanta, Georgia, May 22, 1932, www.presidency.ucsb.edu/documents/ address-oglethorpe-university-atlanta-georgia.
14 Elliot A. Rosen, Roosevelt and the Brains Trust: An Historiographical Overview 87 Pol. Sci. Q. 531 (1972).
15 Fernando J. Cardim de Carvalho, Economic Planning Under Capitalism: The New Deal and Postwar France Experiments, Working Paper, Levy Institute, Bard College, February, 2019, at 2, www.levyinstitute.org/pubs/wp_923.pdf.
16 Tate Museum of Art, Lifestyle and Legacy of the Bloomsbury Group, www.tate.org.uk/ art/art-terms/b/bloomsbury/lifestyle-lives-and-legacy-bloomsbury-group; Anna Louie Sussman, Keynes's Art Collection Shows Why Art Investing Is Like the Lottery, April 5, 2017, www.artsy.net/article/artsy-editorial-keyness-art-collection-art-investing-lottery.
17 Alan Brinkley, The End of Reform: New Deal Liberalism in Recession and War (1995).
18 Homeowners Loan Act of 1933, Pub. L. 33, 73rd Congress (1933).
19 National Housing Act, Pub. L. 479(1934).
20 Farm Credit Act of 1933, Pub. L. 75(1933).
21 Emergency Relief Appropriation Act of 1935 (creating the Works Progress Administration); Emergency Conservation Work (ECW) Act of 1933 (creating the Civil Conservation Corps).
22 Robert Stammers, The History of the FDIC, Federal Deposit Insurance Corporation, August 31, 2021, www.investopedia.com/articles/economics/09/fdic-history.as.
23 Emergency Banking Act, Pub. L. 73–1 (1933).
24 William L. Silber, Why Did FDR's Bank Holiday Succeed? 15 Eco. Pol. Rev. 19 (2009); Stephen Greene, Federal Reserve History, Emergency Banking Act of 1933, March 9, 1933, www.federalreservehistory.org/essays/emergency_banking_act_of_1933.
25 Sarah Pruitt, How FDR's Fireside Chats' Helped Calm a Nation in Crisis, The History Channel, April 7, 2020, www.history.com/news/fdr-fireside-chats-great-depression-world-war-ii; "The Fireside Chats" – President Franklin D. Roosevelt (1933–1944), www.loc.gov/ static/programs/national-recording-preservation-board/documents/FiresideChats.pdf.
26 Banking Act of 1935, Pub. L. 74–305 (1935).
27 Federal Reserve Bank, Overview: The History of the Federal Reserve 1913 to Today, www .federalreservehistory.org/essays/federal-reserve-history.
28 First Inaugural Address of Franklin D. Roosevelt, March 4, 1933, https://avalon.law.yale .edu/20th_century/froos1.asp.
29 Celina Resendez, Frank Capra's Cinematic Therapy, October 4, 2016, SMU Research Scholars, https://stmuscholars.org/frank-capras-cinematic-therapy/.
30 Id.
31 Franklin D. Roosevelt Presidential Library and Museum, First Inaugural Address, www .fdrlibrary.org/documents/356632/390886/First+Inagural+Address+Curriculum+Hub+ Documents.pdf/55c42890-6b80-4d34-b68a-b4a30f2797d5.
32 Jean Edward Smith, FDR 343 (2008).
33 Jill Lepore, These Truths: A History of the United States 437 (2018).
34 Smith, supra note 32, at 345.
35 Id. at 345–46.
36 National Archives, Archives Library Information Center (ALIC), New Deal Arts available at www.archives.gov/research/alic/reference/new-deal-arts.html.
37 Smith, supra note 32, at 321.
38 Civilian Conservation Corps, October 17, 2010, www.history.com/topics/great-depression/ civilian-conservation-corps.

39 de Carvalho, supra note 15, at 2.
40 Lepore, supra note 33, at 437.
41 Agricultural Adjustment Act, Pub. L. 73–10 (1933).
42 Kenneth Finegold, From Agrarianism to Adjustment: The Political Origins of New Deal Agricultural Policy, 11 Pol. & Soc. 1, 1, 5 (1982).
43 Id. at 6.
44 James T. Young, The Origins of New Deal Agricultural Policy: Interest Groups' Role in Policy Formation, 21 Pol. Studies J. 190, 197 (1993).
45 United States v. Butler, 297 U.S. 1 (1936).
46 Agricultural Adjustment Act, Pub. L. 75–430 (1938).
47 National Industrial Recovery Act, Pub. L. 73–67 (1933).
48 Mark Chicu, Chris Vickers & Nicolas L. Ziebarth, Cementing the Case for Collusion Under the National Recovery Administration, 50 Explorations in Eco. Hist. 487, 487 (2013).
49 Smith, supra note 32, at 343.
50 Anthony J. Badger, The New Deal: The Depression Years, 1933–1940, at 73 (2002) (check this).
51 A.L.A. Schechter Poultry Corp. v. U.S., 295 U.S. 495 (1935); Panama Refining Co. v. Ryan, 293 U.S. 388 (1935).
52 Robert L. Rabin, Federal Regulation in Historical Perspective 38 Stan. L. Rev. 1189, 1252–53 (1986).
53 Securities Act of 1933, 48 Stat. 74 (1933).
54 Securities Exchange Act of 1934, 48 Stat. 881 (1934).
55 Public Utilities Holding Company Act, Publ. L. 74–687 (1935).
56 Banking Act of 1933 (Glass-Stegall), Pub. L. 73–66 (1933).
57 National Labor Relations Act, Pub. L. 74–198 (1935).
58 Ahmed A. White, Industrial Terrorism and the Unmaking of the New Deal Labor Law, 11 Nevada L. Rev. 561, 561 (2011).
59 Federal Water Power Act, 41. Stat. 1063.
60 Public Utility Act, 74–333 (1935).
61 Natural Gas Act, Pub. L. 75–688 (1938).
62 The Communications Act of 1934, Pub. L. 73–416 (1934).
63 Air Mail Act, Pub. L. 68–359 (1925).
64 Richard Green, Daring Deliveries: The U.S. Post Office and the Birth of Commercial Aviation, National Archives, September 30, 2014, https://unwritten-record.blogs.archives .gov/2014/09/30/daring-deliveries-the-u-s-post-office-and-the-birth-of-commercial-aviation/; Airmail: A Brief History, About the Post Office Service, https://about.usps.com/ who/profile/history/pdf/airmail.pdf.
65 How Air Travel Has Changed in Every Decade from the 1920s Until Today, Love Exploring, www.loveexploring.com/gallerylist/86315/how-air-travel-has-changed-in-every-decade-from-the-1920s-to-today.
66 Civil Aeronautics Act, 52 Stat. 973 (1938).
67 Federal Aviation Administration, A Brief History of the FAA, www.faa.gov/about/history/ brief_history.
68 Daniel T. Rodgers, The American Welfare System in Transition, in Futures for the Welfare State 298 (Norman Furniss ed., 1986).
69 Social Security Act, Pub. L. 74–271 (1935).
70 Arthur L. Berney, Joseph Goldberg, John A. Dooley, III, and David W. Carroll, Legal Problems of the Poor 591 (1975).

71 Bryan W. Miller & John McCarthy, Last Persson to Receive Pension from Civil Was, $73.13 Monthly, Dies at Age 90, USA Today (June 16, 2020); Peter David Blanck, Before Disability Civil Rights, 52 Ala. L. Rev. 1 (2000).

72 Aid to Families With Dependent Children Act, 42 U.S.C. §§ 1101-09.

73 Rauchway, supra note 1, at 121.

74 Michael Kazin, What It Took to Win: A History of the Democratic Party ch.6 (2022); Gary Gerstle, The Rise and Fall of the Neoliberal Order: America and the World in the Free Market Era 48–49 (2022).

75 Jill Watts, The Black Cabinet: The Untold Story of African Americans and Politics During the Age of Roosevelt (2020).

76 Adolph Reed, Jr., Race and the New Deal Coalition, The Nation (March 20, 2008).

77 Franklin Roosevelt's Annual Address to Congress – The "Four Freedoms," January 6, 1944, http://docs.fdrlibrary.marist.edu/od4freed.html.

78 Id.

79 Franklin D. Roosevelt, State of the Union Message to Congress January 11, 1944, www .fdrlibrary.marist.edu/archives/pdfs/state_union.pdf.

6 DWIGHT EISENHOWER'S AMERICA

1 Marcus Lu, Is the American Dream Over? Here's What the Data Says, World Economic Forum (September 2, 2020); Center for Budget and Policy Priorities, A Guide to Statistics on Historical Trends in Income Inequality (January 13, 2020); Claudia Golden & Robert A. Margo, The Great Compression: The Wage Structure in the United States at Mid-Century (1991).

2 Richard Rhodes, The Making of the Atomic Bomb (1987).

3 Atomic Energy Act of 1946, Pub. L. 79–585.

4 Stephen E. Ambrose, Eisenhower: Soldier and President 342 (1990).

5 Atomic Energy Act of 1954, Pub. L. 83–703.

6 Joseph P. Tomain, Nuclear Power Transformation 8 (1987) (quoting the report).

7 Id. at 9 (quoting Weaver).

8 Price-Anderson Act, Pub. L. 85–256.

9 National Aeronautics and Space Act of 1958, Pub. L. 85–568.

10 Mariana Mazzucato, Mission Economy: A Moonshot Guide to Changing Capitalism ch. 4 (2021).

11 Id.

12 Mariana Mazzucato, The Entrepreneurial State: Debunking Public vs. Private Sector Myths (2013).

13 Servicemen's Readjustment Act of 1944, Pub. L. 113–11.

14 David Stebenne, Promised Land: How the Rise of the Middle Class Transformed America, (1929–1968) 101 (2020).

15 Steven A. Ramirez, The Law & Macroeconomics of the New Deal at 70, 62 Md. L. Rev. 515, 557 (2003).

16 Michael Bennet, When Dreams Came True: The G.I. Bill and the Making of Modern America 8 (1996).

17 Id. at 33 (quoting Schlesinger).

18 Id. at 30.

19 The Postwar Housing Boom Wasn't All Sunshine and Roses, Daily Beast, September 25, 2018, www.thedailybeast.com/the-postwar-housing-boom-wasnt-all-sunshine-and-roses;

Barbara Kelly, The Suburban Revolution, The New York Times, February 1, 1987, www.nytimes.com/1987/02/01/nyregion/the-suburban-revolution.html.

20 Melissa Murray, When War Is Work: The G.I. Bill, Citizenship, and the Civic Generation, 96 Cal. L. Rev. 967, 974 (2008).

21 Id. at 21.

22 Id.

23 Id. at 23.

24 Susan Metler, Soldiers to Citizens: The GI Bill and the Making of the Greatest Generation (2005).

25 Gunnar Myrdal, An American Dilemma: The Negro Problem and Modern Democracy (1944).

26 Richard Rothstein, The Color of Law: A Forgotten History of How Government Segregated America (2017).

27 Noah Sheidlower, The Controversial History of Levittown, America's First Suburb, Untapped New York (July 31, 2020).

28 David Wilma, Seattle Civic Unity Committee Denounces Restrictive Covenants That Discriminate against African Americans, Jews, and Asians in February 1948, www.historylink.org/File/3153.

29 Daily Beast, The Postwar Housing Boom Wasn't All Sunshine and Roses, September 12, 2018, www.thedailybeast.com/the-postwar-housing-boom-wasnt-all-sunshine-and-roses/

30 Robert A. Dentler, Barriers to Northern School Desegregation, 95 Daedalus 45 (Winter 1966).

31 Michael O'Donnell, Commander v. Chief: The Lessons of Eisenhower's Civil Rights Struggle with his Chief Justice Earl Warren, The Atlantic (April 2018).

32 Pedro da Costa, Housing Discrimination Underpins the Staggering Wealth Gap Between Blacks and Whites, Economic Policy Institute, April 8, 2019, www.epi.org/blog/housing-discrimination-underpins-the-staggering-wealth-gap-between-Blacks-and-whites/.

33 National Association of Realtors, Racial Disparities in Homeownership Rates, March 3, 2022, www.nar.realtor/blogs/economists-outlook/racial-disparities-in-homeownership-rates.

34 This disparity in funding has been upheld by the United States Supreme Court in *San Antonio School District* v. *Rodriguez*, 411 U.S. 1 (1973). The Court has also rejected busing across school district to achieve balance in *Milliken* v. *Bradley*, 418 U.S. 717 (1974).

35 Federal-Aid Highway Act of 1956, Pub. L. No. 84-627.

36 Deborah N. Archer, "White Men's Roads Through Black Men's Homes": Advancing Racial Equity through Highway Reconstruction, 73 Vand. L. Rev. 1259, 1264–65 (2020).

37 Id. at 1265 (quoting Sam Ross-Brown, Transportation Secretary Foxx Moves to Heal Scars of Urban Renewal, Am Prospect (Sept. 30, 2016)).

38 Robert Caro, The Power Broker: Robert Moses and the Fall of New York (1974); Jane Jacobs, The Death and Life of Great American Cities (1961).

39 Ambrose, supra note 4, at 541 (quoting Ewald).

40 University of Virginia, Miller Center, McCarthyism and the Red Scare, https://millercenter.org/the-presidency/educational-resources/age-of-eisenhower/mcarthyism-red-scare.

41 *Brown v. Board of Education*, 347 U.S. 483 (1954).

42 Rosie the Riveter, History, www.history.com/topics/world-war-ii/rosie-the-riveter.

43 John Kenneth Galbraith, The Affluent Society 187–88 (1998 ed.).

44 Todd Gitlin, The Sixties: Years of Hope, Days of Rage chs. 4–6 (1993 ed.).

45 The Sixties Project, Port Huron Statement, www2.iath.virginia.edu/sixties/HTML_docs/Resources/Primary/Manifestos/SDS_Port_Huron.html.

46 Id.
47 F. A. Hayek, The Road to Serfdom (1944).
48 Milton Friedman, Free to Choose (1980); Milton Friedman, Capitalism and Freedom (1962).
49 Ronald Coase, The Nature of the Firm, 4 Economica 386 (1937).
50 Ronald Coase, The Problem of Social Cost, 3 J. Law & Econ. 1 (1960).
51 Thomas Piketty, Capital and Ideology (2019); Heather Boushey, Unbound: How Inequality Constricts Our Economy and What We Can Do about It (2019); Katharina Pistor, The Code of Capital: How the Law Creates Wealth and Inequality (2019); Thomas Piketty, Capital (2013).
52 Thomas Philippon, The Great Reversal: How America Gave Up on Free Markets (2019)
53 George Packer, Celebrating Inequity, The New York Times, May 19, 2013, www.nytimes .com/2013/05/20/opinion/inequality-and-the-modern-culture-of-celebrity.html.
54 Id.
55 Ambrose, supra note 4, at 536–37.

7 RACHEL CARSON'S AMERICA

1 Rachael Carson, Silent Spring (1962).
2 NRDC, The Story of Silent Spring, www.nrdc.org/stories/story-silent-spring.
3 Zygmunt J.B. Plater, From the Beginning, A Fundamental Shift of Paradigms: A Theory and Short History of Environmental Law, 27 Loy. L.A. L. Rev. 981, 982 (1994).
4 Thorstein Veblen, The Theory of the Leisure Class (2016) (1899).
5 Sarah Paolantonio, Bob Dylan's "The Times They Are A-Changin" Turns 55: Anniversary Retrospective, January 9, 2019, Albumism, https://albumism.com/features/bob-dylan-the-times-they-are-a-changin-turns-55-anniversary-retrospective.
6 Cal Jillson, Pursuing the American Dream: Opportunity and Exclusion over Four Centuries 220 (2004).
7 Michael Pertschuk, Revolt against Regulation: The Rise and Pause of the Consumer Movement 5 (1982); Murray Weidenbaum, Business, Government and the Public 7–10 (2d ed. 1981).
8 National Women's History Museum, Rachael Carson 1907–1964 (ed. Debra Michaels) (quoting the reporter and Kennedy), www.womenshistory.org/education-resources/ biographies/rachel-carson.
9 JoAnne L. Dunec, On a Further Shore: The Life and Legacy of Rachael Carson, 27 Nat. Resources & Env't 62, 62 (2013).
10 Terry Tempest Williams, One Patriot, in Rachael Carson, Legacy and Challenge 21 (Lisa H. Sideris & Kathleen Dean Moore eds. 2008).
11 David Prindle, The Paradoxes of Democratic Capitalism: Politics and Economics in American Thought 183 (2006).
12 Peter Manus, One Hundred Years of Green: A Legal Perspective on Three Twentieth Century Nature Philosophers, 59 U. Pitt. L. Rev. 557, 626 (1998).
13 Beth Gillin & James C. Young, 30,000 Mark Earth Day at Fairmont Park Rally, Phila. Inquirer, April 23, 1970, at 1.
14 Adam Rome, The Genius of Earth Day, 15 Env't Hist. 194, 195 (2010).
15 Gillin & Young, supra note 13.
16 Rome, supra note 14.
17 Id.

18 Paul Sabin, Public Citizen: The Attack on Big Government and the Remaking of American Liberalism ch. 3 (2021).

19 Livia Albeck-Ripka and Kendra Pierre-Louis, American before Earth Day: Smog and Disasters Spurred the Laws that Trump Wants to Undo, The New York Times, April 21, 2018, www.nytimes.com/2018/04/21/climate/environmental-disasters-earth-day.html.

20 NBC News, 1969 Santa Barbara Oil Spill Was Galvinizing for the Environment Movement, May 20, 2015, www.nbcnews.com/news/us-news/1969-oil-spill-near-santa-barbara-was-galvanizing-environmentalism-n361911.

21 Dr. Jordan Kleiman, Love Canal: A Brief History, SUNY Genesco, Love Canal: A Brief History | SUNY Geneseo.

22 Eden Gauteron, Songs about the Burning of the Cuyahoga River, July 29, 2021, https://edengauteron.medium.com/songs-about-the-burning-of-the-cuyahoga-river-a6ecdea68a9a.

23 "Burn On," track 8 on Randy Newman, Sail Away, Warner Bros. Records, 1972.

24 John H. Hartig, Burning Rivers: Revival of Four Urban Industrial Rivers That Caught Fire (2010).

25 Robert Bullard, Dumping in Dixie: Race, Class, and Environmental Quality 35–38 (1990); Renee Skelton & Vernice Miller, The Environmental Justice Movement, NRDC (March 17, 2016); www.nrdc.org/stories/environmental-justice-movement; United Church of Christ, A Movement Is Born: Environmental Justice and the UCC, www.ucc.org/what-we-do/justice-local-church-ministries/justice/faithful-action-ministries/environmental-justice/a_movement_is_born_environmental_justice_and_the_ucc/.

26 Clean Water Act of 1965, Pub. L. 89–234.

27 Clean Water Act Amendments of 1972, Pub. L. 92–500 (1972).

28 1966 Clean Air Act, Pub. L. 89–865.

29 Federal Environmental Pesticide Control Act of 1972, Pub. L. 92–516.

30 1974 Safe Drinking Water Act, Pub. L. 93–523.

31 Toxic Substances Control Act of 1976, Pub. L. 94–469.

32 Resource Recovery and Conservation Act of 1976, Pub. L. 94–580.

33 1980 Comprehensive Environmental Response, Compensation, and Liability Act, Pub. L. 96–510.

34 Alexis C. Madrigal, Why Nixon Created the EPA, Atlantic Magazine, December 2, 2010, www.theatlantic.com/technology/archive/2010/12/gallery-why-nixon-created-the-epa/67351/.

35 Meir Rindle, Richard Nixon and the Rise of Environmentalism, June 2, 2017, Science History Institute, www.sciencehistory.org/distillations/richard-nixon-and-the-rise-of-american-environmentalism.

36 Wilderness Act of 1964, Pub. L. 88–577 (1964).

37 National Environmental Policy Act of 1979, Pub. L. 91–190.

38 Marine Mammal Protection Act of 1972, Pub. L. 92–522.

39 Marine Protection, Research, and Sanctuaries Act of 1972, Pub. L. 92–532.

40 Endangered Species Act of 1973, Pub. L. 93–205.

41 Levin Center, Wayne State University School of Law, Portraits in Oversight: Abraham Ribicoff and the Traffic Safety Hearings, www.levin-center.org/wp-content/uploads/2021/12/7-Portraits-in-Oversight-Abraham-Ribicoff-the-Trafic-Safety-Hearings-Levin-Center-at-Wayne-Law-1.pdf.

42 Nicholas Lemann, The Last Battle over Big Business: Ralph Nader, General Motors, and What We Get Wrong about Regulation, New Yorker, May 31, 2021, www.newyorker.com/magazine/2021/06/07/the-last-battle-over-big-business.

43 Id.

44 Julius Duscha, Nader's Raiders Is Their Name, and Whistle-Blowing Is Their Game, The New York Times, March 21, 1971, www.nytimes.com/1971/03/21/archives/stop-in-the-public-interest-stop-in-the-public-interest.html.

45 Id.

46 Harrison Wellford, Sowing the Wind: A Report for Ralph Nader's Center for the Study of Responsive Food Safety and Chemical Harvest (1973); David Zwick and Marcy Benstock, Master Wasteland: Ralph Nader's Study Group Report on Water Pollution (1971); Robert C. Fellmeth, Edward F. Cox, & John E. Schutz, The Nader Report on the Federal Trade Commission (1970); Jim Turner, The Chemical Feast: Ralph Nader's Study Group Report on the Food and Drug Administration (New York: Grossman Publishers, 1970); and Robert C. Fellmeth, The Interstate Commerce Commission: Ralph Nader's Study Group Report on the Interstate Commerce Commission & Transportation (New York: Grossman Publishers, 1970).

47 Milton Silverman & Phillip R. Lee, Pills, Profits, and Politics 95–96 (1974); Robert D. McFadden, & Frances Oldham Kelsey, Who Saved U.S. Babies from Thalidomide, Dies at 10, The New York Times, April 7, 2015, www.nytimes.com/2015/08/08/science/frances-oldham-kelsey-fda-doctor-who-exposed-danger-of-thalidomide-dies-at-101.html.

48 Thomas O. McGarity & Sidney A. Shapiro, Workers at Risk: The Failed Promise of the Occupational Safety and Health Administration 34 (1993).

49 Id.

50 National Traffic and Motor Vehicle Safety Act, Pub. L. 89–563 (1966).

51 Occupational Safety and Health Act, Pub. L. 91–596 (1971).

52 Consumer Product Safety Act, Pub. L. 92–573 (1972).

53 Mine Safety and Health Act, Pub. L. 95–164 (1977).

54 Food and Drug Act Amendments, Pub. L. 87–781 (1962).

55 Michael Harrington, The Other America 2 (1962).

56 Maurice Isserman, Michael Harrington: Warrior on Poverty, The New York Times, June 19, 2009 (quoting Harrington).

57 Antonio De Loera-Brust, Revisiting R.F.K. 's Poverty Tour, America: The Jesuit Rev., June 1, 2018 (quoting Kennedy).

58 Lyndon Johnson, Great Society Speech (1964), available at www.americanrhetoric.com/speeches/lbjthegreatsociety.htm.

59 Peter B. Edelman, Toward A Comprehensive Strategy: Getting beyond the Silver Bullet, 81 Geo. L. J. 1697, 1710 (1993).

60 Equal Opportunity Act of 1964, Pub. L. 88–452.

61 Legal Services Corporation, History: The Founding of LSC, www.lsc.gov/about-lsc/who-we-are/history.

62 Medicare Care and Medicaid Act, Pub. L. 89–97 (1965).

63 Elementary and Secondary Education Act of 1965, Pub. L. 89–10.

64 Robert Caro, Master of the Senate (2019).

65 Civil Rights Act of 1964, Pub. L. 88–352.

66 1965 Higher Education Act, Pub. L. 89–329.

67 Voting Rights Act of 1965, Pub. L. 89–110.

68 Jill Lapore, These Truths: A History of the United States (2018).

69 Charles A. Reich, The Greening of America (1970).

70 Id. at 111.

71 Id. at 102.

72 Id. at 88.

73 Id. at 229.

74 University of Virginia, Miller Center, The Kennedy Commitment, September 18, 2017, https://millercenter.org/the-presidency/educational-resources/kennedy-commitment.

75 U.S. Department of State, Office of the Historian, U.S. Involvement in the Vietnam War: The Gulf of Tonkin and Escalation, 1964, https://history.state.gov/milestones/1961-1968/gulf-of-tonkin.

76 Kent Germany, Lyndon Johnson, Foreign Affairs, Miller Center, https://millercenter.org/president/lbjohnson/foreign-affairs.

77 Anti-Vietnam War Demonstration Held, Learning Network, The New York Times, November 15, 2011, https://learning.blogs.nytimes.com/2011/11/15/nov-15-1969-anti-vietnam-war-demonstration-held/.

78 Genius, Lyrics: Pete Seeger, Waist Deep in the Big Muddy, https://genius.com/Pete-seeger-waist-deep-in-the-big-muddy-lyrics.

79 Id.

80 David Paul Kuhn, The Hardhat Riot; Nixon, New York City, and the Dawn of the White Working Class Revolution chs. 5–7 (2020).

81 Id. at chs. 13–20.

82 Id. at 160.

83 Michael McCann, Taking Reform Seriously: Perspectives of Public Interest Liberalism 78 (1986).

84 Andrew S. McFarland, Public Interest Lobbies: Decision-Making on Energy 16–17 (1976).

85 Richard Stewart, The Reformation of American Administrative Law, 88 Harv. L. Rev. 1667 (1975).

86 Michael E. McLachlan, Democratizing the Administrative Process: Toward Increased Responsiveness, 4 Ariz. L. Rev. 848 (1971).

87 McCann, Taking Reform Seriously, note 65 at 52, citing Public Citizen's 1979 Annual Report.

88 Id. at 68 (citing Nadar).

89 Id. at 68 (citing Reilly).

90 Garrett De Bell, The Environmental Handbook: Prepared for the First National Environmental Teach-In 285 (1970).

91 Michael P. Smith, Alienation and the Bureaucracy: The Role of Participatory Administration, 31 Pub. Admin. Rev. 658 (1971).

92 Charles A. Reich, The New Property, 73 Yale L. J. 733 (1964): Charles A. Reich, Midnight Welfare Searches and the Social Security Act, 72 Yale L. J. 1347 (1963); Charles A. Reich, Individual Rights and Social Welfare: The Emerging Legal Issues, 74 Yale L.J. 1245 (1965).

93 Sidney A. Shapiro, Pragmatic Administrative Law, Article 1, Issues in Legal Scholarship, The Reformation of American Administration Law (2005), www.degruyter.com/journal/key/ils/5/1/html.

8 JOHN LEWIS'S AMERICA

1 Gene Sperling, Economic Dignity 45 (2020) (quoting Adams).

2 Edmund Fawcett, Liberalism: The Life of an Idea ch. 7 2d ed. (2018).

3 Sperling, supra note 1, at 45 (quoting Adams).

4 Sydney Trent, John Lewis Nearly Died on the Edmund Pettus Bridge: Now It May Be Renamed for Him, Washington Post, January 26, 2020, www.washingtonpost.com/history/2020/07/26/john-lewis-bloody-sunday-edmund-pettus-bridge/; Stanford University,

The Martin Luther King, Jr. Research and Education Institute, Selma to Montgomery March 21–25, 1965, https://kinginstitute.stanford.edu/encyclopedia/selma-montgomery-march.

5 John Lewis, Together, You Can Redeem the Soul of Our Nation, The New York Times (July 30, 2020).

6 Poetry Foundation, Phillis Wheatley, www.poetryfoundation.org/poets/phillis-wheatley.

7 Michael S. Harper & Anthony Walton, The Vintage Book of African American Poetry: 200 Years of Vision, Struggle, Power, Beauty, and Triumph from 50 *Outstanding Poets* 14 (2000).

8 African American Poetry: 250 Years of Struggle & Song 10 (Kevin Young ed., 2020).

9 Matthew Desmond, In Order to Understand the Brutality of American Capitalism, You Have to Start on the Planation, The New York Times (Aug. 14, 2019), www.nytimes.com/interactive/2019/08/14/magazine/slavery-capitalism.html.

10 Zoe Thomas, The Hidden Links between Slavery and Wall Street, BBC News (August 28, 2019), www.bbc.com/news/business-49476247.

11 Dina Gerdeman, The Clear Connection between Slavery and American Capitalism, FORBES (March 3, 2017); Sven Beckert & Seth Rockman (eds), Slavery's Capitalism: A New History of American Economic Development (2016).

12 MIT Libraries, MIT and Slavery, https://libraries.mit.edu/mit-and-slavery/universities-and-slavery/.

13 Danielle Allen, Our Declaration: A Reading of the Declarations of Independence in Defense of Equality (2014); Pauline Maier American Scripture: Making the Declaration of Independence (1997).

14 Allen, supra note 13, at 71.

15 William M. Weicek, The Sources of Anti-Slavery Constitutionalism in American, 1760–1848, 62–63 (1977).

16 Joseph P. Tomain, Creon's Ghost, Law, Justice and the Humanities 126 (2009).

17 U.S. Constitution, Article IV, Section 2, Clause 3.

18 Fugitive Slave Act of 1793, 1 Stat. 302.

19 Toni Morrisoni, Beloved (1987).

20 *Prigg* v. *Pennsylvania*, 16 Pet. (41 U.S.) 539, 611 (1842).

21 Id. at 612.

22 Id. at 611.

23 Fugitive Slave Act of 1850, Pub. L. 31–60.

24 James McPherson, Battle Cry of Freedom: The Civil War Era 76–79 (1988).

25 *Dred Scott* v. *Sandford*, 60 U.S. 393, 394, 407 (1857).

26 Frederick Douglass, The Meaning of July Fourth for the Negro (July 5, 1852), https://masshumanities.org/files/programs/douglass/speech_complete.pdf.

27 Frederick Douglas, What the Black Man Wants? (April 1865), www.blackpast.org/african-american-history/1865-frederick-douglass-what-black-man-wants/.

28 Ta-Nehisi Coates, We Were Eight Years in Power: An American Tragedy xiii (2017) (quoting Thomas Miller).

29 Id. at xiv.

30 Jill Lepore, These Truths: A History of the United States 323 (2018).

31 W.E.B. Dubois, Black Reconstruction in America 1860–1880 (1992 ed.).

32 Eric Foner, Reconstruction: America's Unfinished Revolution 1863–1877, at 582 (2014 ed.)

33 Ferris State University, The Origins of Jim Crow, https://jimcrowmuseum.ferris.edu/origins.htm.

34 Cambell Robinson, A Lynching Memorial Is Opening: The Country Has Never Seen Anything Like It, The New York Times, April 25, 2018, www.nytimes.com/2018/04/25/us/lynching-memorial-alabama.html.

35 1875 Civil Rights Act, 18 Stat. 335.

36 The Civil Rights Cases, 109 U.S. 3 (1883).

37 Id. at 57.

38 *Plessy v. Ferguson*, 163 U.S. 537, 551 (1896).

39 Id. at 560.

40 *State of Missouri v. Canada*, 305 U.S. 337 (1938).

41 Nation Archives, Timeline of Events Leading to the *Brown v. Board of Education* Decision of 1954, www.archives.gov/education/lessons/brown-v-board/timeline.html.

42 Lucius J. Barker, Thurgood Marshall, The Law and the System: Tenants of an Enduring Legacy, 44 Stan. L. Rev. 1237, 1237 (1992).

43 *McLaurin v. Oklahoma State Regents*, 339 U.S. 637 (1950); *Brown v. Board of Education*, 337 U.S. 483 (1954); *Bolling v. Sharpe*, 347 U.S. 497 (1954).

44 *Cooper v. Aaron*, 358 U.S. 1 (1958).

45 347 U.S. at 494–95.

46 *Plessy v. Ferguson*, supra note 38, at 551.

47 NPR, Read Martin Luther King Jr.'s 'I Have a Dream' Speech in Its Entirety, January 14, 2022, www.npr.org/2010/01/18/122701268/i-have-a-dream-speech-in-its-entirety.

48 Taylor Branch, Parting the Waters: America in the King Years 1954–1963 869–76 (1988); Jon Meacham, His Truth Is Marching On: John Lewis and the Power of Hope 134–42 (2020).

49 Original Draft of John Lewis' Speech at the March on Washington, chrome-extension:// efaidnbmnnnibpcajpcglclefindmkaj/https://njsbf.org/wp-content/uploads/2021/12/ Original-Draft-of-John-Lewis-Speech-at-the-March-on-Washington-Handout.pdf.

50 John Lewis, Speech at the March on Washington, August 28, 1963, https:// voicesofdemocracy.umd.edu/lewis-speech-at-the-march-on-washington-speech-text/.

51 Malcolm X, God's Judgment (December 4, 1963).

52 John Herbers, Violence: It Is as American as Cherry Pie, The New York Times (June 8, 1969).

53 American Radio Works, Malcom X: The Ballot or the Bullet, https://americanradioworks .publicradio.org/features/blackspeech/mx.html.

54 Malcolm X, The Bullet or the Ballot (April 12, 1964), www.edchange.org/multicultural/ speeches/malcolm_x_ballot.html.

55 Gunnar Myrdal, An American Dilemma: The Negro Problem and Modern Democracy (1944); see also Andrew Hacker, Two Nations: Black and White, Separate Hostile, Unequal (1992).

56 The American Presidency Project, Lyndon B. Johnson, Commencement Address at Howard University: "To Fulfill these Rights" (June 4, 1965) available at www.presidency .ucsb.edu/documents/commencement-address-howard-university-fulfill-these-rights.

57 Civil Rights Act of 1964, Pub. L. 88–352.

58 Lyndon Baines Johnson, On Signing the Civil Rights Act of 1964 (June 2, 1964).

59 The American Presidency Project: Commencement Address at Howard University, June 4, 1965, www.presidency.ucsb.edu/documents/commencement-address-howard-university- fulfill-these-rights.

60 Voting Rights Act of. 1965, Pub. L. 89–110.

61 U.S. Const., 15th Amendment.

62 Gunnar Myrdal, An American Dilemma: The Negro Problem and Modern Democracy (1944); Andrew Hacker, Two Nations: Black and White, Separate Hostile, Unequal (1992).

63 Transcript of Amanda Gorman's Inaugural Poem, January 20, 2021, The Hill, https://docs .google.com/document/d/1ejvmoupoR-uFzBafEudRQgjBOLyqSBdA/edit.

9 ALFRED KAHN'S AMERICA

1 Gary Gerstle, The Rise and Fall of the Neoliberal Order: America and the World in the Free Market Era (2022).

2 Andrew Downer Crain, Ford, Carter, and Deregulation in the 1970s, 5 J. Telecomm. & Hight Tech. L. 413 (2007).

3 Alfred E. Kahn, The Economics of Regulation: Institutions and Principles (1 vol. ed. 1988); Stephen Breyer, Regulation and Its Reform (1982).

4 Susan S. Lang, Economist Alfred Kahn, Father of Airline Deregulation and Former Presidential Adviser, Dies at 93, Cornell Chronicle, December 27, 2010, https://news .cornell.edu/stories/2010/12/alfred-kahn-father-airline-deregulation-dies-93.

5 Samuel P. Huntington, The Marasmus of the ICC: The Commission, The Railroads, and the Public Interest, 61 Yale L. J. 467 (1952); George J. Stigler, The Theory of Economic Regulation, 2 Bell J. Econ. & Mgmt. Sci. 3 (1971).

6 Lang, supra note 4.

7 Letters of Note, On Bureaucratese and Gobbledygook, April 26, 2011 (reprinting the memo), https://lettersofnote.com/2011/04/26/on-bureaucratese-and-gobbledygook/.

8 Lang, supra note 4.

9 Interstate Commerce Act, Pub. L. 49–41 (1887).

10 Hepburn Act, Pub. L. 59–337 (1906).

11 Motor Carrier Act, Pub. L. 74–255 (1935).

12 Civil Aeronautics Act, 52 Stat. 973 (1938).

13 Gabriel Kolko, Railroads and Regulation 1877–1916 (1965).

14 Simple Flying, The History of Southwest Airlines, June 5, 2022, https://simpleflying.com/ southwest-airlines-history/.

15 Carole Shiffrin, Carter Would Let Airlines Compete by Cutting Fares, Washington Post, March 5, 1977, www.washingtonpost.com/archive/politics/1977/03/05/carter-would-let-airlines-compete-by-cutting-fares/00decf4d-adf3-4b7b-95ba-b5312b1716cb/.

16 Airline Deregulation Act of 1978, Pub. L. No. 95-504.

17 Paul Stephen Dempsey, Airline Deregulation and Laissez-Faire Mythology: Economic Theory in Turbulence, 56 J. Air L. & Commerce 305 (1990); Phil Weiser, Alfred Kahn as a Case Study of a Political Entrepreneur: An Essay in Honor of His 90th Birthday, 4 Rev. Network Econ. 603 (2008).

18 Staggers Rail Act, Pub. L. 96–448 (1980).

19 Motor Carrier Act, Pub. L. No. 96-296 (1980).

20 Natural Gas Act, Pub. L. 75–688 (1938).

21 National Energy Act of 1978, Pub. L. 95-618.

22 Natural Gas Regulatory Policy Act, Pub. L. 95-621(1978).

23 Economic Stabilization Act, Pub. L. 91–379 (1970).

24 William N. Walker, Nixon Taught Us How Not to Fight Inflation, Wall St. J., August 13, 2021, www.wsj.com/articles/nixon-fight-inflation-price-controls-stagflation-gas-shortages-biden-democrats-reconciliation-bill-federal-reserve-11628885071.

25 Id.

26 Public Utilities Regulatory Policies Act of 1978, Pub. L. No. 95-17.

27 Kenneth J. Robinson, Federal Reserve History: Savings and Loan Crisis: 1980–1989, www.federalreservehistory.org/essays/savings-and-loan-crisis#:~:text=A%20Turbulent%20 History,-The%20relatively%20greater&text=As%20inflation%20accelerated%20and%20 interest,Losses%20began%20to%20mount.

28 Depository Institutions Deregulation and Monetary Control Act, Pub. L. No. 96-221 (of 1980).

29 Dustin Ryan Walker, Unleashing the Financial Sector: Home Loan Deregulation and the Savings and Loan Crisis, 1966–1989 (June 2018).
30 Financial Institutions Reform, Recovery and Enforcement Act, Pub. L. No. 101–73 (1989); Robinson, supra note 27.

10 RONALD REAGAN'S AMERICA

1 The West Wing: He Shall from Time to Time … (NBC television broadcast January 12, 2000), www.westwingtranscripts.com/search.php?flag=getTranscript&id=12.
2 Ronald Reagan, Inaugural Address, January 20, 1981, www.reaganfoundation.org/media/128614/inaguration.pdf.
3 America's Bill of Rights, Ronald Reagan Library, July 3, 1987, www.reaganlibrary.gov/archives/speech/americas-economic-bill-rights.
4 President William Jefferson Clinton, State of the Union Address, January 23, 1966, https://clintonwhitehouse4.archives.gov/WH/New/other/sotu.html.
5 Id.
6 Lewis F. Powell Jr., Attack on American Free Enterprise System 1 (August 23, 1971), chrome-extension://efaidnbmnnnibpcajpcglclefindmkaj/https://law2.wlu.edu/deptimages/Powell%20Archives/PowellMemorandumTypescript.pdf.
7 David Vogel, Fluctuating Fortunes: The Political Power of Business in America (1989).
8 Sidney A. Shapiro & Joseph P. Tomain, Achieving Democracy: The Future of Progressive Politics 49 (2014).
9 Lee Edwards, Barry M. Goldwater: The Most Consequential Loser in American Politics, July 3, 2014, www.heritage.org/political-process/report/barry-m-goldwater-the-most-consequential-loser-american-politics.
10 Id.
11 Matthew Continetti, The Right: The Hundred Year War for American Conservatism (2022).
12 Lou Cannon, Ronald Reagan: Life before the Presidency, University of Virginia Miller Center, https://millercenter.org/president/reagan/life-before-the-presidency.
13 Id.
14 Jeffery Kahn, Ronald Reagan Launched Political Career Using Berkeley Campus as a Target, UC Berkeley News, June 8, 2004, www.berkeley.edu/news/media/releases/2004/06/08_reagan.shtml.
15 Edwin Meese, III, The Law of the Constitution, Tulane University (October 21,1986), www.justice.gov/ag/speeches-attorney-general-edwin-meese-iii.
16 Jorge M. Farinacci-Fernós, Looking for the Correct Tool for the Job: Methodological Models of Constitutional Interpretation and Adjudication, 52 Rev. Jur. U.I.P.R. 213, 244 (2018).
17 Meese, supra note15, at 49.
18 Paul Brest, The Misconceived Quest for the Original Understanding, 60 B. U. L. Rev. 204, 204 (1980).
19 Ann Southworth, Lawyers and the Conservative Counterrevolution, 43 L. & Soc. Inquiry 1698 (2018).
20 William J. Haun, The Philosopher in Action: A Tribute to the Honorable Edwin Meese III, 13 Engage 4 (March 2012).
21 Id. at 7.
22 Lawrence B. Solum, What Is Originalism? The Evolution of Contemporary Originalist Theory, in The Challenge of Originalism: Essays in Constitutional Theory (Grant J. Huscroft & Bradley W. Miller eds., 2011).

23 J. Craig Jenkins & Craig M. Eckert, The Right Turn in Economic Policy: Business Elites and the New Conservative Economics, 15 Sociological Forum 307 (2000).

24 Sherman Antitrust Act of 1890, 26 Stat. 209; Clayton Antitrust Act of 1914, 38 Stat. 730.

25 Richard Schmalensee, Bill Baxter in the Antitrust Arena: An Economist's Appreciation, 51 Stan. L. Rev. 1317 (1999); Lawrence J. White, Present at the Beginning of a New Era for Antitrust: Reflections on 1982–1983, 16 Rev. Industrial Org. 131 (2000).

26 Robert H. Bork. The Antitrust Paradox: A Policy at War with Itself (1978).

27 Tim Wu, The Curse of Bigness ch. 4 (2018).

28 Lina M. Khan, Book Review: The End of Antitrust History Revisited, 133 Harv. L. Rev. 1655 (2020); Herbert Hovenkamp, Is Antitrust's Consumer Welfare Principle Imperiled? 45 J. Corp. L. 101, 102 (2019).

29 DOJ, 1982 Merger Guidelines, www.justice.gov/archives/atr/1982-merger-guidelines#:~: text=The%20unifying%20theme%20of%20the,if%20the%20market%20were%20competitive.

30 Shreille Ismail, Transformative Choices: A Review of 70 Years of FCC Decisions, FCC Staff Working Paper (October 2010).

31 Telecommunications Reform Act of 1996, Pub. L. 104–104.

32 *FCC* v. *Prometheus Radio Project*, 141 S. Ct. 1150 (2021).

33 Gramm-Leach-Bliley Act, Pub. L. 106–102 (1999).

34 Suanne Craig, The Weekend Wall Street Died, The Wall Street Journal, December 29, 2008.

35 Andrew Ross Sorkin, Too Big to Fail: The Inside Story of How Wall Street and Washington Fought to Save the Financial System – and Themselves (2009); Simon Johnson & James Kwak, Thirteen Bankers: The Wall Street Takeover and the Next Financial Meltdown 175 (2010); Bethany McLean & Joe Nocera, All the Devils Are Here: The Hidden History of the Financial Crisis (2012).

36 Id.

37 Edmund L. Andrews, Greenspan Concedes Error on Regulation, The New York Times (October 23, 2008).

38 Congressional Oversight Panel, December Oversight Report: Taking Stock: What Has the Trouble Asset Program Achieved? (2009).

39 Better Markets, The Cost of the Crisis, $20 Trillion and Counting, October 29, 2018, available at https://bettermarkets.com/resources/20-trillion-and-counting-cost-wall-street-caused-financial-crisis.

40 Tam Harbert, Here's How Much the 2008 Bailouts Really Cost, MIT Sloan School, Feb 21, 2019, https://mitsloan.mit.edu/ideas-made-to-matter/heres-how-much-2008-bailouts-really-cost.

41 *Seila Law LLC* v. *Consumer Financial Protection Bureau*, 140 S.Ct. 2183 (2020); *Consumer Financial Protection Bureau* v. *Community Financial Services of America, Inc.*, 51 F4th 616 (5th Cir. 2022).

42 George Gilder, Wealth and Poverty (1981).

43 Sidney A. Shapiro & Joseph P. Tomain, Regulatory Law and Policy: Cases and Materials 581 (1998) (quoting Charles Murray, Losing Ground: America's Social Policy (1984)).

44 Ronald Regan, Radio Address to the Nation on Welfare Reform, August 1, 1987, www.reaganfoundation.org/media/128766/welfare.pdf.

45 Jeremy Lybarger, The Price You Pay: The Life and Times of the Women Known as the Welfare Queen, The Nation, July 2, 2019.

46 Personal Responsibility and Work Opportunity Act of 1996, Pub. L. 104–193.

47 Americans with Disabilities Act of 1990, Pub. L. 101–336.

48 Lilly Ledbetter Fair Pay Act, Pub. L. 111–2 (2009).

49 Student Aid & Fiscal Responsibility Act of 2009, 124 Stat. 1071.

50 Dodd-Frank Wall Street Reform and Consumer Protection Act of 2010, Pub. L. No. 111–203 (2010).

51 Patient Protection and Affordable Care Act of 2010, Pub. L. No. 111–148 (2010).

52 About the Office, The Office of Barak and Michelle Obama, https://barackobama.com/about/.

53 10 Ways the ACA Has Improved Health Care in the Past Decade, Center for American Progress, March 23, 2020, www.americanprogress.org/article/10-ways-aca-improved-health-care-past-decade/.

54 Stephen Neukam, The 10 States That Have Not Expanded Medicaid, The Hill, March 23, 2023, https://thehill.com/homenews/state-watch/3914916-these-10-states-have-not-expanded-medicaid/#:~:text=Wyoming%2C%20Kansas%2C%.

55 Matthew Titolo, Privatization and the Market Frame, 60 Buffalo L. Rev. 493, 525 (2012).

56 Paul Verkuil, Valuing Bureaucracy: The Case for Professional Government (2017).

57 Steven Pearlstein, The Federal Outsourcing Boom and Why It Is Failing Americans, The Washington Post, January 31, 2014, www.washingtonpost.com/business/the-federal-outsourcing-boom-and-why-its-failing-americans/2014/01/31/21d03c40-8914-11e3-833c-33098f9e5267_story.html.

58 Verkuil, supra note 56.

59 Pearlstein, supra note 57.

60 Jessica Bulman-Pozen, Administrative States: Beyond Presidential Administration, 98 Tex. L. Rev. 265 (2019).

61 Sidney A. Shapiro & Ronald F. Wright, The Future of the Administrative Presidency: Turning Administrative Law Inside-Out, 65 U. Miami L. Rev. 577 (2011).

62 1993 Regulatory Planning and Review, Executive Order 12866, 58 Fed. Reg. September 30, 1993, www.archives.gov/files/federal-register/executive-orders/pdf/12866.pdf.

63 Economic Wealth Recovery Tax Act, Pub. L. 97–34 (1981); Economic Growth and Tax Relief Reconciliation Act, Pub. L. 107–16 (2001); Job Creation and Worker Assistance Act, Pub. L. 107–147 (2002); Jobs and Growth Tax Relief Reconciliation Act, Public Law No. 108–27 (2003).

64 Christopher Ingraham, The Top Tax Rate Has Been Cut Six Times since 1980 – Usually with Democrats' Help, www.washingtonpost.com/us-policy/2019/02/27/top-tax-rate-has-been-cut-six-times-since-usually-with-democrats-help/.

65 Barack Obama's Remarks to the Democratic National Convention, The New York Times, July 27, 2004, www.nytimes.com/2004/07/27/politics/campaign/barack-obamas-remarks-to-the-democratic-national.html.

66 The Second Inauguration of Barack Obama, January 21, 2013, https://obamawhitehouse.archives.gov/blog/2013/01/21/second-inauguration-barack-obama.

11 MITCH McCONNELL'S AMERICA

1 *New York State Rifle & Pistol Assn. v. Bruen*, 142 S.Ct. 2111 (2022).

2 *Dobbs v. Jackson Women's Health Org.*, 142 S.Ct. 2228 (2022).

3 *West Virginia v. EPA*, 142 S.Ct. 2587 (2022).

4 Ron Elving, What Happened with Merrick Garland in 2016 and Why It Matters Now, NPR (June 29, 2018), www.npr.org/2018/06/29/624467256/what-happened-with-merrick-garland-in-2016-and-why-it-matters-now.

5 Id.

6 Amanda Hollis-Brusky, Ideas with Consequences: The Federalist Society and the Conservative Counterrevolution (2015); Steven Teles, The Rise of the Conservative Legal Movement: The Battle for Control of the Law (2008); Sheldon Whitehouse, The Scheme: How the Right Wing Used Dark Money to Capture the Supreme Court (2022); Chris McGreal, Leonard Leo: The Secretive Rightwinger Using Billions to Reshape America, The Guardian, September 4, 2022.

7 Alexander M. Bickel, The Least Dangerous Branch (1962).

8 Stuart Hampshire, Justice is Conflict (2000).

9 Jeffrey M. Jones, Confidence in U.S. Supreme Court Sinks to Historic Low, Gallup (June 23, 2022), https://news.gallup.com/poll/394103/confidence-supreme-court-sinks-historic-low.aspx.

10 Richard A. Posner, Divergent Paths: The Academy and the Judiciary (2016); Richard A. Posner, The Supreme Court 2004 Term: Forward: A Political Court, 119 Harv. L. Rev. 31 (2005).

11 *McCulloch* v. *Maryland*, 17 U.S. (4 Wheat.) 316 (1819).

12 *Dartmouth College* v. *Woodward*, 17 U.S. (4 Wheat.) 518 (1819).

13 U.S. Const. Art. 1, Sec. 10.

14 *Gibbons* v. *Ogden*, 22 U.S. (9 Wheat.) 1 (1824).

15 *Charles River Bridge* v. *Warren Bridge*, 36 U.S. (11 Pet.) 420 (1837).

16 Michael Lind, Land of Promise: An Economic History of the United States 106–09 (2012).

17 *Dred Scott* v. *Sandford*, 60 U.S. 393 (1857).

18 *Lochner* v. *New York*, 198 U.S. 45 (1905).

19 *Holden* v. *Hardy*, 169 U.S. 366 (1898); *Allgeyer* v. *Louisiana*, 165 U.S. 578 (1897); *Gundling* v. *Chicago*, 177 U.S. 183 (1900).

20 Lochner, 198 U.S. at 70; David E. Bernstein, *Lochner* v. *New York*: A Centennial Retrospective, 83 Wash. U. L. Q. 1469, 1479–81 (2005).

21 Id. at 69.

22 Roscoe Pound, Liberty of Contract, 18 Yale L. J. 454 (1908).

23 Adam Cohen, Supreme Inequality: The Supreme Court's Fifty-Year Battle for a More Unjust America xv, xxi (2020).

24 Herbert Hovenkamp, Enterprise and American Law 1836–1937 (1991).

25 Geoffrey P. Miller, The Tue Story of Carolene Products, 1987 Sup. Ct. Rev. 397 (1987).

26 *United States* v. *Carolene Products*, 304 U.S. 144 (1937).

27 Miller, supra note 25, at 416.

28 Carolene Products, 304 U.S.144, 147 (1938).

29 Id. at 152.

30 Id. at 152–53 n. 4.

31 John Hart Ely, Democracy and Distrust: A Theory of Judicial Review (1980).

32 Wickard v. Filburn, 317 U.S. 111 (1942).

33 U.S. Const, Art. I, Sec. 10.

34 *Ashwander* v. *TVA*, 297 U.S. 288 (1936).

35 Barry Sullivan & Christine Kexel Chabot, The Science of Administrative Change, 52 Conn. L. Rev. 1 (2020); Jon Michaels, Revitalize the Bureaucracy, in American Constitution Society, Rethinking Admin Law: From APA to Z (2019); Nicholas O. Stephanopoulus, The Anti-Carolene Court, 2019 Sup. Ct. Rev (2019).

36 Danielle Allen, Our Declaration: A Reading of the Declaration of Independence in Defense of Equality (2014).

37 Evan Andrews, The Green Book: The Black Travelers' Guide to Jim Crow America, March 13, 2019, History Chanel, www.history.com/news/the-green-book-the-black-travelers-guide-to-jim-crow-america (quoting the Green Book).

38 *Katzenbach v. McClung*, 379 U.S. 294, 299 (1964).
39 Andrew Yeager, Forced to Seat Blacks, Ala. Restaurant Complied with History, NPR WFIU (December 13, 2014).
40 *United States v. Lopez*, 514 U.S. 549 (1995).
41 *United States v. Morrison*, 529 U.S. 598 (2000).
42 *Industrial Union Dept. v. American Petroleum Institute*, 448 U.S. 607 (1980).
43 *J.W. Hampton, Jr. & Co. v. United States*, 276 U.S. 394 (1928).
44 *Gideon v. Wainwright*, 372 U.S. 335 (1963).
45 Ciara Torres-Spelliscy, The Cautionary Tale of Abe Fortas, Brennan Center, Feb. 6, 2018, www.brennancenter.org/our-work/analysis-opinion/cautionary-tale-abe-fortas.
46 Carl Hulse, How Mitch McConnell Delivered Justice Amy Coney Barret's Rapid Confirmation, The New York Times (November 3, 2020); Patricia Taddonio, On Night of Ginsburg's Death, McConnell Pushed Trump to Nominate Amy Coney Barrett, Frontline (November 24, 2020); Aris Folley, McConnell Pushed Trump to Nominate Barrett on the Night of Ginsburg's Death: Report, The Hill (November 24, 2020).
47 Noah Feldman with Lidia Jean Kott, Takeover: How a Conservative Student Club Captured the Supreme Court (2021).
48 See Gillian Metzger, The Supreme Court, 2016 Term – Forward: 1930s Redux: The Administrative State Under Siege, 131 Harv. L. Rev. 1 (2017); Sophia Z. Lee, Our Administered Constitution: Administrative Constitutionalism from the Founding to the Present, 167 U. Penn. L. Rev. 1699 (2019); Richard L. Hasen, The Supreme Court's Pro-Partisan Turn, 109 Georgetown L. J. On-Line 50 (2020).
49 *Chevron v. NRDC*, 467 U.S. 837 (1984).
50 Id.
51 Jonathan H. Adler, Shunting Aside Chevron Deference, Regulatory Rev., August 7, 2018.
52 *Biden v. Nebraska*, 2023 WL 4277210 (2023).
53 Lisa Heinzerling, The Power Canons, 58 Wm & Mary L. Rev. 1933 (2017).
54 Id. at 1939–40 and 1980–2003.
55 *West Virginia v. EPA*, 142 S.Ct. 258 (2022).
56 *National Federation of Independ. Businesses v. OSHA*, 142 S.Ct. 661 (2021) (per curium and concurrence).
57 *FDA v. Brown & Williamson Tobacco Corp.*, 529 U.S. 120 (2000).
58 *Department of Education v. Brown* (2023).
59 Higher Education Relief Opportunities for Students Act of 2003, Pub. L. 107–122.
60 *Baker v. Carr*, 369 U.S. 186 (1962); *Reynolds v. Sims*, 377 U.S. 533 (1964).
61 *Citizens United v. Federal Election Comm'n.*, 558 U.S. 310 (2010).
62 *Crawford v. Marrion Cty. Election Bd.*, 553 U.S. 181 (2008).
63 *Husted v. A. Philip Randolph Institute*, 138 S.Ct. 1833 (2018).
64 *Parents Involved in Community Schools v. Seattle*, 551 U.S. 701 (2007).
65 *Allen v. Miligan*, 2023 WL 3937599 (2023); Michael Wines, Supreme Court Gives the Voting Rights Act a Tenuous New Lease on Life, The New York Times, June 8, 2023; Richard L. Hasen, John Roberts Throws a Curveball, The New York Times, June 8, 2023.
66 *Shelby City. v. Holder*, 570 U.S. 529 (2013).
67 *Brnovich v. Democratic National Committee*, 141 S.Ct. 2321 (2021).
68 *Rucho v. Common Cause*, 139 S.Ct. 2484 (2019).
69 Adam Liptak, Supreme Court Won't Extend Wisconsin's Deadline for Mailed Ballots, The New York Times, October 26, 2020, www.nytimes.com/2020/10/26/us/supreme-court-wisconsin-ballots.html.

70 Teran Powell, 40 Coronavirus Cases in Milwaukee County Linked to Wisconsin Election, Health Officials Say, WUWM 89.7, Milwaukee's NPR (April 24, 2020).
71 Brandon Tensley, America's Long History of Back Voter Suppression, CNN Politics.
72 Theodore R. Johnson & Max Feldman, The New Voter Suppression, Brennan Center for Justice, January 16, 2020.
73 Brennan Center for Justice, Debunking the Voter Fraud Myth, January 31, 2017; Resources on Voter Fraud Claims, June 26, 2017.
74 Christiana A. Cassidy, Far Too Little Voter Fraud to Tip Election to Trump, AP Finds, AP, December 14, 2021.
75 Josh Gerstein & Alexander Ward, Supreme Court Has Voted to Overturn Abortion Rights, Draft Opinion Shows, Politico, May 2, 2022, www.politico.com/news/2022/05/02/supreme-court-abortion-draft-opinion-00029473.
76 *Dobbs v. Jackson Women's Health Org.*, 142 S.Ct. 2228 (2022).
77 William Baude, Precedent and Discretion, 2019 S. Ct. Rev. 313 (2020).
78 *Janus v. State, County, and Municipal Employees*, 138 S.Ct. 2448 (2018); *Ramos v. Louisiana*, 140 S.Ct. 1390 (2020) (Kavanaugh, J. concurring); Adam Liptak, Precedent, Meet Clarence Thomas, You May Not Get Along, The New York Times A13, March 4, 2019.
79 *Dobbs v. Jackson Women's Health Org.*, 140 S.Ct. 1390 (2022) (Thomas, J., concurring).
80 *Students for Fair Admissions v. Harvard University*, 2023 WL 4239254 (2023).
81 Id. (Sotomayer, J. dissenting).
82 Id.
83 July 4, 1861: July 4th Message to Congress, Miller Center, https://millercenter.org/the-presidency/presidential-speeches/july-4-1861-july-4th-message-congress.
84 *303 Creative v. Aubrey Elenis*, 2023 WL 4277208 (2023).
85 Jack M. Balkin, The Cycles of Constitutional Time (2020).
86 Linda Greenhouse, The Supreme Court Has Crossed the Rubicon, The New York Times, February 9, 2022.
87 Daniel A. Farber, The Misuse of History to Undercut the Modern Regulatory State, Regulatory Rev., February 1, 2022; David M. Driesen, Major Questions and Juristocracy, Regulatory Rev., January 31, 2022.

12 DONALD TRUMP'S AMERICA

1 Glenn Kessler, Salvador Rizzo & Meg Kelly, Trump's False or Misleading Claims Total 30,573 over 4 years, The Washington Post, January 24, 2021, www.washingtonpost.com/politics/2021/01/24/trumps-false-or-misleading-claims-total-30573-over-four-years/; David Montgomery, The Abnormal Presidency, The Washington Post, November 10, 2020, www.washingtonpost.com/graphics/2020/lifestyle/magazine/trump-presidential-norm-breaking-list/.
2 Thomas B. Edsall, 'Gut-level Hatred' Is Consuming Our Political Life, The New York Times, July 19, 2023, www.nytimes.com/2023/07/19/opinion/polarization-nationalism-patriotism-history.html.
3 Id.
4 Nolan D. McCaskill, Trump Tells Wisconsin: Victory Was a Surprise, Politico, December 13, 2016, www.politico.com/story/2016/12/donald-trump-wisconsin-232605.
5 George Packer, Head of the Class: How Donald Trump Is Winning over the White Working Class, The New Yorker, May 16, 2016, www.newyorker.com/magazine/2016/05/16/how-donald-trump-appeals-to-the-white-working-class.

6   Arlie Hochschild, Strangers in Their Own Land: Anger and Mourning on the American Right (2016).

7   Katherine J. Cramer, The Politics of Resentment: Rural Consciousness in Wisconsin and the Rise of Scott Walker 221–22 (2016).

8   Ben Jacobs, Hillary Clinton Calls Half of Trump Supporters Bigoted "Deplorables," The Guardian, September 10, 2016, www.theguardian.com/us-news/2016/sep/10/hillary-clinton-trump-supporters–bigoted-deplorables.

9   Elizabeth Lowry, Demon Copperhead by Barbara Kingsolver Review – Dickens Updated, The Guardian, November 10, 2022, www.theguardian.com/books/2022/nov/10/demon-copperhead-by-barbara-kingsolver-review-dickens-updated.

10   Jordan Weismann, 60 Years of American Economic History, Told in 1 Graph, The Atlantic, August 23, 2012, www.theatlantic.com/business/archive/2012/08/60-years-of-american-economic-history-told-in-1-graph/261503/.

11   Id.

12   Id.

13   Juliana Menasce Horowitz, Ruth Igielnik, & Rakesh Kochhar, Pew Research Center, Trends in Income and Wealth Inequality, January 9, 2020, www.pewresearch.org/social-trends/2020/01/09/trends-in-income-and-wealth-inequality/.

14   Opinion: The U.S. Is Growing More Unequal, The Washington Post, June 16, 2021, www.washingtonpost.com/opinions/2021/07/16/us-is-growing-more-unequal-thats-harmful-fixable/.

15   Irving Bernstein, Guns and Butter: The Presidency of Lyndon Johnson (1996); Art Pine, War in Vietnam Started 13-Year Spiral of Prices, The Washington Post, October 25, 1978, www.washingtonpost.com/archive/politics/1978/10/25/war-in-vietnam-started-13-year-spiral-of-prices/eb322c1f-d1a2-4e40-bfbd-bccae51a9efc/.

16   Louis D. Johnston, Why Today's Inflation Is Nothing Like the Inflation of the 1970s, MinnPost, November 19, 2021, www.minnpost.com/macro-micro-minnesota/2021/11/why-todays-inflation-is-nothing-like-the-inflation-of-the-1970s/#:~:text=Inflation%20in%20the%201970s%20was,were%2C%20in%20retrospect%2C%20clear.

17   Art Pine, War in Vietnam Started 13-Year Spiral of Prices, The Washington Post, October 25, 1978, www.washingtonpost.com/archive/politics/1978/10/25/war-in-vietnam-started-13-year-spiral-of-prices/eb322c1f-d1a2-4e40-bfbd-bccae51a9efc/.

18   Al Broaddus, President, Reserve Bank of Richmond, Guns and Butter, Region Focus, Summer 2003, www.richmondfed.org/publications/research/econ_focus/2003/summer/~/media/D9A67A72BB58486EB26609B0D1CD7BD9.ashx.

19   Richard Cohen, Guns or Butter, The Washington Post, September 22, 2005, www.washingtonpost.com/archive/opinions/2005/09/22/choose-guns-or-butter/6001be20-e3b0-43c8-9bae-c1ad9093b1c3/.

20   Julian E. Zelizer, The Nation: Guns and Butter; Government Can Run More Than a War, The New York Times, December 30, 2001, www.nytimes.com/2001/12/30/weekinreview/the-nation-guns-and-butter-government-can-run-more-than-a-war.html (quoting Johnson).

21   Globalization, Growth and Poverty: Building an Inclusive Economy, A World Bank Policy Research Report 23 (2002), documents1.worldbank.org/curated/en/954071468778196576/pdf/multiopage.pdf.

22   Kathryn Watson, "You All Just Got a Lot Richer," Trump Tells Friends, Referencing Tax Overhaul, CBSNews, December 24, 2017, www.cbsnews.com/news/trump-mar-a-lago-christmas-trip/.

23   Scott Horsley, After 2 Years, Trump Tax Cuts Have Failed to Deliver on GOP's Promises, NPR, December 20, 2019.

24 William Greider, The Education of David Stockman, The Atlantic, December 1981, www
    .theatlantic.com/magazine/archive/1981/12/the-education-of-david–stockman/305760/.

25 Cory Jannsen, Stock Buyback: A Breakdown, Investopedia (March 24, 2021).

26 Peter Cary & Allan Holmes, The Secret Saga of Trump's Tax Cuts, Center for Public
    Integrity, April 30, 2019, https://publicintegrity.org/inequality-poverty-opportunity/
    taxes/trumps-tax-cuts/the-secret-saga-of-trumps-tax-cuts/; Peter Cary & Allan Holmes,
    Workers Barely Benefited from Trump's Sweeping Tax Cuts, Investigation Shows, The
    Guardian, April 30, 2019; www.theguardian.com/us-news/2019/apr/30/trump-tax-cut-law-
    investigation-worker-benefits.

27 Committee for a Response Budget, President Trump's $4 Trillion Debt Increase, July 25,
    2019, www.crfb.org/blogs/president-trumps-4-trillion-debt-increase.

28 Adam Looney, Brookings Institute, Funding Our Nation's Priorities: Reforming the
    Tax Code's Advantageous Treatment of the Wealthy, May 12, 2021, www.brookings
    .edu/testimonies/funding-our-nations-priorities-reforming-the-tax-codes-advantageous-
    treatment-of-the-wealthy/; Thomas Piketty and Emmanuel Saez, How Progressive Is
    the U.S. Federal Tax System? A Historical and International Perspective, 21 J. Econ.
    Perspectives 3 (2007); www.aeaweb.org/articles?id=10.1257/jep.21.1.3.

29 Scott Horsley, After 2 Years, Trump Tax Cuts Have Failed to Deliver on GOP's Promises,
    NPR, December 20, 2019, www.npr.org/2019/12/20/789540931/2-years-later-trump-tax-
    cuts-have-failed-to-deliver-on-gops-promises; Tax Policy Center, Distributional Analysis
    of the Conference Agreement for the Tax Cuts and Jobs Act, December 18, 2017, www
    .taxpolicycenter.org/publications/distributional-analysis-conference-agreement-tax-cuts-
    and-jobs-act/full.

30 Institute of Tax and Economic Policy, Who Pays? 6th Edition, October 2018, https://itep
    .org/whopays/.

31 Warren Buffett and His Secretary on Their Tax Rates, ABC News, January 25, 2012,
    https://abcnews.go.com/blogs/business/2012/01/warren-buffett-and-his-secretary-talk-
    taxes.

32 Id.

33 Eric York, Tracking the Economic Impact of U.S. Tariffs and Retaliatory Actions,
    Tax Foundation, October 19, 2021, https://taxfoundation.org/tariffs-trump-trade-war/;
    Ross Hass & Abraham Denmark, More Paint Than Gain: How the US-China Trade
    War Hurt America, Brookings, August 7, 2020, www.brookings.edu/blog/order-from-
    chaos/2020/08/07/more-pain-than-gain-how-the-us-china-trade-war-hurt-america/.

34 Philip Rucker & Robert Costa, Bannon Vows a Daily Fight for "Deconstruction of the
    Administrative State," The Washington Post, February 23, 2017, www.washingtonpost
    .com/politics/top-wh-strategist-vows-a-daily-fight-for-deconstruction-of-the-administrative-
    state/2017/02/23/03f6b8da-f9ea-11e6-bf01-d47f8cf9b643_story.html.

35 Exec. Order 13771, 82 Fed. Reg. 9339 (Feb. 3, 2017).

36 Joseph P. Tomain, Executive Orders Reforming Regulation and Reducing Regulatory
    Costs, Trends, July/August 2017.

37 Office of Mgmt. & Budget, 2017 Draft Report to Congress on the Benefits and Costs of
    Federal Regulations and Agency Compliance with the United Mandates Reform Act 2
    (2017); Amy Siden, The Cost-Benefit Boomerang, The American Prospect, July 25, 2019,
    https://prospect.org/economy/cost-benefit-boomerang/.

38 Lola Fadulu, Trump Targets Michelle Obama's School Nutrition Guidelines on
    Her Birthday, The New York Times, January 17, 2020; Savannah Behrman, Trump
    Administration Roll Back School Lunch Regulations on Fruits and Vegetables, USA
    Today, January 17, 2020.

39 Nadja Popovich, Livia Albeck-Ripka, & Kendra Pierre-Louis, The Trump Administration Rolled Back More Than 100 Environmental Rules. Here's the Full List, The New York Times, January 20 2021, www.nytimes.com/interactive/2020/climate/trump-environment-rollbacks-list.html.

40 Rebecca Hersher, U.S. Officially Leaving Paris Climate Agreement, National Public Radio, November 3, 2020, www.npr.org/2020/11/03/930312701/u-s-officially-leaving-paris-climate-agreement.

41 Eric Wolff, Energy Department Climate Office Bans Use of Phrase "Climate Change," Politico, March 29, 2017, www.politico.com/story/2017/03/energy-department-climate-change-phrases-banned-236655.

42 Fourth National Climate Assessment, November 2018, https://nca2018.globalchange .gov/chapter/front-matter-about/; Akshit Sangomla, US Elections 2020: A History of Trump's Climate Change Denial, Down to Earth, November 3, 2020, www .downtoearth.org.in/news/climate-change/us-elections-2020-a-history-of-trump-s-climate-change-denial-74075.

43 Does Regulation Kill Jobs (Cary Coglianese, Adam F. Finkel & Christopher Carrigan eds., 2014).

44 Sarah Okeson, Trump's Record in Federal Courts Is the Worst of Any Recent President, Salon, September 25, 2020, www.salon.com/2020/09/25/trumps-record-in-federal-courts-is-the-worst-of-any-recent-president_partner/.

45 Michael Lewis, The Fifth Risk 21 (2018).

46 David A. Graham, The President Who Doesn't Read, The Atlantic, January 5, 2018, www .theatlantic.com/politics/archive/2018/01/americas-first-post-text-president/549794/.

47 Marc Fisher, Donald Trump Doesn't Read Much, The Washington Post, July 17, 2016, www .washingtonpost.com/politics/donald-trump-doesnt-read-much-being-president-probably-wouldnt-change-that/2016/07/17/d2ddf2bc-4932-11e6-90a8-fb84201e0645_story.html.

48 NBC News, "I'm a Very Stable Genius," President Donald Trump Says as NATO Summit Ends https://youtube.com/watch?v=yJm-uqbNUqQ&feature=share.

49 Linda Qiu, Ryan Zinke Broke Ethics Rules as Interior Secretary, Inquiry Finds, The New York Times, February 16, 2022.

50 Peter Baker, Trump Ramps Up Effort to Install Only Those Loyal, The New York Times (January 23, 2020).

51 George Packer, The President Is Winning His War on American Institutions, The Atlantic, April 2020, www.theatlantic.com/magazine/archive/2020/04/how-to-destroy-a-government/606793/.

52 Michael D. Shear & Maggie Haberman, Health Dept. Official Says Doubts on Hydroxychloroquine Led to His Ouster, The New York Times, April 22, 2020, www.nytimes .com/2020/04/22/us/politics/rick-bright-trump-hydroxychloroquine-coronavirus.html.

53 Elizabeth Magill & Adrian Vermeule, Allocating Power within Agencies, 120 Yale L. J. 1032, 1037–38 (2011).

54 Michael Koncewicz, The GOP Appointees Who Defied the President, The Atlantic, November 19, 2019, www.theatlantic.com/ideas/archive/2019/11/the-gop-appointees-who-defied-the-president/602230/.

55 Bartleby.com available at www.bartleby.com/73/1514.html.

56 Jon Michaels, How Trump Is Dismantling a Pillar of the American State, November 7, 2017, The Guardian, www.theguardian.com/commentisfree/2017/nov/07/donald-trump-dismantling-american-administrative-state.

57 Annie Gowen et al., Science Ranks Grow Thin in Trump Administrations, The Washington Pos (January 23, 2020); see also Brad Plumer & Coral Davenport, Science

under Attack: How Trump Is Sidelining Researcher and Their Work, The New York Times Magazine (December 28, 2019).

58 Brian Naylor, Trump Administration Announces Plans to Move Hundreds of Federal Jobs Out of D.C., National Public Radio, July 19, 2019, www.npr.org/2019/07/19/743599320/ trump-administration-announces-plans-to-move-hundreds-of-federal-jobs-out-of-d-c; Damien Paletta, Trump Budget Expected to Seek Historic Contraction of Federal Workforce, The Washington Post, May 12, 2017, www.washingtonpost.com/ business/economy/through-his-budget-a-bottom-line-look-at-trumps-new-washingt on/2017/03/12/29739206-05be-11e7-b9fa-ed727b644a0b_story.html?tid=ss_fb&utm_ term=.01b1d3dd4392.

59 Juliet Eilperin, Trump Officials Moved Most Bureau of Land Management Positions Out of D.C., The Washington Post, January 28, 2021, www.washingtonpost.com/climate-environment/2021/01/28/trump-blm-reorganization/.

60 Jon Michaels, How Trump Is Dismantling a Pillar of the American State, The Guardian, November 7, 2017, www.theguardian.com/commentisfree/2017/nov/07/donald-trump-dismantling-american-administrative-state.

61 Select Committee to Investigate the January 6th Attack on the United States Capitol, Final Report 20–21 (December 22, 2022).

62 Jamie Raskin, Unthinkable: Trauma, Truth, and the Trials of American Democracy 152 (2022).

63 John F. Kennedy Presidential Library and Museum, 2022 Profile in Courage Award: Liz Cheney (May 22, 2022) available at www.jfklibrary.org/events-and-awards/profile-in-courage-award/award-recipients/defending-democracy-2022/liz-cheney.

64 Fareed Zakaria, Republicans Care More about Tribal Loyalty Than Conservative Principles, The Washington Post, May 13, 2021, www.washingtonpost.com/opinions/ global-opinions/republicans-care-more-about-tribal-loyalty-than-conservative-princ iples/2021/05/13/753abf64-b42b-11eb-ab43-bebddc5a0f65_story.html; Heritage Action for America, https://heritageaction.com/scorecard/members/C001109/116/; League of Conservation Votes, National Environmental Scorecard, https://scorecard.lcv.org/ moc/liz-cheney.

65 Select Committee to Investigate the January 6th Attack on the United States Capitol at xvi–xvii.

66 Iowa State University Archives of Women's Political Communication, Liz Cheney Concession Speech (August 16, 2022) available at https://awpc.cattcenter.iastate .edu/2022/08/17/concession-speech-aug-16-2022/.

67 U.S. News Staff, Ranking America's Worst Presidents, November 6, 2019, www.usnews .com/news/special-reports/the-worst-presidents/articles/ranking-americas-worst-presidents.

13 ANTHONY FAUCI'S AMERICA

1 Morgan Chalfant, Jill Biden Recognizes Fauci as an "American Hero," The Hill, May 20, 2021, https://thehill.com/homenews/administration/554617-jill-biden-recognizes-dr-fauci-as-an-american-hero.

2 Editorial, Fauci Is an American Hero Trying to Save Lives – Everything Trump Is Not, Houston Chronicle, October 21, 2020, www.houstonchronicle.com/opinion/editorials/ article/Editorial-Fauci-is-an-American-hero-trying-to-15662717.php.

3 Daniel Yarwood, Stop Bashing the Bureaucracy, 56 Pub. Admin. Rev. 611, 611 (1996).

4 Rena Steinzor & Sidney Shapiro, The People's Agents and the Battle to Protect the American Public 126 (2010).

5 Rena Steinzor, Bureaucracy Bashing, Obama Style, Huff Post, April 10, 2012, www .huffpost.com/entry/bureaucracy-bashing-obama_b1265608.

6 Wisconsin Historical Society, Proxmire, William. Golden Fleece Awards: 1975–1987, www.wisconsinhistory.org/turningpoints/search.asp?id=1742.

7 Avalon Project, Yale Law School, Inaugural Address of John F. Kennedy, January 20, 1961, https://avalon.law.yale.edu/20th_century/kennedy.asp.

8 Partnership for Public Service, Samuel J. Heyman Service to American Medals, Program Overview & History, https://servicetoamericamedals.org/about/; Partnership for Public Service, Service for America Medals, 2019, https://servicetoamericamedals.org/honorees/?fwp_year=2019.

9 Service to American Medals, Honorees, Partnership for Public Service, https://servicetoamericamedals.org/honorees/.

10 Elizabeth Fisher & Sidney A. Shapiro, Administrative Competence: Reimagining Administrative Law 130–32 (2020).

11 Patricia Wallace Ingraham, The Foundation of Merit: Public Service in American Democracy 20 (1995) (quoting Jackson).

12 Jerry L. Mashaw, Administration and "The Democracy": Administrative Law from Jackson to Lincoln, 1829–1861, 117 Yale L. J. 1568, 1615–16 (2008).

13 Woodrow Wilson, The Study of Administration, 2 Political Sci. Q. 197, 216 (1887).

14 Herbert Croly, Progressive Democracy 359 (1915).

15 Id. at 356.

16 B. Guy Peters, Institutional Theory in Political Science: The New Institutionalism 30 (3d ed. 2012); James March & Johan P. Olsen, Rediscovering Institutions 23–24 (1989); Sidney A. Shapiro, Why Administrative Law Misunderstands How Government Works: The Missing Institutional Analysis, 53 Washburn L.J. 1, 5–8 (2013).

17 Sidney A. Shapiro & Ronald F. Wright, The Future of the Administrative Presidency: Turning Administrative Law Inside-Out, 65 U. Miami L. Rev. 577, 586–589 (2011).

18 Hebert Kaufman, The Forest Ranger: A Study in Administrative Behavior (1960).

19 Paul C. Light, Government's Greatest Achievements in the Past Half Century: From Civil Rights to Homeland Defense 2 (2002).

20 Id.

21 Logan Harper, Our 10 Favorite Public Servants from Popular Culture, UNC School of Government, June 28, 2013, https://onlinempa.unc.edu/public-servants-pop-culture/.

22 Mihriye Mete, Bureaucratic Behavior in Strategic Environments: Politicians, Taxpayers, and the IRS, 64 J. Pol. 384, 384 (2002); see also B. Dan Wood & Richard W. Waterman, The Dynamics of Political-Bureaucratic Adoption, 37 Am. J. Pol. Sci. 497, 497 (1993).

23 Marissa Martino Golden, What Motivates Bureaucrats: Politics and Administration During the Reagan Years 151–52 (2000).

24 Logan Harper, Our 10 Favorite Public Servants from Popular Culture, UNC School of Government, June 28, 2013, https://onlinempa.unc.edu/public-servants-pop-culture/.

25 Michael McFaul, The Deeply Dedicated State, The New York Review of Books, www .nybooks.com/daily/2019/10/31/the-deeply-dedicated-state/?fbclid=IwAR3lVn8mziVhum TG23HN2Xu8nK8O50ZxngwHNd8T–O4Zh5AVT30yo2R9Q4.

26 Id.

27 Michael Lewis, The Fifth Risk 54 (2018) (quoting McWilliams).

28 Donald Kettl, et. al., No Time to Wait: Building a Public Service for the Twenty-First Century, National Academy of Public Administration White Paper, July 2017, at 3, www .napawash.org/uploads/Academy_Studies/No-Time-to-Wait_Building-a-Public-Service-for-the-21st-Century.pdf.

29 Id. at 18.

30 Id. at 9.

31 Molly Jahn, et. al., Are Declines in the U.S. Federal Workforce Capabilities Putting Government at the Risk of Failing?, Senior Executives Association Report, January 2019, at 1, https://cdn.ymaws.com/seniorexecs.org/resource/resmgr/government_at_the_risk_of_fa.pdf.

32 Id. at 2.

33 The Voelker Alliance, Preparing Tomorrows Public Service: What the Next Generation Needs 9 (2018), www.volckeralliance.org/sites/default/files/attachments/Preparing%20 Tomorrow%27s%20Public%20Service.pdf.

34 Donald Kettl, et. al., supra note 61, at 5.

35 Id. at 6.

36 Report of the National Commission on the Public Service, Urgent Business for America: Revitalizing the Federal Government for the Twenty-First Century 1 (January 2003), https://ourpublicservice.org/wp-content/uploads/2003/01/7dd93d98ebc51f44548885f502dd 13a7-1414078938.pdf.

37 President Kennedy's Special Message to the Congress on Urgent National Needs, MAY 25, 1961, John F. Kennedy Presidential Library and Museum, www.jfklibrary .org/archives/other-resources/john-f-kennedy-speeches/united-states-congress-special- message-19610525.

14 JOE BIDEN'S AMERICA

1 Dan Merica, Jeff Zeleny & Arlette Saenz, "Amtrak Joe" Could Arrive for His Inauguration by Train, CNN, December 7, 2020, https://edition.cnn.com/2020/12/07/politics/biden- amtrak/index.html.

2 Steven Livingston, Joe Biden: Life before the Presidency, Miller Center, https:// millercenter.org/joe-biden-life-presidency.

3 Jeff Zeleny, Arlette Saenz & Kate Sullivan, Biden No Longer Taking Amtrak to Inauguration Amid Security Concerns, CNN, January 13, 2021, www.cnn.com/2021/01/13/ politics/biden-amtrak-inauguration-security/index.html.

4 Thomas Beaumont, Joe Biden's Decision to Run in 2020: The Inside Story of His Deliberation Over Three Years, Delaware Online, April 28, 2019, https://edition.cnn .com/2020/12/07/politics/biden-amtrak/index.html.

5 Inaugural Address by President Joseph R. Biden, Jr., January 20, 2021, www.whitehouse .gov/briefing-room/speeches-remarks/2021/01/20/inaugural-address-by-president-joseph-r- biden-jr/.

6 IMBDtv, The American President, Michael Douglas: Andrew Shepherd (1995), www .imdb.com/title/tt0112346/characters/nm0000140.

7 Inaugural Address, supra note 5.

8 Nan Lin, Biden Promised a Historically Diverse Cabinet. Was He Able to Deliver? NBCDWF, April 29, 2021, www.nbcdfw.com/news/politics/biden-administration/biden- cabinet-breakdown-by-gender-age-ethnicity/2619324/.

9 Victory Institute, LGBTQ Appointments in the Biden-Harris Administration, April 29, 2021, https://victoryinstitute.org/programs/presidential-appointments-initiative/lgbtq-appointments- in-the-biden-harris-administration/.

10 Mariel Padilla, Biden Promised the Most Diverse Administration Ever: Here's How Is He Doing? Gov'n Exec., May 3, 2021, www.govexec.com/management/2021/05/biden- promised-most-diverse-administration-ever-heres-how-hes-doing/173757/; Amirah Ismail,

The Biden-Harris Administration Is the Most Diverse Ever, ShareAmerica, May 10, 2021, https://share.america.gov/biden-harris-administration-most-diverse/.

11   Peter Baker, Biden Seeks Shift in How the Nation Serves Its People, The New York Times, April 28, 2021, www.nytimes.com/2021/04/28/us/politics/joe-biden-government-plans.html.

12   Jonathan Weisman & Reid J. Epstein, G.O.P. Declares January 6 Attack "Legitimate Political Discourse," The New York Times, Feb. 4, 2022.

13   Lee Drutman, How Much Longer Can This Era of Political Gridlock Last?, FiveThirtyEight (March 4, 2021), https://fivethirtyeight.com/features/how-much-longer-can-this-era-of-political-gridlock-last/.

14   Id.

15   Center for Budget & Policy Priorities, Chart Book: Tracking the Recovery from the Pandemic Recession, July 28, 2022, www.cbpp.org/research/economy/tracking-the-recovery-from-the-pandemic-recession#pandemic_recession_deeper.

16   Gabe Alpert, A Breakdown of the Fiscal and Monetary Responses to the Pandemic, April 12, 2022, www.investopedia.com/government-stimulus-efforts-to-fight-the-covid-19-crisis-4799723.

17   Lauren Gambino & Maanvi Singh, US Senate Passes Historic $2tn Relief Package as Coronavirus Devastates Economy, The Guardian, March 25, 2020, www.theguardian.com/world/2020/mar/25/senate-passes-coronavirus-stimulus-package.

18   American Rescue Plan Act of 2021, Pub. L. No. 117-2; Albert, supra note 16; Barbara Sprunt, Meeting with Republicans on COVID-19 Relief, White House Says Biden "Will Not Settle," NPR, January 31, 2021, www.npr.org/sections/coronavirus-live-updates/2021/01/31/962554923/10-senate-republicans-plan-to-detail-slimmed-down-covid-19-counteroffer.

19   Allan Smith, McConnell Says He's "100 Percent" Focused on "Stopping" Biden's Administration, NBC News, May 5, 2021.

20   Libby Cathey, Biden Taunts McConnell for "Bragging" about Relief Bill He Voted Against, ABC News, July 7, 2021, https://abcnews.go.com/Politics/biden-taunts-mcconnell-bragging-relief-bill-voted/story?id=78718155; Steven Peoples, Republicans Promote Pandemic Relief They Voted Against, ABC News, May 6, 2021, https://abcnews.go.com/Business/wireStory/republicans-promote-pandemic-relief-voted-77527236.

21   Albert, supra note 16.

22   Center for Disease Control and Prevention, CDC Issues Eviction Moratorium Order in Areas of Substantial and High Transmission, August 3, 2021, www.cdc.gov/media/releases/2021/s0803-cdc-eviction-order.html.

23   The Commonwealth Fund, The U.S. COVID-19 Vaccination Program at One Year: How Many Deaths and Hospitalizations Were Averted? December 14, 2021, www.commonwealthfund.org/publications/issue-briefs/2021/dec/us-covid-19-vaccination-program-one-year-how-many-deaths-and.

24   Emily Cochrane, Senate Passes $1 Trillion Infrastructure Bill, Handing Biden a Bipartisan Win, The New York Times, August 10, 2021, www.nytimes.com/2021/08/10/us/politics/infrastructure-bill-passes.html.

25   Katie Rogers, How 'Infrastructure Week' Became a Long-Running Joke, The New York Times, May 22, 2019, www.nytimes.com/2019/05/22/us/politics/trump-infrastructure-week.html.

26   David Schaper, 10 Years after Bridge Collapse, America Is Still Crumbling, NPR, August 1, 2017, www.npr.org/2017/08/01/540669701/10-years-after-bridge-collapse-america-is-still-crumbling.

27 James McBride & Anshu Siripurapu, The State of U.S. Infrastructure, Council of Foreign Relations, November 8, 2021, www.cfr.org/backgrounder/state-us-infrastructure.

28 Catie Edmondson, Senate Passes $280 Billion Industrial Policy Bill to Counter China, The New York Times, July 27, 2022, www.nytimes.com/2022/07/27/us/politics/senate-chips-china.html; Amy B. Wang & Marianna Sotomayor, House Passes Bill to Subsidize U.S.-Made Semiconductor Chips in Win for Biden, The Washington Post, July 28, 2022, www.washingtonpost.com/politics/2022/07/28/house-vote-semiconductor-chips-bill/.

29. Louise Boyle, Meet Biden's Climate Crisis Army, Indep., January 18, 2021, www .independent.co.uk/environment/climate-change/biden-climate-change-hires-white-house-b1788976.html [https://perma.cc/39UL-QB6F]; Grp. of Thirty, Mainstreaming the Transition to a Net-Zero Economy 6–7 (2020), https://group30.org/images/uploads/ publications/G30_Mainstreaming_the_Transition_to_a_Net-Zero_Economy_2.pdf [https://perma.cc/XHL5-4J2S]; Hannah Wiseman, Jennifer Granholm and the Energy Department Can Usher in a Just Transition to Clean Energy: Here's How, CPRBlog (Dec. 17, 2020), http://progressivereform.org/cpr-blog/jennifer-granholm-and-energy-department-can-usher-just-transition-clean-energy-heres-how/ [https://perma.cc/BC4E-QQ6S]; Jeff Turrentine, Biden's Choice for the Council on Environmental Quality: Brenda Mallory, Nat. Res. Def. Council (Dec. 22, 2020), www.nrdc.org/stories/bidens-choice-council-environmental-quality-brenda-mallory [https://perma.cc/NGC7-22XV].

30 Inflation Reduction Act of 2022, Pub. L. 117–169.

31 Comment, Climate Change, The New Yorker, August 22, 2022.

32 Fred Krup, The Biggest Thing Congress Has Ever Done to Address Climate Change, NRDC, August 12, 2022, www.edf.org/blog/2022/08/12/biggest-thing-congress-has-ever-done-address-climate-change.

33 Andrew Thompson, What Scientists Say about the Historic Climate Bill, Scientific American, August 12, 2022, www.scientificamerican.com/article/what-scientists-say-about-the-historic-climate-bill/.

34 Fred Krup, The Biggest Thing Congress Has Ever Done to Address Climate Change, NRDC, August 12, 2022, www.edf.org/blog/2022/08/12/biggest-thing-congress-has-ever-done-address-climate-change.

35 Nadja Popovich & Brad Plumer, How the New Climate Bill Would Reduce Emissions, The New York Times, August 12, 2022, www.nytimes.com/interactive/2022/08/02/climate/ manchin-deal-emissions-cuts.html.

36 Rachel Garfield, Kendal Orgera, & Anthony Damico, The Uninsured and the ACA: A Primer – Key Facts about Health Insurance and the Uninsured Amidst Changes to the Affordable Care Act, Kaiser Family Foundation, January 25, 2019, www.kff.org/report-section/the-uninsured-and-the-aca-a-primer-key-facts-about-health-insurance-and-the-uninsured-amidst-changes-to-the-affordable-care-act-how-many-people-are-uninsured/.

37 Carl Hulse, McCain Provides a Dramatic Finale on Health Care: Thumb Down, The New York Times, July 28, 2017, www.nytimes.com/2017/07/28/us/john-mccains-real-return.html.

38 Id.

39 President Biden Signs the PACT Act and Delivers on His Promise to America's Veterans, The White House, August 20, 2022, www.whitehouse.gov/briefing-room/statements-releases/2022/08/10/fact-sheet-president-biden-signs-the-pact-act-and-delivers-on-his-promise-to-americas-veterans/.

40 By the Numbers: The Inflation Reduction Act, The White House, August 15, 2022, www.whitehouse.gov/briefing-room/statements-releases/2022/08/15/by-the-numbers-the-inflation-reduction-act/.

41 Juliette Cubanski, Tricia Neuman, Meredith Freed & Anthony Damico, How Will the Prescription Drug Provisions in the Inflation Reduction Act Affect Medicare Beneficiaries? Kaiser Family Foundation, August 18, 2022, www.kff.org/medicare/issue-brief/how-will-the-prescription-drug-provisions-in-the-inflation-reduction-act-affect-medicare-beneficiaries/.

42 Kaiser Family Foundation, How Will the Prescription Drug Provisions in the Inflation Reduction Act Affect Medicare Benefits, January 24, 2023, www.kff.org/medicare/issue-brief/how-will-the-prescription-drug-provisions-in-the-inflation-reduction-act-affect-medicare-beneficiaries/#:~:text=Prior%20to%20consideration%20by%20the,years%20(2022%2D2031).

43 President Biden Announces Student Loan Relief for Borrowers Who Need It Most, The White House, August 24, 2022, www.whitehouse.gov/briefing-room/statements-releases/2022/08/24/fact-sheet-president-biden-announces-student-loan-relief-for-borrowers-who-need-it-most/.

44 *Biden v. Nebraska*, 2023 WL 4277210 (2023).

45 Federal Student Aid (DOE), The Biden-Harris Administration's Student Debt Relief Plan (2023) https://studentaid.gov/debt-relief-announcement.

46 Kevin M. Guthrie, Challenges to Higher Education's Most Essential Purposes, April 9, 2019, https://sr.ithaka.org/publications/challenges-to-higher-educations-most-essential-purposes/; John Ebersole, Going Private: Why Public Institutions Are Considering Crossing Over (Part 1), November 11, 2014, https://evolllution.com/opinions/private-public-institutions-crossing-part-1/.

47 Thomas Adam, College Was Once Free and for the Public Good – What Happened? Yes Magazine, July 20, 2017, www.yesmagazine.org/economy/2017/07/20/college-was-once-free-and-for-the-public-good-what-happened.

48 Susan Dynarski, Why I Changed My Mind on Student Debt Forgiveness, The New York Times, August 30, 2022, www.nytimes.com/2022/08/30/opinion/student-loan-debt-relief-biden.html.

49 Id.; Susan Dynarski, New Data Gives Clearer Picture of Student Debt, The New York Times, September 10, 2015, www.nytimes.com/2015/09/11/upshot/new-data-gives-clearer-picture-of-student-debt.html.

50 Luke Herrine, The Future of the Education Department's Power to Cancel Student Loan Debt, The Regulatory Review, January 6, 2017, www.theregreview.org/2017/01/06/herrine-future-educations-power-to-cancel-debt/.

51 Ryan Bort, 'Deadbeats' Don't Pay Debts, Says Trump Fed Pick Held in Contempt for Not Paying Debts, Rolling Stone, August 26, 2022, www.rollingstone.com/politics/politics-news/stephen-moore-debt-deadbeats-republican-hypocrisy-1234582294/.

52 L. Z, Granderson, Is Biden's Student Debt Forgiveness Fair? Orleans Times Herald, August 30, 2022, www.oleantimesherald.com/opinion/is-bidens-student-debt-forgiveness-fair/article_76440a1d-7912-5a17-b633-dcf30271986d.html.

53 Dynarski, supra note 47.

15 CONCLUSION

1 Sidney A. Shapiro & Joseph P. Tomain, Achieving Democracy: The Future of Progressive Regulation (2014).

2 David McCullough, The American Spirit: Who We Are and What We Stand For (2017).

3 Preamble, U.S. Constitution, https://constitution.congress.gov/constitution/preamble/.

4 Id.

5 Jill Lepore, This America: The Case for the Nation 137 (2019).

Index

Printed in the United States
by Baker & Taylor Publisher Services